MW01199811

[*f* R *i* E N d S h *i* p]
[C O U N S E L I N G]

Jesus' Model
for Speaking
Life-Words to
Hurting People

[fRiENdShip
COUNSELING]

KEVIN D. HUGGINS, PH.D.

NAVPRESS

Bringing Truth to Life
P.O. Box 35001, Colorado Springs, Colorado 80935

OUR GUARANTEE TO YOU

We believe so strongly in the message of our books that we are making this quality guarantee to you. If for any reason you are disappointed with the content of this book, return the title page to us with your name and address and we will refund to you the list price of the book. To help us serve you better, please briefly describe why you were disappointed. Mail your refund request to: NavPress, P.O. Box 35002, Colorado Springs, CO 80935.

The Navigators is an international Christian organization. Our mission is to reach, disciple, and equip people to know Christ and to make Him known through successive generations. We envision multitudes of diverse people in the United States and every other nation who have a passionate love for Christ, live a lifestyle of sharing Christ's love, and multiply spiritual laborers among those without Christ.

NavPress is the publishing ministry of The Navigators. NavPress publications help believers learn biblical truth and apply what they learn to their lives and ministries. Our mission is to stimulate spiritual formation among our readers.

ISBN 1-57683-299-6

Cover design and photograph by Kelly Noffsinger
Creative Team: Brad Lewis, Darla Hightower, Glynese Northam

Some of the anecdotal illustrations in this book are true to life and are included with the permission of the persons involved. All other illustrations are composites of real situations, and any resemblance to people living or dead is coincidental.

Library of Congress Cataloging-in-Publication Data
Huggins, Kevin.
    Friendship counseling : Jesus' model for speaking life-words to hurting people / Kevin D. Huggins.
    p. cm.
Includes bibliographical references.
    ISBN 1-57683-299-6
    1. Jesus Christ — Counseling methods. 2. Pastoral counseling — Biblical teaching. I. Title.
    BT590.C78 H84 2003
    253.5 — dc21   2002012208

Printed in the United States of America

1 2 3 4 5 6 7 8 9 10 / 06 05 04 03

CONTENTS

$$\begin{bmatrix} P \text{ A r T } o \text{ N } e : \\ \text{JESUS AND HUMAN SUFFERING} \end{bmatrix}$$

$$\begin{bmatrix} P \text{ A r T } t \text{ w } O : \\ \text{JESUS AND HUMAN CHANGE} \end{bmatrix}$$

$$\begin{bmatrix} P \text{ A r T } t \text{ H } \textbf{r} \text{ E } e : \\ \text{JESUS AND HUMAN COUNSELING} \end{bmatrix}$$

ACKNOWLEDGMENTS

I want to thank the students and alumni of the Masters of Christian Counseling Program at Philadelphia Biblical University. Our interactions together over the past ten years served as my catalyst in developing the vision, motivation, and concepts for *Friendship Counseling*. I'm especially indebted to faculty colleagues Mike Dittman, Penny Freeman, Jim Meyer, and Lisa Kuzma who have labored with me to develop effective ways to train men and women for biblical counseling ministries. I'm also indebted to the staff and administration of our University for the support they provided while I wrote this book. Our Provost, Dr. Donald MacCullough, and my academic assistant, Diane Minor, provided special assistance and encouragement to me.

My wife, Vicky, provided invaluable conceptual, editorial, technical, and emotional support to me at each stage of writing this book. She sacrificed and invested hundreds of hours of her life over a three-year period to help me see this book to fruition. I couldn't have completed this project without her encouragement through each stage of the arduous writing process.

I also want to acknowledge the large role that Dr. Larry Crabb's teaching, writing, and mentoring have played in shaping my own perspective and approach to friendship-counseling. Anyone familiar with his contributions to the field of biblical counseling will recognize his influence on my thinking.

Finally, I want to thank Matthew, Mark, Luke, and John — the four biblical authors who allowed God to use them to provide the written record of Jesus' life-words to hurting people.

It's been a privilege to spend thousands of hours over the last ten years pouring through their rich accounts of our Lord's counseling interactions.

GUIDE TO UNDERSTANDING
SCRIPTURE REFERENCES

When I make references to a passage of Scripture without quoting the words of that passage, I cite only the book of the Bible, the chapter, and/or the verse of the passage.

When I quote the actual words of a passage of Scripture, I cite the translation or version I've taken the quotation from along with the book, chapter, and verse of the passage.

In the few instances when the words of a passage appear but I've not cited the version or translation, the words are my own translation from the 21st edition of Eberhard Nestle's *Novum Testamentum Graece* text used in *The Interlinear NASB-NIV Parallel New Testament in Greek and English*.

I use the following abbreviations when citing the sources of biblical quotations in this book:

NASB   Marshall, A., *The Interlinear NASB-NIV Parallel New Testament in Greek and English* (Grand Rapids, MI: Zondervan, 1993)

NIV   Marshall, A., *The Interlinear NASB-NIV Parallel New Testament in Greek and English* (Grand Rapids, MI: Zondervan, 1993)

AMP   The Lockman Foundation, *The Amplified New Testament* (Grand Rapids, MI: Zondervan, 1958)

TLB   Tyndale House Publishers, Inc., *The Living Bible* (Wheaton, IL: Tyndale, 1971)

MSG   Peterson, E., *The Message* (Colorado Springs, CO: NavPress, 1993)

PH   Phillips, J.B., *The New Testament in Modern English* (New York: MacMillan, 1958)

INTRODUCTION

At one point many of Jesus' disciples deserted him. "Do you want to leave me too?" Jesus asked the twelve. Simon Peter answered, "Lord, to whom would we go? You alone have the words of life." (John 6:66-67)

During the past decade, I've experienced suffering like never before. A string of events brought hardships into my life I never thought I could endure. I turned to my friends — other pastors, counselors, and Christian leaders — for help.

I wanted them to take away my pain, to tell me how to make everything right again, to show me how to end my suffering. With the best of intentions, they spoke many words to me. Those who'd been through great suffering themselves spoke the most helpful words — things I would have paid little attention to in other circumstances. Their words didn't accomplish any of the things I wanted, yet they provided me with the hope and guidance I needed. Without the life-words of my friends — words God gave them to speak to me — I'd have a very different story to tell today.

This book is about using our words to offer hope and guidance to those who struggle, whether with physical or psychological pain. This includes people who struggle as innocent victims of circumstances and people who struggle with problems they helped to create.

When friends are suffering, instinctively we first reach out to them through a physical gesture or touch, acts of kindness, or a shoulder to lean on. Oswald Chambers writes, "There are some types of suffering before which the only thing you can do is keep your mouth shut."[1] This book doesn't speak to all the nonverbal ways we can reach out to people to lessen their suffering. Instead, it speaks to how we can use words to offer hope and life to those who are experiencing loss, anguish, or affliction that can't be alleviated by nonverbal interventions.

When that well-known sufferer from the Bible, Job, was struggling with multiple afflictions and excruciating pain, his counselors chose not to say a word to him for seven days. Instead, they displayed their concern by sitting with him in silence. When Job spoke, his counselors listened for a long time before they uttered a word. Finally, Job (like all sufferers) needed to hear words from his friends to understand what was happening to him and how to respond to it.

In his book *Wounded Healer*, Henri Nouwen describes the kind of counselor that sufferers need:

> A minister [friendship-counselor] is not a doctor whose primary task is to take away pain . . . the main task of the minister [friendship-counselor] is to prevent people from suffering for the wrong reasons. Many people suffer because of the false supposition . . . that there should be no fear or loneliness, no confusion or doubt. . . . When we become aware that we do not have to escape our pains, but that we can mobilize them into a common search for life, those very pains are transformed from expressions of despair into signs of hope.[2]

Our society dedicates whole industries to train professional helpers to talk to hurting people. We've come to believe that only professionals can craft healing words. We call what they do therapy, misleading those in the best position to help sufferers — those in their own communities and churches — into thinking that they have little to offer and could even do sufferers harm. But what do people in the throes of suffering really need — professionally trained strangers to talk with? When tragedies occur, like the ones at Columbine High School or the World Trade Center, most people turn to one another for words of comfort and life rather than to professional counselors.

God calls us as Christians to come alongside each other as we struggle and offer words very different from the world's: "[B]e God's children, blameless, sincere and wholesome, living in a warped and diseased world, and shining there like lights in a dark place. For you hold in your hands the very word of life" (Philippians 2:14-16, PH). We're called to speak life-words to our suffering friends.

Too many of today's approaches to counseling focus on telling struggling people what they're doing wrong and what to change to make their circumstances more fulfilling or less painful. But these are death-words; they reinforce in people the belief that their lives depend on making their self-centered existence more effective, comfortable, or fulfilling.

Life-words do the opposite. They show how to use a suffering to exchange our self-centered existence for a completely different life. Jesus' conversations with hurting people provide us with the only clear model for doing this. When he spoke to sufferers, his goal was much greater than improving their circumstances or rescuing them from their troubles. In fact, his counsel often encouraged people to make choices that led them into deeper suffering.

The ultimate goal of Jesus' words to hurting people was character transformation. His words showed individuals how to acquire the kind of character that enabled them to use their pain and problems to live in ways that give their lives eternal value, meaning, and joy.

Beth, a student of mine, struggled with self-centered family members and coworkers. None of the important people in her life seemed to change even though, with God's help, she was loving them better than she'd ever dreamed. She questioned why she should let God change her if it wasn't going to lessen her suffering. In desperation, she prayed: "God, if you're not going to change the people in my world, you're going to have to change me even more. I need a heart that not only loves people who don't love back, but one that finds all I need in you alone." When she started praying this way, Jesus' promise in John 7:38 started to become real to her: "Whoever depends on me, as the Scripture has said, will experience a river of life flowing right into his heart." She began to feel stronger and more alive, even around those who disappointed her. And she experienced real freedom and joy in being the person she wanted to be in their presence, regardless of their responses.

Jesus' words show struggling people how to change the very nature of their existence: through a change of their own heart. That's what makes them life-words. They're words that guide people to build their lives upon what God's power can do in their hearts, instead of on what they can do for themselves in their own power.

We can speak these kinds of words only by following Jesus' example. Peter observed that Jesus, alone, "has the words of life" (John 6:68). **The purpose of this book is to equip Christians to speak to people in their struggles like Christ did — to offer words that help their hurting friends acquire and display his character in the midst of whatever pain or problems they are experiencing.**

Jesus' model for speaking life-words adapts to any setting where we encounter hurting people.* It's effective in formal counseling settings, as well as in less-structured discipleship settings like churches, homes, schools, hospitals, and prisons. It's also effective in informal friendship conversations held over coffee or the telephone. In essence, this model is "friendship-counseling." It shows us how to come alongside hurting people and help them live as Christ's disciples in the midst of their troubles.

Jesus' model for counseling hurting people is built on five core truths in his teachings.

THE INDISPENSABILITY OF CHRIST

He who abides in Me and I in him, he bears much fruit, for apart from Me you can do nothing. (Jesus, John 15:5, NASB)

Life-words point to Christ as the ultimate source of life and health. No one can experience health, psychologically or spiritually,[†] without knowing Christ intimately and obeying him unconditionally. As Creator and Lord, he alone can give us the power and freedom to live and love as healthy people. Our souls wither and psychological symptoms develop when we're not connected to him.

THE SUPREMACY OF THE BIBLE

Man does not live on bread alone, but on every word that comes from the mouth of God. (Jesus, Matthew 4:4, NIV)

Life-words point to the Bible as the only reliable and accurate framework for understanding how psychological[‡] or spiritual problems develop and how they're resolved. The Bible alone provides the wisdom troubled people need to find hope and direction. It's the operating manual for our hearts.

THE IMPERATIVE TO LOVE

As I have loved you, so you must love one another. By this all men will know that you are my disciples. (Jesus, John 13:34-35, NIV)

Life-words communicate our responsibility to love others as

Christ does, no matter how difficult that may be. This is the best indicator of psychological health: how lovingly we relate to those around us. Of course, loving others as Christ does is impossible without God's help. Life-words help us acquire the heart and strength we need to love people around us.

THE NECESSITY OF SUFFERING

In this world you will have trouble. But take heart! I have overcome the world. (Jesus, John 16:33, NIV)

Life-words communicate that while suffering is an inescapable part of human experience, it's not the source of our psychological problems. Choosing to respond inappropriately to suffering is. The goal of life-words isn't to help others escape suffering, but to acquire the character to respond to suffering the way Jesus did. Suffering is an integral part of God's strategy for reproducing Christ's character in our hearts.

THE NEED FOR INNER TRANSFORMATION

You clean the outside of the cup and dish, but inside they are full of greed and self-indulgence . . . First clean the inside of the cup and dish, and then the outside also will be clean. (Jesus, Matthew 23:25-26, NIV)

Life-words communicate that we can't grow psychologically or spiritually without addressing the forces that govern our hearts. This means using spiritual disciplines such as reflection, repentance, prayer, and worship to forge a relationship with God that revolutionizes our inner lives. Behavior change can't be lasting or substantial unless preceded by a transformation of what controls us at the deepest levels.

Built on these core truths, this book unfolds in three parts.

Part One presents Jesus' perspective of human suffering to help you look into the eyes and hearts of hurting people the way Jesus did. These chapters help you understand how Jesus uses human suffering to accomplish his purposes in people's lives.

Part Two explores how Jesus helped people change in the midst of their suffering. It sheds light on what Jesus was doing when he talked with hurting people—both how he related to them and how he spoke to them. These chapters introduce you to Jesus' model for using life-words to help people grow and change.

Part Three gives specific guidelines for using Jesus' model in your own friendship-counseling ministry. These chapters use counseling transcripts and exercises to teach you when and how to speak life-words to hurting friends at different stages in their spiritual journeys.

Friendship Counseling grows out of my commitment to train Christians for counseling ministries that imitate Christ's. I've chosen each principle, passage, illustration, question, and exercise to get you working as you read. Answer every question. Complete every exercise. Work through every issue raised in your own heart. It's my earnest prayer that you'll use *Friendship Counseling* as a tool to develop and enhance your own relationship with God as well as your counseling ministry to hurting people.

---

* This model fosters and facilitates mentor-mentoree relationships. Whether you have a pre-existing relationship with someone or not, you should use this model to counsel them only if both of you understand and agree that you are entering into a non-reciprocal, mentor-mentoree, helping relationship.

† In this book I use the terms "psychological" and "spiritual" synonymously. Since psychology is nothing more than the study of how the human psyche or soul functions ("psyche" being the Greek word used in the New Testament for the human soul or spirit), we can't really separate it from the concept of spiritual functioning. The Bible makes no distinction between psychological

health and spiritual health. Both speak of the same immaterial part of people that accounts for the character they display in their choices and behavior.

‡ When I speak of psychological functioning, I'm referring to the "soulish" capacities of longing, thinking, choosing, and feeling that all people possess and use when responding to life's circumstances. This book is about how to speak to struggling people who still have good use of these capacities. It's not a book about helping those who have lost control of these capacities due to biological disorders or illnesses.

[*p* A r T *o* n e :
JESUS AND HUMAN
SUFFERING]

Jesus went through all the towns and villages, teaching in their synagogues, preaching the good news of the kingdom and healing every disease and sickness. When he saw the crowds, he had compassion on them, because they were harassed *and* helpless, *like sheep without a shepherd.*
Matthew 9:35-36, NIV, emphasis added

Jesus never held himself aloof from hurting people. As he walked among them and witnessed their struggles, he reached out to them. Christ knew that every person he encountered struggled with both "harassment" (trouble in the world) and "helplessness" (trouble in the heart).

Harassed was Jesus' way of describing the trouble we experience in the world. The world regularly disappoints and hurts us. Whatever form our troubles take (relational difficulties, physical infirmities, natural disasters, economic setbacks, ethical dilemmas), they remind us daily that we're not living in heaven yet.

Troubles in our world create tremors in our hearts. We can't suffer externally without it affecting us internally. The older we get, the more we realize our world isn't the kinder, gentler place we'd like it to be. We feel like we're fighting a losing battle — *helpless* to protect what's most important to us. A sense of futility assaults our hearts, and the struggle to master our world degenerates into a battle to protect our souls. Holding onto our dignity and integrity becomes harder with each round of suffering. In Jesus' words, we're like sheep without a shepherd, watching helplessly as the wolves in our world sweep in to rob us of our joy and vitality.

This is the challenge of human existence — finding a way to keep the troubles in our world from devouring our hearts. That's why we need shepherds — skilled counselor-friends who come alongside us as we suffer and show us how to use the trouble in our world to seek the only one who can protect and restore our troubled hearts.

1

$$\left[\begin{array}{c} t \text{ R o U } b \text{ L e} \\ \text{IN THE WORLD} \end{array}\right]$$

In this world you will have trouble.
Jesus, John 16:33, NIV

Counseling relationships begin with people in pain asking for help with the trouble they're experiencing. Listen as Michelle describes her troubles to her counselor:

Michelle: My problem is so embarrassing, but it's always on my mind. It's my marriage. No one else really knows what's going on. I've told my sister that we're going through a rough time right now, adjusting to the kids' absence. But it's ridiculous. We've been "empty nesters" for a couple of years now. What's our problem? Anyway, I feel like such a hypocrite. Here I am, a ministry leader, and my marriage is falling apart.

Counselor: It sounds like you've kept this inside for a long time.

Michelle: Yes, I guess I have. I talk to God about it, but that doesn't seem to change anything.

Counselor: I know this is difficult, but could you describe what's happening in your relationship with your husband?

Michelle: Actually, that's easy—*nothing!* There's nothing there. I feel dead toward him. I'm not sure I want to live like this the rest of my life. Our marriage started off so strong; I never thought it would come to this. We're like two strangers living in the same house. We're both busy—he does his thing and I do mine. We never do anything together anymore. All he wants to do is watch TV, and he expects me to sit there with him. He never talks to me about anything but his job; lately, he hasn't been talking at all, except what's needed to navigate through the busyness of life. At least when the kids were home, we talked about them.

We're supposed to be a Christian couple, but we never talk about spiritual things or pray together. He acts like he's mad at me, but he won't tell me what's wrong. We just kind of stay out of each other's way right now. It's driving me crazy. I've begged him to tell me what's wrong, but he won't. I've even yelled at him, thinking maybe I could get his attention and make him see how serious this is. Nothing works. I feel like giving up. I've been praying for him for years, but he doesn't seem to change. I feel like I mean absolutely nothing to him. I really want to please the Lord, but I want something more.

How do you make sense of Michelle's suffering?

Why would God allow a woman like Michelle, obviously trying to do the right thing, to suffer so much in her marriage?

THE OLDEST QUESTION IN THE BOOK

His disciples asked him, "Teacher, who sinned, this man or his parents, that he was born blind?" "Neither this man nor his parents sinned," said Jesus, "but this happened so that the work of God might be displayed in his life." (John 9:2-3, NIV, emphasis added)

Why does God allow people to experience trouble, especially when they're trying to live good lives? People have struggled with this question from the beginning. It's the question Job and his counselors debated in the oldest book of the Bible. And it's a question anyone who wants to help hurting people must be prepared to answer.

Job began asking this question after he began experiencing great trouble. Within a matter of days he suffered the catastrophic death of all of his children, servants, and livestock, and an outbreak of painful boils over his whole body. Then his family and friends deserted him when he needed them the most. He asked his counselors, "Why is a man allowed to be born if God is only going to give him a hopeless life of uselessness and frustration? . . . I was not fat and lazy, yet trouble struck me down" (Job 3:23,26, TLB).

We know from Jesus' teachings (see John 16:33) that suffering is an inevitable part of life. When humans chose to rebel against God, he chose to subject the most precious of his creations to a hostile environment where suffering is unavoidable (see Romans 8:19-22). God doesn't do this to frustrate or punish us. God has a much higher purpose than that. According to Jesus, it's "so that his work might be displayed" in us.

Can you think of a time when God used a difficulty or hardship to display his work in you? What was he displaying?

VIEWING SUFFERING AS THE SOLUTION, NOT THE PROBLEM

We do not want you to be uninformed, brothers, about the hardships we suffered in the province of Asia. We were under great pressure, far beyond our ability to endure, so that we despaired even of life.

Indeed, in our hearts we felt the sentence of death. But this happened that we might not rely on ourselves but on God, who raises the dead. He has delivered us from such a deadly peril, and he will deliver us. (Paul, 2 Corinthians 1:8-10, NIV)

God knows it's unhealthy for sinful human beings to live the pain-free existence they once enjoyed in Eden. If we operated in that environment, we'd choose to live independently of God. The Bible calls this "arrogance" — the belief that we can make our lives work apart from God.

God once told the nation of Israel his prescription for human arrogance: "I will lead you into the desert where no one can rescue you. There I will speak tenderly to you . . . until in your misery you earnestly seek me" (Hosea 2:14; 5:15). God wants to be our oasis. But outside a desert, we don't feel much need for an oasis. That's what makes the troubles in our world necessary and beneficial. They form the desert that leads us to seek out and enjoy the oasis we would otherwise pass by. C. S. Lewis observed, "It is a dreadful truth that the state of (as you say) 'having to depend solely on God' is what we all dread the most. And of course that just shows how very much, how almost exclusively, we have been depending on things. But trouble goes so far back in our lives, and is now so deeply ingrained, we will not turn to him as long as He leaves us anything else to turn to."[1]

The apostle Paul discovered firsthand how God uses suffering as the antidote for arrogance. Reflecting on his own trials, he observed, "But this happened to us so that we might not rely on ourselves but on God, who raises the dead." (2 Corinthians 1:9, NIV). We could paraphrase Paul's words this way: "If God didn't allow our troubles to destroy us, and instead he used them to bring us to a place of deeper dependence on him, then we don't have to be afraid of any troubles that come our way in the future. We can count on the same God who kept suffering from destroying us back then to not only protect us, but to deliver us from the deadly tendency to operate independently from him. This frees us to live more boldly than before!"

What happens when you attempt to make your life work apart from God?

MORE PAINFUL THAN IT HAS TO BE

But this precious treasure — this light and power that now shine within us — is held in a perishable container, that is, in our weak bodies, (so that) everyone can see that the glorious power within must be from God and is not our own. (Paul, 2 Corinthians 4:7, TLB)

Like Michelle and Job, we're all tempted to think that our suffering is pointless. What does it accomplish? So we live our lives to minimize suffering, avoiding certain people or situations. We restrict our freedom and conduct our lives with caution. Tragically, this makes us weaker psychologically.

In the wake of his own trials, Paul could have concluded: "You know what suffering means? We can't be carefree anymore. If God let this happen once and it almost destroyed us, we certainly can't trust him again. If it happens again, it will destroy us! We have to watch our own backsides. Our lives depend on never letting anything like this happen again." This conclusion would have filled Paul's heart with fear and pressure and caused him to lead a very different life. Such a view of suffering would have left Paul (as it would us) self-absorbed and psychologically impaired!

Fear of suffering needlessly multiplies our pain. It adds "virtual suffering" to our lives because we live in a constant state of dread, scanning the horizon for any number of things we imagine will destroy us. We make our suffering even harder to bear than it has to be.

Leah Henderson, a former student of mine, serves as a mental health advocate. In a recent e-mail she described to me the self-protective cycle that magnifies the suffering of hurting people:

I see it all the time, Kevin, people so self-absorbed in their hurt and pain that they're paralyzed to live. In fact, their hurt and pain *are* their life! They organize their day around their hurts. The deeper the pain, the more protection they think they need. The more protection they think they need, the more self-absorbed they become. The more self-absorbed they become, the less they're able to love. The less they're able to love, the less lovable they are. The less lovable they are, the more they are likely to be hurt . . . and the cycle starts all over again.

What effect does past suffering have on the way you live your life? Do you try to avoid suffering in any way that makes your life harder?

AN OPERATING THEATER FOR OUR HEARTS

Since Jesus went through everything you're going through and more, learn to think like him. Think of your sufferings as a weaning from that old sinful habit of always expecting to get your own way. Then you'll be able to live out your days free to pursue what God wants instead of being tyrannized by what you want. (Peter, 1 Peter 4:1-2, MSG)

The apostle Peter wrote an entire letter to Christians to give them reasons for welcoming suffering instead of fearing it. He said, "Do not fear what [people who don't know Christ] fear . . . After you have suffered a little while [the God of all grace] will himself restore you and make you strong, firm and steadfast" (1 Peter 3:14; 5:10, NIV). According to Peter, suffering is God's graduate school of maturity for Christians where he equips us to be the kind of people he created us to be.

In this letter, Peter describes three ways suffering can have incredible value and meaning in our lives:

(1) It deepens **our faith** — our conviction that God is trustworthy and sufficient when we have nothing else to sustain us (1:6-7);

(2) It matures **our love** — our capacity to endure hardships and difficulties for the purpose of furthering God's purposes in other people's lives (2:21 – 3:3);

(3) It purifies **our hope** — our confidence that the suffering he asks us to endure for him now is small compared to the benefits it will reap later (3:13-16).

Peter explains that suffering is both God's crucible and fish bowl. He uses our troubles to shape us into the kind of people he wants us to be *while our world watches*. When we allow him to, he turns any difficult circumstance into an operating theater for our hearts.

Even though Job chose to spend a great deal of his time and energy complaining bitterly about the troubles in his world, his heart was ultimately transformed by the new way he encountered God in the midst of his troubles (Job 42:1-6). When Job was finally granted an audience with God, he could hardly speak (40:3-5). His suffering, complaints, questions, and needs suddenly melted into insignificance. The few words he managed to speak to God said it all: "My ears had heard of you but now my eyes have seen you. Therefore I despise myself and repent in dust and ashes" (42:5-6, NIV). Job became a changed man because his suffering gave him the opportunity to see both himself and God in a new light. This wouldn't have happened apart from suffering.

Speaking from her wheelchair to a large gathering of Christian counselors about her own suffering, Joni Eareckson Tada explained: "Our problems are not about something. They're about someone . . . You don't start believing with answers, but with assurances . . . assurances that there is an order to our painful reality that makes sense . . . that God allows suffering to come between [him] and us, so that nothing else comes between [him] and us."[2]

God wants to use our suffering to produce unimaginable changes in our hearts. He doesn't do this by answering our questions when we suffer. Instead, he becomes the solution to the problem that suffering exposes in our hearts — the trouble that comes from trying to make our lives work apart from him.

What's the most important thing suffering has taught you about yourself and God?

MAKING SENSE OF OUR SUFFERING

To keep me from becoming conceited . . . there was given me a thorn in my flesh . . . Three times I pleaded with the Lord to take it away from me. But he said to me, "My grace is sufficient for you, for my power is made perfect in weakness." (2 Corinthians 12:7-9, NIV)

Suffering makes no more sense to someone who thinks his soul is in fine shape than surgery does to someone who has no physical ailments. In a prosperous or pain-free environment, we can maintain the illusion that our souls need no major surgery. This is why God places us in a world where happiness is precarious; it's his way of making us look outside ourselves for something to make us complete. He wants us to learn that real life is found only in him, rather than in the gifts he gives us for sustenance and pleasure.

Our arrogance makes it tricky for God to give us gifts. As sinners, we invariably take credit for any good thing he does for us. We even use it to maintain our independence from him. No wonder then, as Paul tells us, when God chooses to grace us with gifts, he ingeniously makes sure "thorns in the flesh" accompany them in order to keep them from strengthening our arrogance (2 Corinthians 12:7).

A "thorn in the flesh" is any kind of suffering or affliction that attacks or weakens our capacity to live independently of God (12:8-9). According to Paul, thorns in the flesh come in at least five varieties (12:10): "weaknesses" (physical infirmities), "insults" (relational difficulties), "hardships" (natural disasters and economic difficulties), "persecutions" (physical violence), and "difficulties" (emotional distress). Sometimes we experience multiple thorns at the same time.

God used thorns to great benefit in a close friend's life. Craig was a gifted pastor, counselor, and author. While he was careful to present himself to others as a humble man, in his heart he took great pride in the way he was able to help others. Contrary to his own teaching, he believed that his success came from his own goodness.

No one would have ever suspected that Craig was an arrogant man until his marriage began to disintegrate. Suddenly, everything Craig depended on for his sense of moral superiority was threatened: his "model" marriage and family, his control over every detail of his life, his status as a pastor and author. Craig panicked. He felt stripped of everything that made life worthwhile and soon withdrew from everyone he knew. "How could anyone respect me if I can't keep my own marriage together? I'm no good to anyone." Craig's troubles exposed how much he was depending on his own accomplishments instead of God.

It took almost a year for Craig to recognize the depth of his arrogance. When he received word that his last appeal for reconciliation with his wife failed, he wanted to scream at God. One night on an empty beach, that's what he did. He fell on his knees and shouted toward heaven, "God! I hate you for taking away everything I loved and depended on!" Then he shook his fist at God and yelled, "I dare you to come down here right now and finish me off! I have no use for you or this life any more."

Then the most remarkable thing happened. God visited Craig, but in a way he didn't expect. Instead of coming to punish, he came to comfort. Jesus spoke with a tenderness that Craig hadn't experienced before: "Now that you know how bad you really are, how much you hate me and deserve nothing but my wrath, maybe you can understand what grace is. I'll be everything you need, not because you deserve it, but because I love you as a son." At that moment Craig experienced the truth of Paul's words: "I count as worthless everything I had to lose in order to gain the priceless experience of knowing Christ Jesus my Lord" (Philippians 3:8).

When God speaks to us in our suffering, he offers us comfort and life in the way we least expect. Instead of delivering us from the *pain* in our world, he delivers us from the *stain* on our soul. He uses our suffering to free us from our dependence on everything but him. Oswald Chambers calls this "the place of destitution." He writes, "It is not that God *will not* do anything for us until we get there, but that he *cannot*. God can do nothing for me if I am sufficient for myself. When we come to the place of destitution spiritually, we find the Lord waiting, and saying, 'If any man thirst, let him come unto Me and drink.'"[3]

What kind of suffering is God using to teach you to depend on him instead of yourself?

BREAKING THE RULES

Friends, when life gets really difficult, don't jump to the conclusion that God isn't on the job. Instead, be glad that you are in the very thick of what Christ experienced. This is a spiritual refining process, with glory just around the corner. (Peter, 1 Peter 4:12, MSG)

Job and his counselors shared the belief that good people shouldn't have to suffer. In their belief system there could be only one purpose for human suffering—to punish wickedness. They believed that they could prevent suffering by living a good life. Before his afflictions struck, Job was a man everyone considered blameless, upright, and God-fearing (Job 1:1). He regularly made sacrifices to atone for sins that he and his children might have unknowingly committed. He kept all the rules! It just didn't make sense that Job, of all people, would have to suffer.

Job and his counselors couldn't conceive of anything beneficial coming from good people suffering (Job 5:17-18). They came to bitterly disagree on why an apparently decent and righteous man would suffer so greatly. Job tried to resolve this contradiction by contending that it was God who'd broken the rules. God must have wronged him and unjustly subjected him to a fate that should only fall to the wicked (19:6-7). Job accused God of being both unjust and unloving toward him (33:8-13).

Job's counselors, however, tried to resolve the contradiction by attacking Job's character instead of God's. They figured that Job must be the one who broke the rules (Job 22:4-5). The longer Job spoke bitterly about God, the more this seemed likely.

Elihu, a younger man who listened for hours as Job and his counselors debated, finally challenged the rules they were applying to human suffering. He reminded them that God uses suffering to great benefit not only in the lives of the wicked, but also in the lives of the godly (Job 33:29-30). Further, God exercises this prerogative without ever compromising his just and loving nature. Whether righteous or wicked, people have no way of choosing when or where their own suffering occurs, no matter what set of rules they follow.

Through a conversation that occurred between God and Satan before Job's trials began (Job 1 and 2), we see why God allowed Job to suffer so greatly (and why God allows us to suffer as well). God was giving Job the opportunity to do something he couldn't do in any other circumstance — attain and display a level of faith that would enable him to trust and worship God even when there was no material reason to do so.

God uses suffering in our lives to accomplish things that paradise or prosperity never can. The benefit doesn't depend on knowing exactly *why* God allows suffering to come into our lives. Rather it depends on knowing *how* God wants us to respond when suffering comes. Whatever the timing and nature of our affliction, we can rest in knowing that when we respond to suffering the way God asks, he will add great maturity, meaning, and joy to our lives.

Elihu spoke life-words to Job when he spoke of the mercy God makes available to sufferers: "Those who suffer he delivers *in* their suffering [note: not *from* their suffering]; he speaks to them *in* their affliction. He is wooing you from the jaws of distress to a spacious place free from restriction, to the comfort of your table laden with choice food" (Job 36:15-16, NIV, emphasis added). Betsy Ten Boom comforted fellow inmates in a concentration camp during World War II, with words reminiscent of Elihu's: "There is no pit so deep, that He is not deeper still."[4]

What question would you like God to answer about a trial or hardship you've experienced?

ASKING A DIFFERENT QUESTION

While he lived on earth, anticipating death, Jesus cried out in pain and wept in sorrow as he offered up priestly prayers to God. Because he honored God, God answered him. Though he was God's Son, he learned trusting-obedience by what he suffered, just as we do. (Hebrews 5:7-8, MSG)

Meaningless suffering is the hardest to endure. If we see no purpose or value in our suffering, we think and act in destructive ways. Our focus becomes relief. When relief doesn't come, we develop what therapists call psychological "symptoms" or "disorders."

But God uses suffering to purposely and lovingly give us the opportunity to deepen our relationship with him, to develop our character, and to serve him in ways we couldn't or wouldn't on our own. God used suffering to accomplish these very things in the life of his own son, Jesus Christ, even though he was sinless: "Though [Christ] was God's Son, he learned trusting-obedience by what he suffered" (Hebrews 5:8, MSG).

When Nazis imprisoned Betsy Ten Boom for giving sanctuary to Jews, her faith in Christ was tried by the most severe of tests. As her puzzled campmates watched her continue to worship and trust God in the midst of unimaginable suffering, they inquired, "Why did your God send you here?" Her faith provided her with the simplest, but most profound of answers: "To obey him. If you love him, you need no other answer."[5]

We'll never find meaning, purpose, or hope in our suffering by asking fault-finding or problem-solving questions, "Why is this happening to me? How can I get relief from it?" Such questions often reflect an arrogance that says, "God has made some kind of mistake. I don't deserve this. I can get myself out of this if I can just figure out the rule I broke and make proper amends."

However, we'll only begin to find meaning, purpose, and hope in our suffering when we ask questions of a different kind — *questions that focus on our responsibility as sufferers rather than on the causes or cures of our suffering.* Elihu, the youngest and wisest of all of Job's friends, tried to shift Job's focus in this way (Job 35:9-16). Job, however, was too busy trying to convince everybody that he *wasn't* responsible for his suffering to focus on what he *was* responsible for in the midst of his suffering.

Richard Wurmbrand, writing about his ordeal in Nazi and Communist prisons, tells about the question he learned to ask in the midst of suffering:

> "Why suffering?" is a wrong question. No right answer exists for wrong questions. Who can tell the melody of a peach? The question is wrong. Ask instead, "What good can I do with my sorrow? How can I use it to become more loving and more understanding towards others?" As for the rest, accept what Jesus said to Peter: "What I am doing you do not understand now, but you will know after this."[6]

What unique opportunities for serving God and displaying his character to others do your present hardships provide you?

THE RESPONSIBILITY OF SUFFERERS

For it has been granted to you on behalf of Christ not only to believe on him, but also to suffer for him, since you are going through the same struggle you saw I had, and now hear that I still have. (Paul, Philippians 1:29-30, NIV)

Debbie Morris is a woman well acquainted with suffering. In 1980, she and her boyfriend were abducted by two men. These men murdered Debbie's boyfriend and raped her multiple times before she was ultimately freed. In her book, *Forgiving the Dead*

Man Walking, Debbie recounts her ordeal and subsequent journey of faith and forgiveness. She writes, "As I came to believe . . . (that) God was there working and watching all along . . . I found that the basic question I had for God changed as well. Instead of, "Why did this terrible thing happen?" I began asking, "What do you want me to do now in this situation?" . . . I began asking God what he wanted me to do and how he wanted to use the circumstances and experiences of my life."[7]

When we're struggling, life-words help us ask the question servants ask: "While I'm in the midst of these circumstances — which I didn't choose and cannot change — what are my responsibilities to God and where can I find the strength to carry them out?" The answer to this question guides sufferers toward what will bring them real hope and purpose (and psychological health). *It helps them view their troubles the way God does — as unique opportunities to accomplish something for him they couldn't accomplish under any other circumstances.*

When we suffer, we can become so preoccupied with finding relief that we forget about the responsibilities we have as servants of God. Instead of excusing us from our servant duties, suffering brings with it new and harder servant duties for us to perform. We ask, "How can this be fair? Surely God can't expect very much from us when we're suffering; can he?" He does because he's merciful. *The high duties he gives us in the midst of our suffering empower us to transform otherwise senseless tragedies into the most sacred and significant assignments of our lives.* Writing to a friend, C. S. Lewis observed, "We are told that even those tribulations which fall upon us by necessity, if embraced for Christ's sake, become as meritorious as voluntary sufferings . . . if taken in the right way."[8]

Can you recall a time when someone you knew used an otherwise "senseless tragedy" to serve God in some significant way?

SUFFERING'S ULTIMATE OBJECTIVE

Do you want more and more of God's kindness and peace? Then learn to know him better and better. For as you know him better, he will give you, through his great power, everything you need for living a truly good life: he even shares his own glory and his own goodness with us! And by that same mighty power he has given us all the other rich and wonderful blessings he promised; for instance, the promise to save us from the lust and rottenness all around us, and to give us his own character. (Peter, 2 Peter 1:2-4, TLB)

No matter how unbearable suffering seems, we can weather it in a way that enables us to emerge as stronger, healthier people. *How we weather it, however, depends on the kind of meaning we attach to it.*

In his letter to the Philippians, Paul says he learned the secret to being content in any and every situation. He said, "contentment is knowing that whatever my circumstances, I have the power in Christ to do all God is asking me to do in that situation" (Philippians 4:12-13). This is also the reason Paul saw "thorns in the flesh" as good. He wrote, "When my 'thorns' stretch me beyond what I can endure in my own power, it provides opportunity to display to the world what I can do through only God's power" (2 Corinthians 12:9-10).

God doesn't want us to view suffering as the roadblock to knowing happiness. He wants us to see it as the avenue to knowing him and becoming like him — acquiring and displaying a heart that resembles Christ's (Romans 8:17-18). The Bible reminds us that even though no hardship seems pleasant at the time, "it produces a harvest of righteousness and peace for those who have been trained by it" (Hebrews 12:11, NIV).

The words that truly offer life to hurting people are those that help them attach the same significance to suffering that God does — seeing suffering as the tool God uses to make them, as C.S. Lewis put it, into "quite a different person than they ever thought they could be":

> When a man turns to Christ and seems to be getting on pretty well (in the sense that some of his bad habits are corrected), he often feels that it would be natural if things went fairly smoothly. When troubles come along—illness, money troubles, new kinds of temptation—he is disappointed. These things, he feels, might have been necessary to rouse him and make him repent in his bad old days; but why now? . . . Imagine yourself as a living house. God comes in to rebuild that house. At first, perhaps, you can understand what he is doing. He is getting the drains right and stopping the leaks in the roof and so on: you knew that those jobs needed doing and so you are not surprised. But presently he starts knocking the house about in a way that hurts abominably and does not seem to make sense . . . throwing out a new wing here, putting on an extra floor there, running up towers, making courtyards. You thought you were going to be made into a decent little cottage: but He is building a palace. He intends to come and live in it Himself. If we let Him."[9]

What surprises you most about the way God uses suffering in your life?

2

[*t* R o U *b* L e]
[IN THE HEART]

Do not let your hearts be troubled.
Jesus to his disciples, John 14:27, NIV

When hurting people turn to us for help, they're usually pretty good at describing the troubles they're experiencing in the world. But embedded in this description is always evidence of a second set of troubles — the ones in their hearts that Jesus warned us about. Listen to Randy, a young man in his thirties, tell his counselor why he came for help. Beyond the trouble he's experiencing in the world, his words point to deeper troubles.

I've been married about three years now. I'm a youth pastor at a church not far from here. Actually this is my second go-around. After I graduated from Bible college, I took my first youth position right away. It was rough. We were there for just ten months before quitting and moving back in with my parents. Then I got a call from this church. I was a little apprehensive about taking it because of the experience I'd just had. But my wife, Mallory, was really enthusiastic and thought this would be a good opportunity. So I took the position, and I've been in it now for six or seven months. Now Mallory is pregnant. This is actually our second pregnancy— we lost the first one about five months ago.

Things in this ministry aren't going very well either. The youth group isn't really bonding, and I feel a lot of stress about Mallory. She's been in the hospital several times. My pastor's told me I really can't talk about the pregnancy because of the nature of it. I have to put on this face every Sunday that everything is fine—that we're doing well—when we're not. The board has already said that I'm on probation. The church isn't aware of it . . . that there's a possibility that I could lose my job, but the board's going to keep me at least until our baby is born.

I guess I made the wrong decision about going into the ministry. And my wife's pregnant. I have no idea about where to go. I'm coming to you because I obviously have two strikes against me . . . before I'm a total failure. So that's why I'm here—to find out what I should do.

If you were counseling Randy, what would your first sentence be after hearing his sad story?

WHEN TROUBLE JUST WON'T GO AWAY

No trial has come upon you that is not experienced by others as well. And even in this God can be trusted. He will never let you be pushed beyond what you can endure without sinning. When you are tried, he will always provide a way for you to endure without losing your integrity. (Paul, 1 Corinthians 10:13)

When our troubles multiply and persist, where does that leave us? As passive reactors—victims with little power to decide what becomes of us? Far from it. Although Jesus teaches that we can do little to escape the troubles in our world (John 16:33), he says that we can do a lot to escape the troubles in our hearts: "My peace I give you. I do not give to you as the world gives. Do not let your hearts be troubled and do not be afraid" (John 14:27, NIV).

No matter how painful or restricting our circumstances, we always retain the freedom to choose how we respond to them. To deny this, as one author observes, means to "reduce people to the level of an animal bound by instinct":

> But I will insist that every adult, no matter how unfortunate a childhood he had or how habit-ridden he may be, is free to make choices about his life. . . . To say of Hitler, to say of the criminal, that he did not choose to be bad but was a victim of his upbringing is to make all morality, all discussion of right and wrong, impossible. It leaves unanswered the question of why people in similar circumstances did not all become Hitlers. But worse, to say "It is not his fault; he was not free to choose" is to rob a person of his humanity, and reduce him to the level of an animal who is similarly not free to choose between right and wrong.[1]

Although our choices may seem limited, we always have a choice available to us that prevents our heart from becoming as troubled as our world. This is why Paul, in the midst of totalitarian oppression and persecution, could write to the Corinthians: "We are afflicted on every side, but not crushed; confused, but not in despair; mistreated, but not abandoned; struck down, but not snuffed out. We always experience sufferings similar to those Jesus experienced, to give God the opportunity to perfect and display the life and character of Jesus in us" (2 Corinthians 4:8-10).

The condition of our hearts isn't determined by the amount or type of suffering we experience or escape. *It's determined by the way we respond to suffering.* As long as we control our mental faculties, no one can rob us of the dignity and privilege of this kind of self-determination.

Our response to suffering shapes our character and determines our psychological or spiritual health. This doesn't mean that all the problems we experience are due to character or spiritual problems. Sometimes, disturbances in thought, behavior, or emotions can be caused by biological problems over which we have little control. But these are rare. Normally, our souls remain very much in control of these faculties, as well-known psychiatrist William Glasser observes:

> We choose essentially everything we do, including the behaviors that are commonly called mental illnesses . . . What is labeled as mental illness, regardless of the causation, are the hundreds of ways people choose to behave when they are unable to satisfy basic genetic needs, such as love and power, to the extent they want.[2]

When are you most tempted to believe, "I don't have a choice. I have to be this kind of person"? What does it mean to you that suffering can't take away your freedom to choose what kind of person you will be?

THE POWER TO DELIGHT GOD

Then the Lord asked Satan, "Have you noticed my servant Job? He is the finest man in all the earth—a good man who fears God and will have nothing to do with evil." (Job 1:8, TLB)

The Bible tells us only people are made in God's image (Genesis 1:26-27). This means God gives us the incredible privilege of exercising sovereignty over our character, choosing what kind of people we want to be.

Like a proud father, God called Satan's attention to the sterling character of Job (Job 1:8). God found particular delight with Job's choice to respond to his gifts with an attitude of thankfulness and service, instead of an attitude of arrogance and self-indulgence.

Our freedom to choose what kind of people we want to be gives us the power to delight God in ways no other creatures do. C. S. Lewis writes, "A world of automata — of creatures that worked like machines — would hardly be worth creating. The happiness which God designs for His higher creatures is the happiness of being free, voluntarily united to Him and to each other . . . And for that they must be free."[3]

What opportunities have you had to bring God delight? How do you know when you're doing this?

SUFFERING AND INTEGRITY

Then the Lord said to Satan, "Have you considered my servant Job? . . . He still maintains his integrity, *though you incited me . . . to ruin him . . ." "Skin for skin!" Satan replied. . . . "Stretch out your hand and strike his flesh and bones, and he will surely curse you to your face." (Job 2:3-5, NIV, emphasis added)*

In the first two chapters of the book of Job we read how Satan, God's sworn enemy, tried to rob God of his joy in Job. Satan asserted that Job's character would change if he were forced to endure great suffering. Satan was banking on the fact that people are usually too weak psychologically to maintain a healthy response to suffering for very long — and often too arrogant to ask for God's help.

It's hard to tell how spiritually or psychologically sound

people really are when we see them in pleasant circumstances. Most people look and sound pretty good when they're getting their own way.

Satan claimed that Job wasn't as psychologically healthy as he seemed. So God agreed to put Job's character to the test by subjecting him to great suffering. God uses suffering to expose the true condition of our hearts. This isn't for his information; it's for ours. He knows what's in our hearts before our troubles expose it. Job's suffering exposed that while he had the maturity to worship and serve God in times of great prosperity, he lacked the maturity or character to do so in times of great suffering.

Early on, Job managed to hold on to his integrity. He called God good, in spite of his physical circumstances. He didn't curse God or sin (see Job 1:22). Even when his wife chided him for continuing to trust God in a situation that was quickly moving from bad to worse, his response to her reflected a soul at peace: "Shall we accept good from God, and not trouble?" (2:10). His response was psychologically sound! Instead of allowing the troubles in his world to govern his life, he chose to be governed by the truths of God. This is the essence of integrity.

But as the suffering wore on day after day, something in Job's soul began to change. Eventually, his arrogance got the best of him, and Job made it his goal to end his suffering. He tried to convince God that the suffering was unfair and should stop (see Job 35:9-16; 36:13). When that didn't work, he defended his character against the charge that he'd brought this misfortune upon himself (27:2-7; 33:8-14; 40:8). Then Job chose to believe his suffering was proof that God was doing something wrong (9:21-24; 10:1-4; 19:6-7). He decided to speak bitterly about God and everyone around him (6:15-17; 10:1-2) and put his own life in jeopardy (13:13-16). He attached feelings of dread (3:25), despair (6:14), shame (10:15), hopelessness (6:11-13; 17:11-16), and terror (23:15-17) to the circumstances God was using to help him and his friends grow. By choosing this response to his suffering, Job made himself psychologically sick! As his response to suffering deteriorated, so did his character.

The privilege of self-determination not only gave Job the power to delight God, it gave him the power to grieve God. Lewis explains why God gives us this kind of power: "God created things which had free will . . . If a thing is free to be good it is also free to be bad. And free will is what has made evil possible. Why, then, did God give them free will? Because free will, though it makes evil possible, is also the only thing that makes possible any love or goodness or joy worth having."[4]

What kind of person are you when you're in pain? What does this reveal about your spiritual or psychological health?

SUFFERING, EVIL, AND PSYCHOLOGICAL PROBLEMS

[Jesus] then began to teach them that the Son of Man must suffer many things . . . and Peter took him aside and began to rebuke him. But when Jesus turned . . . he rebuked Peter. "Get behind me, Satan. . . You do not have in mind the things of God, but the things of men." (Mark 8:31-33, NIV, emphasis added)

The Bible attributes the genesis of psychological problems to the choices we make when we suffer. When we make it our priority to avoid pain or seek our own comfort, our thoughts, behaviors, and emotions become servants of this cause alone. When Peter tried to convince Jesus to avoid suffering as his top priority, Jesus called him "Satan." In choosing to put "the things of men before the things of God," Peter became his own worst enemy. At that moment, his character reflected Satan's, not Christ's.

As his sufferings wore on, Job felt justified to choose thoughts and behaviors he wouldn't have under other circumstances. As a result, he created for himself the kind of psychological disturbance that Paul warned the early Christians to avoid: "For those who are self-seeking and who reject truth and follow evil, there will be wrath and anger. There will be trouble and distress for every human being who does evil" (Romans 2:8-9, NIV).

People are amazingly resourceful and ingenious when it comes to inventing ways to control or minimize the troubles in their world. They use a number of strategies. Here are the four most common (there are many others):

Option 1: Try to remove themselves from the source of their suffering (primarily using avoidance behaviors).

Option 2: Try to get others to rescue them from their suffering (using dependent behaviors).

Option 3: Try to gain a sense of control over their suffering by making other people hurt like they're hurting (using abusive behaviors).

Option 4: Inflict themselves with another kind of suffering, one that they can control, in order to distract themselves from suffering they cannot control (primarily using self-effacing behaviors).

When we try to avoid or escape suffering we literally make ourselves sick. People who choose *option one* often develop anxiety or substance-abuse problems. *Option two* makes people vulnerable to mood and personality problems. Those who choose *option three* often develop antisocial traits and impulse control problems. *Option four* fuels obsessive-compulsive and psychosomatic symptoms.

No matter what strategies we use to try to lessen our pain and satisfy our needs, they ultimately backfire. Instead of creating peace and serenity, we end up making our inner world as empty and destructive as our outer world. James, the brother of Jesus, observed: "For where you have envy and selfish ambition, there you find disorder and every evil practice" (James 3:16, NIV).

When are you tempted to make pain relief your highest priority? What strategy do you use? What does it do to your suffering?

THE PICTURE OF HEALTH

Now my heart is troubled, and what shall I say? "Father, save me from this hour?" No, it was for this very reason I came to this hour. Father, glorify your name!" (Jesus, John 12:27, NIV)

Psychologists have real trouble agreeing on what it means to be psychologically healthy. Hundreds of theories abound about what psychological health looks like and how to achieve it. Apart from the Bible they really have no definitive or authoritative way of determining this.

Observing how Jesus Christ responded to suffering gives us our clearest picture of what it means to be psychologically healthy. The night before Christ went to the cross he was in great agony (see Matthew 26:36-46; Luke 22:39-46). He would soon face the pain of betrayal, desertion, slander, humiliation, and crucifixion. In preparing for this ordeal, he was in so much pain that he perspired blood! Yet he chose to respond to this crisis in every way God wanted him to. This is the true definition of psychological health.

Jesus depended on God for the wisdom and strength he needed (see Luke 22:40-43). He believed that he could trust God to determine when and how he would suffer (see Luke 22:42). He chose to act lovingly and responsibly toward the people around him — including those who contributed to his suffering (see Luke 22:45-51). He experienced feelings (sorrow and joy at the same time) that reflected the true significance of the events that were unfolding — the same significance God was attaching to them (see Hebrews 12:2).

This is how God wants us to respond to suffering. But he won't force us. He lets us choose, even though he knows we'll likely respond as Job did — by hardening our hearts, behaving destructively, injuring our psychological health, and needlessly adding to our own suffering.

Lewis helps us understand why God extends this incredible freedom to us:

> God has made it a rule for Himself that He won't alter people's character by force. He can and will alter them — but only if people let Him . . . He would rather have a world of free beings, with all its risks, than a world of people who did right like machines because they couldn't do anything else. The more we succeed in imagining what a world of perfect automatic beings would look like, the more, I think, we shall see His wisdom.[5]

How does Christ's response to suffering affect you? How do you feel knowing that God can give you the power to respond to suffering as Christ did?

THE ONLY LIMIT TO HUMAN FREEDOM

For I have the desire to do what is good, but I cannot carry it out. For what I do is not the good I want to do; no, the evil I do not want to do — this I keep on doing. Now if I do what I do not want to do, it is no longer I who do it, but it is sin living in me that does it. So I find this law at work: When I want to do good, evil is right there with me. (Paul, Romans 7:18-21, NIV)

One of the oldest debates among psychologists revolves around the strength of the human heart. Do people have hearts or wills strong enough to act independently of adverse influences, or do they have weak hearts that can only react to these influences? In other words, is human character the product of individual choice or the product of forces outside its control? This is really a question about freedom. How free is the human heart to act on its own?

The Bible weighs in on this debate with an answer that differs from all the psychological theories. It teaches that human hearts are free to choose and act independently of every influence except one. We are not free to act independently of our own sinful nature, except with God's help (see Romans 7:24-25).

Because of our sinful nature, we don't have the power to use our rational, volitional, or emotional capacities to serve any long-term cause except one — our own self-gratification (see Ephesians 2:1-3). Our sinful nature uses any hardship or adversity to make the most selfish and cruel acts feel both justifiable and irresistible to us.

When have you experienced the sinful nature restraining your freedom the way Paul did — having the desire to do what is good, but not able to carry it out?

THE COUNSELOR WITHIN US

It wasn't so long ago that we ourselves were stupid and stubborn, dupes of sin, ordered every which way by our glands, going around with a chip on our shoulder, hated and hating back. But when God, our kind and loving Savior God, stepped in, he saved us from all that. It was all his doing; we had nothing to do with it. He gave us a good bath, and we came out of it new people, washed inside and out by the Holy Spirit. Our Savior Jesus poured out new life so generously. God's gift has restored our relationship with him and given us back our lives. (Paul, Titus 3:3-7, MSG)

Jesus knows we have no hope of functioning the way God created us to function as long as we're left to our own devices. As he prepared his disciples for his death and ascension into heaven, he promised to give them an able guide and counselor — someone who would enable them to live free of the demands of their sinful nature: "And I will ask the Father, and he will give you another Counselor to be with you forever — the Spirit of truth. The world cannot accept him, because it neither sees him nor knows him. But you know him, for he lives with you and will be in you . . .The Counselor, the Holy Spirit, whom the Father will send in my name, will teach you all things and will remind you of everything I have said to you" (John 14:16-17,26, NIV).

All of us who know Jesus Christ as our Savior and Lord have this counselor, the Holy Spirit, living within us. His mission is to give us the wisdom and power to live and love like Christ in whatever circumstances we find ourselves.

Having this counselor living within us frees us from dependence upon human teachers and counselors to tell us how to run our lives. Human experts often disagree with one another and change their minds as societal values and opinions shift. Seldom are they bold enough to encourage us to do the unconventional and creative things that serving God and loving others requires. Can you imagine a human counselor advising Moses' mother to put her son in a basket and float him down a river into the hands of her enemy? That, no doubt, was the creative counsel of the Holy Spirit.

Counsel from the Holy Spirit and counsel from people often conflict. The Holy Spirit has a fundamentally different goal — to teach us how to live free of the self-protective demands of our human nature instead of how to satisfy them more effectively. Even when human counselors do encourage us to take courageous and selfless steps, they're not able to give us the power to carry them out. Only the Holy Spirit does that.

What does it mean to you to have the wisest and strongest of all counselors living within you? How does it affect the way you live your life?

THE FOUR STRONGEST FORCES IN THE HUMAN HEART

For at the same time I am delighting in my inner being in the law of God, *this other law is at work in me waging war against the* law of my mind *and making me a prisoner to the* law of sin *which has such a strong grip on me. What a wretched man I am! Who will rescue me from this spiritual death? Thanks be to God . . . because through Christ Jesus the* law of the Spirit of Life *frees me from the* law of sin and death. *(Paul, Romans 7:22-25; 8:2, emphasis added)*

In his letter to the Roman Christians, Paul describes a struggle that typifies the same struggle we all experience. In his intimate reflections (see Romans 7:22–8:2), Paul identifies the four forces (he calls them "laws") that vie for dominion of our hearts.

The first force is *the law of God* or the Bible. The law of God arouses our conscience and persuasively calls us to live the way God commands. The Bible describes itself as "living and active and sharper than any two-edged sword, and piercing as far as the division of soul and spirit, of both joints and marrow, and able to judge the thoughts and intentions of the heart" (Hebrews 4:12,

NASB). As powerful and persuasive as this "sword-to-the-heart" can be, Paul tells us there are other forces at work in our hearts that are even stronger. They can resist the law of God and overrule it.

The second force is *the law of our minds*. This force is strong enough to say "no" to the law of God. Our minds can choose to bow to God's authority or to live independently of it. We can serve our own self-interests according to a "bible" of our own making, or we can choose to serve God according to the Bible he has given us. This choice becomes the basis by which we govern our lives.

The two working together, the law of God and the law of our minds, can be a formidable force. Think of it — our minds agreeing with the Bible and resolving to obey it no matter what! We might be tempted to think that nothing could defeat this dynamic duo. However, the third force — *the law of sin and death* — is more formidable than the first two combined. No amount of willpower to keep God's law can resist the gravitational pull of the law of sin and death. Paul tells us the law of sin and death can take our souls hostage and make us do evil no matter how much we'd rather do good. It compels us to sin against others even when we don't want to. In its pursuit of pleasure and power, this dark force separates us from God and kills our capacity to love anyone but ourselves.

Christ alone has the power to release the fourth force, the most powerful of all, into our hearts. When we turn to Christ, surrendering our lives to him and admitting our total inability to be anything but destructive to ourselves and others, he unleashes *the law of the Spirit of life* in our hearts. It comes in like a jet stream, picking us up and giving us the power to defy the gravitational pull of our sinful nature. God's Spirit, the Spirit of life, enables us to be and do things for God we can't do in our own power.

When was the last time you attempted to serve God in a way that you couldn't in your own power? What happened?

TWO COMPETING VOICES

*So I say, live by the Spirit, and you will not gratify the desires of the
sinful nature. For the sinful nature desires what is contrary to the
Spirit, and the Spirit what is contrary to the sinful nature. They are
in conflict with each other, so that you do not do what you want
(Paul, Galatians 5:16-17, NIV)*

Every time we make a decision, two voices compete for our
allegiance: the voice of our sin nature (the law of sin and death)
and the voice of our personal counselor, God's Holy Spirit (the
law of the Spirit of life).

Once the Spirit of life has been unleashed within us, the law
of sin and death loses its power in our lives, but not its voice. It
still calls, from the grave, beckoning us to put the pursuit of
power and pleasure before the pursuit of God and love. While it
no longer has the power to force us, it still uses adversity in our
lives to build a convincing case for living selfishly.

The voice of sin and death always claims to have our best
interest at heart and is masterful at making the "road to death"
look like the "road to life." It tries to convince us that we have
only two options when we're in a painful situation. One option
clearly puts us needlessly in the path of great harm. The other
option is still very selfish, but obviously less dangerous and
more reasonable. The objective is to coax us to choose the lesser
of two evils and even to feel noble about it! This is how sin and
death deceives us into calling evil good.

In the case of Craig, the friend I mentioned in the last
chapter, the voice of sin and death convinced him that he had
only two options: turn a blind eye to his wife's continuing
unfaithfulness or force her to change. Confronted with only
these options, Craig felt justified trying to force his wife to do
what he wanted her to do. Of course, this backfired and only
made her heart harder toward him.

When we listen to the voice of sin and death, we fail to recognize or consider the myriad of options outside of the two it offers. Choosing more creative ways to serve God and to love others doesn't even occur to us.

When was the last time the voice of sin and death convinced you that it was a good idea to do evil? How do you know when this voice is speaking to you?

DEVELOPING AN EAR FOR GOD'S VOICE

Therefore everyone who hears these words of mine and puts them into practice is like a wise man who built his house on the rock. The rain came down, the streams rose, and the winds blew and beat against that house; yet it did not fall, because it had its foundation on the rock. (Jesus, Matthew 7:24-27, NIV)

Often, it's hard to distinguish between the voice of sin and death and the voice of the Spirit of life. The best way to tell the two apart is to listen to what each tells you to do with your fears. Paul gives us this tip in his letter to the Roman Christians: "For you did not receive a spirit that makes you a slave again to fear, but you received the Spirit of sonship" (Romans 8:15, NIV).

The Spirit of life often calls us to walk down roads that seem dangerous. He wants to fill us with the power to live and love in the same courageous ways Jesus does. The voice of sin and death tells us to let our fears rule our lives. The Spirit of life tells us to acknowledge our fears and use them to deepen our dependence on God. Sin and death warn us to protect ourselves because nobody else will. The Spirit of life urges us to boldly do the things that further Christ's purposes in our world, trusting God to protect us. Sin and death tells us to put our own safety and well-being before the interests of others.

As the story of Job unfolds, it's obvious to all of Job's neighbors that he has serious troubles in his world. However, few realize that even more serious troubles are brewing in his heart. A battle is raging for Job's integrity. In the midst of unspeakable suffering, will Job listen to the voice of the God he says he worships and loves? Or will he listen to the voice of his own sinful nature and do whatever's necessary to lessen his suffering?

The hardships each of us experience ignite the same kind of battle in our hearts. We can only win this battle if we do what Job finally chose to do (see Job 42:4) in the midst of suffering: listen to God's voice instead of the voice of sin and death.

Richard Wurmbrand describes what happened when, while starving in a Communist prison, he listened to the Spirit's voice instead of the voice of sin and death:

In the solitary cell under what later became the headquarters of the Central Committee of the Communist Party, I remembered Jesus' words: "When men hate you and revile you, rejoice and leap for joy" (Luke 6:23). It occurred to me that I had neglected a duty. I had rejoiced but not leaped for joy, as Jesus had taught us to do. So I began to dance around the cell. The warden, who kept an eye on me through the peephole in the door, was sure I had gone mad. Guards had orders to behave well toward madmen so that they would not disturb the silence of the prison. To quiet me down, he brought a large loaf of bread, cheese, and two pieces of sugar. Romania should do what all believers are intended to do when in distress. Do nothing practical to remedy a situation that is irremediable. Just praise the Lord, sing and dance in his honor. Angels can take care of the rest. . . . Some will discard such advice as foolishness. But surely it is more practical to be a fool in Christ than to be a "wise" man foolishly angry about what he cannot change.[6]

We speak life-words when we help each other tune in to the voice of the Spirit of life and tune out the voice of sin and death. That's exactly what Elihu offered his friend Job: "God is speaking to you in your affliction . . . He is wooing you from the jaws of distress . . . to the comfort of his table laden with choice food . . . *Listen to his voice!*" (Job 36:15-16; 37:2). Life-words like these have a dual impact. They dispute the counsel that comes from the sinful nature, and they affirm the counsel that comes from the Spirit of life.

How do you know when your counselor within, the Holy Spirit, is speaking to you? How do you help people who are suffering hear his voice?

LOVING OUR ENEMIES INSTEAD OF TRYING TO CHANGE THEM

If you're treated badly for good behavior and continue in spite of it to be a good servant, that is what counts with God. This is the kind of life you've been invited into, the kind of life Christ lived. He suffered everything that came his way so you would know that it could be done, and also know how to do it, step by step. (Peter, 1 Peter 2:21, MSG)

Many times in Scripture, people came to Jesus asking him to change others (see Luke 10:38-41 and 12:13-15). As we often do, they assumed that the character and conduct of those around them were the greatest threat to their well being. Jesus teaches, however, no one has the power to ruin our lives, except one — *ourselves*. We ruin our own lives when we allow our sinful nature to control our character and conduct.

Jesus longs for people to bring the troubles in their hearts, instead of the troubles in their world, to him as the object of their greatest concern. This is what Paul did when he cried out, "What a wretched man that I am. Who can rescue me from my own sinful nature?" (Romans 7:24). Paul acknowledged that rescue from himself was a much greater need than rescue from anyone else. This is the same way Nikolai Horev, a Romanian Christian, learned to pray when he was jailed for his faith:

> Lord, you are my shepherd forever, and I am your sheep forever. May your rod always be in your hand so that when I am in danger, you will protect me from my enemies, or when I stray from your way into wrong paths, either through temptation or through the fear of difficulties, you will use your rod to bring me back to the right way. And should I ever ask you, O Lord, for anything different from what I am asking you now, please ignore it.[7]

This is the kind of heart God wants us to seek from him — one bent on serving him and loving others even when it keeps us in harm's way. The road to life for sufferers requires loving others instead of changing them. While we're ready for God to remove our antagonists, through his Spirit he calls us to love them in ways that promise only to increase our suffering. This is what God asked of both Job (see Job 42:7-9) and Christ (see Matthew 26:40-41) while they were in great pain — to minister to those who were adding to their suffering. This is why life-words to sufferers can easily be mistaken as death-words.

When have you been tempted to believe that another person would ruin your life if you couldn't get him or her to change? How did this affect your relationship with that person?

LIFE-WORDS TO PRISONERS

Those who oppose him [the Lord's servant] must gently instruct, in the hope that God will grant them repentance leading them to a knowledge of the truth, and that they will come to their senses and escape from the trap of the devil, who has taken them captive to do his will. (2 Timothy 2:25-26, NIV)

When I served as a chaplain with the Federal Bureau of Prisons, I often counseled new inmates who were beside themselves with despair — serving the first days of a twenty- or thirty-year sentence. Most new inmates seek solace in any assurances they can get from God or their attorneys that their sentences might be shortened or overturned. Although these assurances might at first seem to be life-words, prisoners who put their hopes in a quick end to their incarceration only grow bitter and more psychologically impaired as their time behind bars accumulates.

People often enter prison enslaved by the darkest of passions — addictions, practices, and perversions of the vilest sorts. Behind bars they have little access to sophisticated rehabilitation programs available outside. Although society calls prisons "correctional institutions," few resources for character correction exist behind their walls. Still, the most secure prison in the world can never deny inmates access to "the way of escape" Jesus offers them. No matter how dark the circumstances, escape is always available from the one thing that has the power to truly ruin their lives — their own sinful human nature.

Jesus' life-words to prisoners are the same as they are for us: "Whoever lays his life down for me will find it" (Luke 9:24). According to Christ, laying down our lives for him (instead of protecting ourselves) is the road to life, whether we're behind physical or figurative bars. We start down this road by taking his hand and letting the same Spirit that empowers him to love, empower us.

For prisoners, walking the road to life means sacrificially loving the staff and inmates that make up their world in whatever ways are available to them. For Craig, struggling with his wife's betrayal, it means laying down his life (instead of trying to get it back) in whatever ways display Christ's love to her.

The Spirit of life stands ready at all times to give us the wisdom and love to walk this road no matter what our circumstances. Speaking life-words to anyone who feels imprisoned by circumstances means helping them discover how the road to life runs right through their present living situation, no matter how restraining it may be.

Joni Eareckson Tada recently told a group of Christian counselors how, as a quadriplegic, she finds the resources to walk this road:

> God has this world rigged for frustration and disappointment so that, tomorrow morning when I wake up . . . and my eyes won't quite be open but I will whisper to God: I don't think I can take another day of this . . . I'm so weary of this pain in the back of my neck and my shoulder. Isn't it enough that I'm paralyzed? I mean, haven't I filled my life's quota for trials? Why do I have to put up with this pain? And so, God, I can't face my friend with a smile this morning. I need you desperately. I require you. I am urgently coming to you for help. Help, Lord Jesus. I don't have a smile for my friend or for anybody this morning. Would you please let me borrow your smile? Cause I don't have one. I need you![8]

Joni's words are reminiscent of something Charles Spurgeon once said: "The Lord's mercy often rides to the door of our hearts upon the black horse of affliction. Jesus uses the whole range of our experience to wean us from earth and woo us to heaven."[9]

When we turn to God for the resources to love in the midst of whatever prison we find ourselves, we experience an intimacy with him that makes whatever it took to get us there seem merciful.

What opportunities do your present difficulties afford you to love others?

What will you need from God to seize these opportunities?

p A *r* T *t* w O :
JESUS AND HUMAN CHANGE

I tell you the truth, unless you change *and become like little children, you will never enter the kingdom of heaven.*
(Jesus to his disciples, Matthew 18:3, NIV, emphasis added)

Jesus' mission is to equip people for a heavenly existence while they're still residents of earth.

While that sounds a bit odd, it's not much different from equipping people for life outside the womb while they're still unborn. They have no idea of the life they're being prepared for once they take their first breath. If life in the womb was the end, no great metamorphosis would be necessary. But it's not. The womb is only a temporary existence for the unborn child. And our earthly life is an incubator — provided by God to prepare us for an existence beyond our wildest imagination.

Interestingly, we're equipped for our heavenly existence the same way we're equipped for our earthly one — by becoming like little children again (Matthew 18:3). Peter describes it this way: "Quit relying on all those things you use to try to make your self-centered existence work (malice, deceit, hypocrisy, envy, and slander). Instead come to God for your nourishment. Feast on his goodness like newborn babies at their mother's breast, so that you'll grow fit and ready for the new existence God wants you to live" (1 Peter 2:1-3).

When we were babies, without our knowing or asking, God carefully fashioned our souls and bodies with everything we needed for our earthly existence. Now he beckons us to let him do it again — prepare us for a much higher level of existence. But this time, he'll only do it with our knowing and asking. God calls us to put ourselves back into his hands — to submit ourselves willingly to a metamorphosis of our inner being that prepares us for a life our minds can barely comprehend.

Jesus' actions and words create in people a willingness and readiness for this kind of existence. His way of relating and speaking emits a magnetic pull, enticing people to seek a radical shift from their self-centered existence to a God-centered one. Those who desire to share in his work must learn to relate and speak as he does.

3

$\big[\,l\,$ I f E - c H a n G i N $g\,\big]$
RELATIONSHIPS

While Jesus was having dinner at Matthew's house, many tax collectors and "sinners" came and ate with him and his disciples. When the Pharisees saw this, they asked his disciples, "Why does your teacher eat with tax collectors and 'sinners'?" On hearing this Jesus said, "It is not the healthy who need a doctor, but the sick. But go and learn what this means: 'I desire mercy, not sacrifice.'"
Matthew 9:10-13, NIV

*J*esus often confused people—especially self-righteous ones—with how he related to those who were considered the dregs of society. The Pharisees, a sect of Jews who sought to be righteous by keeping strict rules requiring separation from anything unrighteous, couldn't understand why Jesus wanted to spend his time with tax collectors and sinners.

For all their faults, the Pharisees did have one thing in common with Jesus: their goal was to get people to live more righteous lives. The conflict between Jesus and the Pharisees centered around *how* people become righteous. The Pharisees wanted to change people through external pressure. They believed, as many behavioral experts do today, that character can be altered by impersonally manipulating environmental forces. The Pharisees couldn't understand why Jesus became so personally involved with people who so obviously needed changing: "Doesn't he know that showing kindness to them will only encourage them to stay the way they are?"

Lacking the courage to speak directly to Jesus, the Pharisees took their concerns to his disciples. But Jesus overheard and answered their question himself. He cited two principles of character change to explain why he works with people the way he does.

THE PRINCIPLE OF NEED

Jesus stood and said in a loud voice, "If anyone is thirsty, let him come to me and drink. Whoever believes in me, as the Scripture has said, streams of living water will flow from within him." By this he meant the Spirit, whom those who believed in him were later to receive. (John 7:37-39, NIV)

First, Jesus mentions the principle of need. He presented it to the Pharisees in a simple observation: "It is not the healthy who *need* a doctor, but the sick." People seek character changes only when convinced they're needed, the same way they seek medical treatment when physically ill.

Of course, the Bible tells us that we all need character changes. We need Jesus to transform our souls because our deeply rooted tendencies are to act in self-serving and destructive ways. Some of us (like the sinners and tax-collectors who ate with Jesus) are acutely aware of this and know we need a soul-doctor. Others of us (like the Pharisees) cling to an illusion that nothing's seriously wrong with our souls. We see no real need for anyone to help us make substantial character changes.

Christ always concentrated his efforts as a "great physician" on the first group. He said, "Blessed are those who hunger and thirst for righteousness" (Matthew 5:6, NIV). He related to people in ways that appealed to their felt-need for a righteous character that only he could give them. The principle of need recognizes that true character change occurs only when we realize something is so desperately wrong with our lives that no one short of God himself—the creator of our souls—can repair them.

What character changes do you need right now? What kind of help do you need from God in order make them?

THE PRINCIPLE OF CHOICE

If anyone chooses *to do God's will, he will find out whether my teaching comes from God or whether I speak on my own. (Jesus, John 7:17, NIV, emphasis added)*

Jesus wrapped his second principle of character change in an expression of his deepest desire for us. He said, "I desire mercy (*voluntary* love), not sacrifice (*forced* love)." In other words, Jesus isn't after coerced acts of compliance. He wants and enjoys freely chosen heartfelt expressions of affection and loyalty.

Relationships that cultivate "voluntary love" are quite different from those that extract "forced love." We cultivate voluntary love by making people aware of their needs and choices; forced love is extracted by making people deny their needs and choices. The second approach can only force people to comply outwardly, but it's powerless to create inward changes. It can never get people to genuinely love.

Parents understand this all too well. We want more from our children than just outward compliance. Through rewards or punishment, we can usually get our kids to alter their behavior and do what we want them to do. But alone, that's never enough to satisfy our parental hearts. We also want their obedience to be voluntary, willing, and even eager. We want them to obey us, help us, and love us — because they want to, not because they have to. Getting our kids to change their conduct is hard enough, but getting them to change the motivations of their heart feels impossible!

This is the principle of choice at work. Like our children, we experience a change of character only when we freely seek it. God never forces it on us, and he doesn't allow anyone else to. Jesus always respects our dignity — our prerogative to choose what kind of people we want to be. Although he has the power to change us at the deepest levels whenever he wants, he chooses to exercise this power only when we invite him to.

The decision to change our character is our own, but the strength to do it is God's. We need a "great physician" for our souls. Even when we resolve to be different, we lack the ability to forge changes in our souls that stand the tests of time, opposition, and adversity. That's why Jesus exhorted Peter to pray for strength (see Matthew 26:41), even after Peter vowed that he would never deny Jesus. On his own, Peter lacked the strength to be the person he vowed he'd be. He ignored Jesus' counsel and ended up denying that he even knew Jesus, his Lord and best friend. He learned the hard way that although God has the power to change people at the deepest levels, he doesn't do it unless he's invited to.

How do you feel about asking God to change you at the deepest levels? What would keep you from doing this?

RELATIONSHIPS AND CHARACTER CHANGE

Jesus said to his disciples: "Things that cause people to sin are bound to come, but woe to that person through whom they come." (Luke 17:1, NIV)

Recent juvenile-crime and school-violence epidemics have awakened a national interest in character development, generating a great deal of literature and research on how families and institutions can foster "good" character. Helping professionals have a growing awareness that the "moral neutrality" they've alleged is a myth. All relationships exert moral influence of one kind or another. Ignoring the moral influence we exert in the lives of students, the people we counsel, or our friends fails to recognize the most important aspect of our relationships: the impact we have on each other's character.

> Neutrality is basically a myth, because therapists' moral biases come through to patients no matter how much they try to hide them. . . . Few seasoned therapists would disagree that the therapist's personality, including what he thinks is important and what he believes about life, are factors which guide the thrust of therapy. Given therapists' considerable moral influence over their patients, it is important that therapists and consumers of the therapy become aware of the values therapists are transmitting.[1]

Paul observed something about the power of human relationships: "Bad friends corrupt good character" (1 Corinthians 15:33). Everyone we encounter is a moral agent of one cause or another. Jesus warns us (see Luke 17:1) to pay close attention to the impact we have on each other's character development. Our relationships are powerful mediums through which we influence each other's moral and spiritual development — for good or for bad.

Which relationships have helped you in your own journey from self-centeredness to God-centeredness? What ingredients made them helpful?

The Secret of Jesus' Relationships

*I am the good shepherd; I know my sheep and my sheep know me — just
as the Father knows me and I know the Father — and I lay down my life for
the sheep. (Jesus' words to the Pharisees, John 10:14-15, NIV, emphasis
added)*

Although all relationships influence character development,
some exert more influence than others. For example, impersonal
relationships (like a high school teacher's relationship with the
150 students she teaches an hour each day) have far less influence on character formation than do more personal relationships (like a parent's relationship with her teenager). We also
know that the ingredients that make relationships most influential in character formation are rarely offered in relationships that
are professional or institutional in nature. This is why children
are generally more influenced in their character development by
their peers than by their teachers, counselors, or pastors. The
more personal the relationship, the more impact it has on character formation.

This is the secret to Jesus' relationships — what makes his
life and words so powerful in our lives. He gets intensely personal with us without violating our dignity (the principle of
choice). His way of relating creates the context for speaking
words that matter — words crafted just for us in our situation.
These are *life-words!*

During a recent interview, well-known pastor and author
Eugene Peterson described the first responsibility of any helper
who desires to speak life-words to someone in distress: "My
task . . . is to get to know her better and to give her life dignity. I
listen. I understand. That's not an insignificant thing in
itself . . . regardless of how bad their problem was or how out of
my depth I was. I wanted to get to know them. They deserve a
pastor who knows them."[2]

People in pain need a spiritual guide who knows them, someone who understands something of the trouble they're having in their world and in their heart, someone who knows how to come alongside them in their suffering and offer very specific hope and direction. In sum, they need a guide who relates to them the way Jesus does.

A clear pattern emerges when we observe Jesus' interactions with troubled people in the Bible. The elements that characterize his pattern of relating to people are the same factors that are most influential in promoting positive character development. Jesus' model of counseling is fundamentally a character-directed model. His goal is always to help people experience a character change in the midst of whatever trouble they're going through. His tool is the relationship he offers them — a relationship characterized by nine character-shaping ingredients.

How would you characterize your own counseling relationships? How are these relationships unique from your other relationships?

INGREDIENT #1: HAND SELECTION

Jesus went out to a mountainside to pray, and spent the night praying to God. When morning came, he called his disciples to him and chose twelve of them, whom he also designated apostles. (Luke 6:12-13, NIV)

Since the work of character-transformation always requires a great investment of time and energy, Jesus exercised great discretion in choosing those he offered the gift of counseling. Before Jesus chose his disciples, he spent time interacting with them and praying (see Luke 6:12-13). Guided by the principles of choice and need, Jesus hand-selected those who demonstrated a willingness and readiness to leave their old way of life and begin a new one (see John 15:16).

Troubled people can find counselors in many places today—mental health centers, social agencies, hospitals, counseling offices, guidance centers. But these counselors are rarely allowed to exercise personal discretion in choosing who they counsel. Arbitrary policies, economic considerations, and insurance restrictions too often dictate the people they can see and for how long.

Counseling relationships are too important and too costly to allow circumstances, economics, or accidents to govern them. Counselors must carefully invest their time and energy where they will bring the greatest return. This is why Jesus' pattern was to prayerfully hand-select those he counseled.

How do you decide whom you will spend time mentoring or counseling? What criteria do you use?

INGREDIENT #2: INTIMATE INVOLVEMENT

Jesus went up on a mountainside and called to him those he wanted, and they came to him. He appointed twelve . . . that they might be with him. *(Mark 3:13-14, NIV, emphasis added)*

In Hebrew, Jesus' name is Immanuel, meaning "God with us." "Withness" goes to the very heart of how Jesus (and anyone who wants to do his work) accomplishes God's mission in people's lives. Instead of standing aloof or detached, Jesus gets intimately involved with those who desire to change.

Paul describes what this looks like in a friendship-counseling relationship: "We were gentle among you, like a mother caring for her little children. We loved you so much that we were delighted to share with you not only the gospel of God but our lives as well" (1 Thessalonians 2:7-8, NIV).

When the practice of psychology first began, the founders intended to promote deep character change in people. To accomplish this, they knew they had to cultivate intensely personal relationships, requiring several hours of intimate conversation each week over a period of years (which, by the way, still doesn't come close to the kind of time Jesus spent with his disciples). Today, most schools of psychology have abandoned character change as a therapeutic goal, admitting that they don't have the resources or knowledge to affect deep changes in people's hearts. Professional boundaries, economic limitations, and the rejection of spiritual resources have reduced the goals of secular psychology to relieving symptoms and stabilizing crises.

This leaves Christian churches and ministries the only places in our society where help to transform character can be found. But we need to be careful not to model our ministries and intervention programs after the impersonal and professional models secular helping institutions use. If we do, we'll fail to provide the intimate, one-on-one relationships and small-group environments that promote character change.

Today, large-group events are the mainstay of church ministries. As these address from a biblical perspective the heart issues people wrestle with, they can help to start the ball of character-change rolling. Jesus often used large-group instruction to awaken people to their needs and choices. Preaching and teaching are like the big guns of a battleship; these large-group events can soften people's defenses and shatter their resistance. But people quickly rebuild their defenses if the "naval bombardment" isn't followed closely by "marines" who storm ashore and take territory yard-by-yard through hand-to-hand combat.

That's what many churches lack today — marines who are trained to get in the trenches with broken people and help them win their hearts back. Jesus' counseling relationships always involved this kind of combat — intimate personal assaults on the things in people's hearts that make them captive to sin and selfishness. Solomon, the wisest of all the Hebrew kings, once observed that "a wise man attacks the city of the mighty and pulls down the stronghold in which they trust" (Proverbs 21:22, NIV). We learn from Jesus' example that this means climbing into the trenches *with* people — getting involved in the troubling details of their lives, and knowing them intimately in their natural surroundings.

The Bible admonishes us to "consider how to spur one another on toward love and good deeds" (Hebrews 10:24). We can't do this without getting to know each other intimately. A gesture or word that spurs one of us to love might be the exact thing that provokes another of us to sin. Friendship counselors never employ a "one-size-fits-all" approach to help people grow.

How has intimate involvement by others in times of trouble contributed to your own character development? How can you offer this kind of involvement to others?

INGREDIENT #3: OPEN MORAL INTENT

Come, follow me . . . and I will make you *fishers of men. (Jesus' invitation to his disciples, Matthew 4:19, NIV, emphasis added)*

Jesus never hid his intentions. From the outset, he made it clear what he was up to. He never invites someone into relationship without fully disclosing his agenda. Paul followed this pattern as well: "With God's help we put our necks on the line to speak truth to you in spite of strong resistance. For our counsel did not spring from error or hidden motives, nor were we trying to trick you . . . We never tried to hide or disguise what we were doing" (1 Thessalonians 2:2-5).

Many psychologists believe that the greatest obstacle to helping people overcome their psychological problems is "resistance." People tend to resist change even when they say they want it. They're afraid to give up their troubling behaviors, thoughts, or emotions because of the dangers it might expose them to. For example, a wife unable to leave her home because of panic attacks may resist getting over them because of the attention they elicit from her husband. She fears that if she gets better, her marriage might return to the same condition it was in before the attacks began.

Psychologists have devised two symptom-directed approaches — direct and indirect — to deal with resistance to change. The direct approach is to make people aware of their resistance by calling it to their attention and helping them face the fears behind it. This doesn't necessarily end the resistance, but it usually softens it. In the case of the woman with the panic attacks, the direct approach is to help her face her fear of losing her husband's love by encouraging her to replace her panic attacks with more direct and assertive ways to improve the quality of her marriage.

The indirect approach attempts to circumvent people's resistance altogether. The counselor keeps the process mysterious, never letting the people he's counseling know what he's up to. When he admonishes them to change a thought or behavior, it's something he really doesn't want them to change at all. The counselor intentionally makes his prescription distasteful so the counselee will resist and do the opposite. He might admonish the panic-phobic wife to do even less for herself to get her husband to give her even more attention. "Without constant pressure on your husband," the counselor might warn, "you may find out that he doesn't really love you — and that would be too horrible to ever face."

Jesus' approach was never symptom-directed. He invited people into a relationship with the open intention of remaking the inner person: "Follow me, and I will make you into something you never dreamed you could be" (Matthew 4:19). When people resisted his invitation, he respected their decision and let them try to make their lives work on their own terms. Meanwhile, he waited with open arms — looking forward to the day they would come to their senses, recognize their bankruptcy, give up their resistance, and return to him willing and ready for change.

Offering this kind of relationship to the wife with panic attacks would mean clarifying that the objective in helping her is not to end her attacks or make her marriage more satisfying. It's to help her use her panic attacks and marriage problems to become a different kind of woman — a woman who loves self-lessly even in the face of great fear and rejection. Accomplishing this would no doubt make a huge impact on her panic attacks and marriage, but only as a by-product of attaining the main objective: the remaking of her character.

Think of a friend you're currently counseling or mentoring. Can you both put into words the objective of your work together? Is it character-directed or symptom-directed?

INGREDIENT #4: PERSONAL MODELING

I have set you an example that you should do as I have done for you. I tell you the truth, no servant is greater than his master. (Jesus' instruction to his disciples, John 13:15-16, NIV)

Jesus always models the things he asks others to do. This is how his disciples were able to write whole books about the intimate details of his life. Jesus invited them to stand right beside him through the trials of his life. They observed what real love looks like in the face of loneliness, poverty, loss, criticism, hunger, separation, disappointment, abandonment, betrayal, injustice, and torture. They studied Jesus in all of these situations — they heard his thoughts, felt his emotions, and observed his choices. Jesus was helping them build a new mental model for living and loving—a model radically different from the consumer model their world extolled.

Cultures and families seldom provide healthy models of what it means to truly love one another. Even Paul, who knew thousands of Christians in his day, was hard-pressed to come up with more than one genuinely loving person he could send to encourage a young church: "I hope in the Lord Jesus to send Timothy to you soon. . . . I have no one else like him, who takes a genuine interest in your welfare. For *everyone looks out for his own interests,* not those of Jesus Christ" (Philippians 2:19-21, NIV, emphasis added).

Paul knew how important it is to give people a model of the life God is calling them to live. He instructed Timothy: "Teach believers with your life: by word, by demeanor, by love, by faith, by integrity. . . . Cultivate these things. Immerse yourself in them. The people will all see you mature right before their eyes! Keep a firm grasp on both your character and your teaching" (1 Timothy 4:11,15-16, MSG).

In counseling relationships, we only have two tools to affect people's lives: our character and our words. Paul admonished Timothy to develop both in plain sight so people could see his progress. Paul was asking Timothy to be a *coping model* for others.

Modeling is one of the most effective ways to teach complex skills. Learning how to love may be the most complex of all skills. That's why Scripture often calls Jesus the "living word of God." In human flesh, Jesus provides us a perfect picture of the character God wants to reproduce in us. Jesus is our *mastery model.*

From the start, mastery models flawlessly demonstrate how to do something complex. Coping models demonstrate the same thing—but with flaws, setbacks, improvements, and gradual mastery. Mastery models help people see the end goal. Coping models show them how to get there.

God provides us with both kinds of models for loving others. Jesus is our mastery model. His servants—like Paul and Timothy, as well as the godly counselors, teachers, and friends he sends into our lives—are our coping models. Both show us the fruit he'll produce in our lives if we let him.

There's no more effective way to give troubled people a model of how God wants to transform them than to let them see him transforming us in the midst of our troubles. C. S. Lewis describes it this way:

> He works on us in all sorts of ways. But above all, He works on us through each other. Men are mirrors, or "carriers" of Christ to other men. Usually it is those who know Him that bring Him to others. This is why the Church, the whole body of Christians, showing Him to one another, is so important.[3]

What coping models have been the most influential in your life? How are you serving as a coping model for the people you are counseling?

INGREDIENT #5: MORAL INSIGHT

Jesus asked [his disciples]: "Why are you talking about having no bread? Do you still not see or understand? Are your hearts hardened? Do you have eyes but fail to see, and ears but fail to hear? And don't you remember? When I broke the five loaves for the five thousand, how many basketfuls of pieces did you pick up?" "Twelve," they replied. "And when I broke the seven loaves for the four thousand, how many basketfuls of pieces did you pick up?" They answered, "Seven." He said to them, "Do you still not understand?" (Mark 8:17-21, NIV)

Everything we say and do reflects the moral condition of our hearts. Even seemingly innocent requests, comments, or actions (like Jesus' disciples discussing their shortage of food provisions) can reflect something about the beliefs that govern us — beliefs about God and his willingness to take care of us. Like Jesus' disciples, we can be so focused on what's going on around us we fail to notice what's going on inside us.

Jesus relates to people in a way that shifts their focus from what's going on in their *world* to what's going on in their *hearts*. Solomon described it this way: "The purposes of a man's heart are deep waters, but a man of understanding draws them out" (Proverbs 20:5, NIV). Jesus' way of working with people "draws out" what controls them at the deepest levels.

Helping people shift their focus is essential to character growth. For example, if parents come to us for help to change their child's behavior, the kind of relationship we offer them is critical. We can either focus on helping them control what they really can't control — the kind of person their child chooses to be. Or we can help them focus on the one thing that they can control — the kind of parent they choose to be. The first choice will only increase the parents' desperation, reinforcing their belief that their child's ultimate well-being is in their hands, not God's. But the second choice helps the parents to grow in character, helping them overcome the things in their own heart that keep them from being the parent their troubled child needs them to be.

While Jesus doesn't want us to dwell only on our own needs and feelings, he actively encourages us to monitor moral forces inside us that control and shape our choices. "Watch out," Jesus once warned a man, "Be on your guard against all kinds of selfish desires" (Luke 12:15). Apart from watching our own hearts, we have no way of knowing what kind of people we really are.

People will never recognize how much they need Christ's healing touch until they get a true glimpse of how their own heart operates. And for that they need a guide—intimate interaction with someone who helps them explore their heart with the same map Jesus uses.

We can't spend time with Jesus without learning more about our own hearts. Jesus never relates to us on the basis of what we look like outside—presentable or unpresentable, poor or rich, old or young, healthy or sick, dark or pale, attractive or ugly, organized or disorganized. None of these indicate the true condition of our hearts. Instead, Jesus relates to us on the basis of the things that give our hearts their character—the directions our lives are going, the causes we're serving, the purposes that motivate us to do what we do. Friendship-counseling relationships that follow Jesus' pattern guide people to reflect on these things.

What kinds of interactions give you the most insight into yourself? How do you use your relationships to help others better understand their own hearts?

INGREDIENT #6: MORAL RESPONSIBILITY

I chose you and appointed you to go and bear fruit—fruit that will last. . . . This is my command: Love each other. *(Jesus' to his disciples, John 15:16-17, NIV, emphasis added)*

Jesus never charged people for his time or services. But that doesn't mean that a relationship with Jesus isn't costly. A relationship with Jesus carries with it one great responsibility: *Get better at loving*—especially in ways that don't come naturally.

The ultimate measure of a friendship-counseling relationship is how effectively it helps people fulfill their responsibility to love others. It is reported that Sigmund Freud's greatest regret about his approach to counseling was that it failed to help people become more loving.[4]

Too often, counseling relationships relieve hurting people of their responsibility to love, encouraging them to think of themselves as victims who have no responsibility to love those who hurt them. When Jesus counsels us, he never lets us use our suffering to exempt ourselves from the responsibility to love — even our enemies! Rather, he shows us how to use our suffering to deepen our love for others.

Above all other virtues, Jesus values love, because love is the root of all other virtues. Love is the only engine strong enough to energize our hearts to think and act the way God designed us to. A relationship with Jesus means being in an environment that constantly spurs us to grow in our capacity to love. Paul described it this way: "Now about brotherly love we do not need to write you, for you yourselves have been taught by God to love each other. . . . Yet we urge you, brothers, to do so more and more" (1 Thessalonians 4:9-10, NIV).

"Loving more and more" means expanding both the depth and breadth of our love — getting better at loving the people we already love and better at expanding our love to include people we find difficult to love. Of course, we're incapable of expanding either without God's help. Lewis once wrote, "No man knows how bad he is till he has tried very hard to be good."[5]

Jesus doesn't expect us to love by "trying really hard to be good." He knows that we can't generate love through mere human effort or ingenuity. God transfuses love from his heart to ours through intimate communion. Peter reminded the early Christians of this: "Now you can have real love for everyone because your souls have been cleansed from selfishness and hatred when you trusted Christ . . . so see to it that you really do love each other warmly, with all your hearts. For you have a new life. It was not passed on to you from your parents, for the life they gave you will fade away. This new one will last forever, for it comes from Christ" (1 Peter 1:22-23, TLB).

One essential element of all nurturing relationships is expectations. For example, without parental expectations, children often fail to develop their potential. In the same way, expectations are essential in relationships that nurture character development. Paul describes it this way: "For you know that we dealt with each of you as a father deals with his own children, encouraging, comforting and urging you to live lives worthy of God, who calls you into his kingdom and glory" (1 Thessalonians 2:11-12, NIV). Jesus constantly calls us to love in ways that are outside our present range of ability. The healthier our character grows, the higher he raises the bar. This is how he keeps our hearts continually growing to resemble his.

How do you measure the effectiveness of your mentoring/counseling relationships? What role does love play in measuring and promoting your friends' health?

INGREDIENT #7: PRESCRIBED SELFLESSNESS

When Jesus had called the Twelve together, he gave them power and authority . . . and he sent them out . . . village to village, preaching the gospel and healing people everywhere. . . . When the apostles returned, they reported to Jesus what they had done. (Luke 9:1,6,10, NIV)

People turn to others for help when they lack the power to control something important to them: their circumstances, the people in their lives, or something about themselves. People think their lives depend upon controlling things that advance their self-interests, and their counselor's job is to give them a prescription to accomplish it. If we give in to this demand, we only help them become more entrenched in their arrogance.

When people come to Jesus looking for a recipe to *advance* their self-interests, he offers a recipe to *transcend* their self-interests.

No matter how painful their circumstances, Jesus never empowers or authorizes them to promote their own self-interests. He warns, "If anyone would come after me, he must deny himself and take up his cross daily and follow me. For whoever tries to find his own life, loses it. But whoever loses his life for my sake, finds it" (Luke 9:23-24). According to Jesus, the pathway to psychological health is not self-advancement. It's self-denial.

God probably gives us more power in marriage than in any other context. The intimacies and privileges of marriage give husbands and wives incredible power in each other's lives. This gives them the ability to do great harm or great good to each other. God doesn't authorize us to use our power to manipulate our partner to meet our own needs. Instead, he prescribes that we use our power to promote our partner's health and growth.

Too many counselors prescribe the opposite: use our power to draw boundaries and assert ourselves for no higher purpose than self-enhancement. They authorize us to put our interests before the interests of anyone else — especially anyone who causes us pain. They give us license to violate love and loyalty if these get in the way of personal happiness. Therapist Mary Pipher describes the impact of this kind of counseling:

> We are trained to focus on the client and ignore the people in the client's life. This can contribute to an "I am the center of the universe" mentality. At its most superficial level, therapy teaches that feeling good is being good, and that duty and obligations are onerous chains, better off broken. . . . While it can be valuable for a person to have a calm, quiet place to talk honestly about problems, too much "massage therapy" can be harmful. At worst it can teach clients to "take care of themselves," without exploring the effects on those not in the room. . . . I remember Bonnie, who had been in therapy with

many other therapists. When we met she said proudly, "I learned from my last therapist that I shouldn't help people. I don't anymore."[6]

Troubled people grant a lot of authority to their counselors. They see them as experts on the problems they're experiencing. They know they need to change something, but they don't know what. So they look to their counselors for a prescription. What counselors say emboldens them to do things they would never do otherwise.

Jesus' prescription for psychological health always calls people to use the power and authority he gives them selflessly. If we want to follow Jesus' pattern when we counsel, our prescriptions must match his. To prescribe anything else is toxic.

What kinds of prescriptions do you give troubled people? Do they match the kinds of prescriptions Jesus gives?

INGREDIENT #8: INWARD ACCOUNTABILITY

One day Jesus sent messengers ahead to reserve rooms for them in a Samaritan village. But they were turned away! The people of the village refused to have anything to do with them. . . . When word came back of what had happened, James and John said to Jesus, "Master, shall we order fire down from heaven to burn them up?" And Jesus said, "You don't realize what your hearts are like. For the Son of Man has not come to destroy men's lives, but to save them." (Luke 9:52-56, TLB)

Accountability lies at the heart of all healthy relationships. Since we carry into all our relationships the power to help or hurt one another, we grow only when we're held accountable for how we use that power. Getting feedback about the way we're using our power in others' lives is essential to our health and growth.

People often want from their counselors a relationship that helps them "get the love they want" without addressing the *kind* of love they *give*. Many self-help books advocate behavior change without heart change — encouraging people to keep the same selfish goals, but find new and improved ways to achieve them.

However, the Bible says that we don't need new and improved strategies for getting our own way. Instead, we need hearts that love. Problems in relationships are the inevitable consequence of using others to satisfy our needs.

> What causes fights and quarrels among you? Don't they come from your desires that battle within you? You want something but don't get it. You kill and covet, but you cannot have what you want. You quarrel and fight. You do not have, because you do not ask God. (James, brother of Jesus, James 4:1-2, NIV)

Fighting and quarreling always begin in the heart with killing and coveting. This is why Jesus holds us accountable for *who we are* inwardly, even more than *what we do* outwardly. When two of his disciples intended to use their authority to get revenge on an inhospitable village, Jesus called attention to their hearts. He said, "You don't see what's energizing your hearts right now. It's not the same thing that energizes mine. I have the desire to love people instead of destroying them!"

Even when people's actions appear kind, friendly, and good-natured, their true intentions can be the opposite. One proverb warns: "He who hates disguises [it] with his lips, but he lays up deceit in his heart. When he speaks graciously, do not believe him, for there are seven abominations in his heart" (Proverbs 26:24-25, NASB). The proverb goes on to explain what our responsibility is toward such a person: "His malice (intentions) may be concealed by deception, but his wickedness will be *exposed in the assembly*" (Proverbs 26:26, NIV, emphasis added).

When we assemble together as God's people (whether in twos, threes, or hundreds) one of our responsibilities is to talk to each other about what energizes us to do what we do, and to hold each other accountable for the way we use our power and authority in other's lives. These are vital ingredients of friendship-counseling relationships.

How do you help the people you counsel trace what they're doing to why they're doing it? Who helps you do this in your life?

INGREDIENT #9: LIFELONG FRIENDSHIP

I no longer call you servants, because a servant does not know his master's business. Instead, I have called you friends, for everything that I learned from my Father I have made known to you. (Jesus to his disciples, John 15:15, NIV)

By their very nature, character-shaping relationships are lifelong. Their goal is not to cure people. It's to recruit them into lifelong partnerships where they're molded into mentors after the likeness of the ones who mentored them. That's what Jesus meant when he said, "A disciple is not above his teacher, but when he is *fully trained* he will be like his teacher" (Luke 6:40, PH, emphasis added).

Jesus' style of counseling is rigorous training. Friendship-counselors train others to live their lives the same way they live their own. This leaves an indelible stamp on people. Not only do their preoccupations come to resemble their mentor's, but so do their hearts.

There's no such thing as a fast approach when it comes to character-transformation. It requires "crock-pot" rather than "microwave" relationships. I was once approached by a group of elders who expressed concern over the lack of mature men in their church. They wanted me to teach them how to disciple other men. I told them that first I would need to disciple them, and that would require meeting weekly in a small group for at least a year. After several seconds of stunned silence, one spoke up: "We were hoping you could train us over breakfast one morning. We're too busy to add another meeting to our week." Puzzled, I inquired, "If you're that busy, how will you find time to disciple others?"

According to Paul, character-directed counseling is a lot like coaching people through the pains of childbirth: "My dear children, for whom I am again in the pains of childbirth until Christ is formed in you" (Galatians 4:19, NIV). Instead of the delivery taking a few hours, however, it takes a period of years. During this time, the coach must stand by to assist whenever the "contractions" of life bring new character struggles. The relationship between a character-coach and his student is never really severed.

The ultimate goal of friendship-counseling is to make colleagues out of the people we counsel. While this is a difficult transition — requiring maturity on the part of both people in the counseling relationship — it's an integral part of the pattern Jesus gives us. The person being counseled must acquire and display faithfulness and skill; the counselor must acquire and display humility and trust. According to Paul, these are essential ingredients of a lifelong partnership: "Everything you have seen me do and say you should entrust to others who have the faithfulness and skill to pass them on to others" (Paul to Timothy, 2 Timothy 2:2).

How can you use your counseling/discipling relationships to train people to do for others what you've done for them?

HELP WANTED: CHARACTER-WORKERS IN
SHORT SUPPLY

Then he [Jesus] said to his disciples, "The harvest is plentiful but the workers are few. Ask the Lord of the harvest, therefore, to send out workers into his harvest field." (Matthew 9:37-38, NIV)

As a counseling educator, I talk frequently to people who've seen God change their lives at deep levels. Many enroll in counselor-training programs because they want to learn how to help others have the same experience. They assume that the most effective way to accomplish this is to become professional counselors.

While there's no question that many dedicated Christians serve God with great effectiveness and distinction as professional counselors, formal, clinical, or institutional settings present many obstacles to helping people experience deep and lasting character changes. Sometimes these obstacles are surmountable. But many times they're not.

Regardless, it's important to recognize that professional counseling is *not* the most effective context for building the kind of relationships with people that promote character change. Few of the ingredients of character-shaping relationships are offered to people in these contexts.

The impact we can have on people's character as professional counselors doesn't compare to the impact we can have as friendship-counselors — sharing community with them in churches, homes, and restaurants, and on campuses, outings, retreats, and missions trips.

Perhaps, in recent years we have come to associate "deep changes" only with professional or clinical contexts because of the limited training provided for friendship-counselors in less-formal contexts. Jesus' way of building friendship-counseling relationships has become a lost practice. Recovering this model, and using the nine ingredients it entails, is the only way we can carry out the character-changing work Christ calls us to do.

Ingredients of a Character-Shaping Relationship	Jesus' Model of Friendship-Counseling	Professional or Clinical Counseling
Hand Selection	Yes	Seldom
Intimate Involvement	Yes	No
Open Moral Intent	Yes	Seldom
Personal Modeling	Yes	No
Moral Insight	Yes	Seldom
Moral Responsibility	Yes	Seldom
Prescribed Selflessness	Yes	Seldom
Inward Accountability	Yes	Seldom
Lifelong Friendship	Yes	No

How many character-shaping ingredients do you incorporate into your counseling/discipling relationships? What limits you from incorporating more?

4

$$\left[\; l \; \text{I} \; f \; \text{E} - c \; \text{H} \; a \; \text{n} \; \text{G} \; i \; \text{N} \; g \;\right]$$

$$\left[\; \text{WORDS} \;\right]$$

As Jesus started on his way, a man ran up to him and fell on his knees before him. "Good teacher," he asked, "what must I do to inherit eternal life?" . . . Jesus answered . . . "You know the commandments. . . ." "'Teacher," he declared, "all these I have kept since I was a boy." Jesus looked at him and loved him. "One thing you lack," he said. "Go, sell everything you have and give to the poor, and you will have treasure in heaven. Then come, follow me." At this the man's face fell. He went away sad, because he had great wealth.

Mark 10:17-22, NIV

When the rich young man approached Jesus asking him for one kind of counseling, he received quite another. This man wanted what most people want from their counselors: advice on how to make his self-centered existence more effective, more rewarding, more secure. He wasn't looking for help to change the self-centered strategy he'd been using since childhood — perfectionism. He just wanted to refine it.

He was asking for *self-improvement* counseling, but he needed *self-deliverance* counseling. Giving him self-improvement counseling would have been death-words. It would have strengthened his belief that life depends upon his own goodness instead of God's.

Instead, Jesus' words invited the young man to do what he couldn't do without God's help—love others in radical and dangerous new ways. He went away disrupted; instead of getting his spiritual pride bolstered as he had expected, Jesus exposed his spiritual poverty. The man began to realize that he couldn't get what he wanted by depending on his own goodness. This was progress—the first step in his journey away from self-centeredness!

Life-words always set the stage for subsequent conversations. As the man left Jesus to reflect on what he was learning about himself, a whole new question formed in his mind. The question, "What can I do to get others to see how good I am?" was replaced by, "What do I do when I can't depend on my own goodness anymore?" Jesus' words not only punctured his arrogance; they inspired brokenness. They made it a matter of time before the man would return to Jesus with a different question and a different attitude—ingredients for an even more life-changing encounter with Jesus.

How do you resist the temptation to give your friends self-improvement counseling? How does your counseling entice them into new encounters with Christ?

THE NATURE OF LIFE-WORDS

Do everything without complaining or arguing, so that you may become blameless and pure, children of God without fault in a crooked and depraved generation, in which you shine like stars in the universe as you hold out the word of life. (Paul to early Christians, Philippians 2:14-16, NIV, emphasis added)

Whenever we counsel a suffering person, we must choose our words carefully. Paul gave a simple rule-of-thumb for choosing the right words: "Use strong words to disrupt those who are arrogant, use soft words to encourage those who are broken, and use actions instead of words to help those who are infirm. But be patient with everyone" (1 Thessalonians 5:14).

We must exercise care and skill with our tongues when we speak to suffering people. Often, we must choose words sufferers don't expect or want — words that seem to add to their suffering by disrupting or wounding them. The Bible teaches us that wounds delivered by a friend can bring healing to the deepest levels of the soul (Proverbs 27:5-6). Words are one of the primary tools God gives us to stimulate character growth in each other: "*Speaking the truth in love*, we will in all things grow up into . . . Christ from whom the whole body . . . builds itself up in love as each part does its work" (Ephesians 4:15-16, NIV). When words carry the right kind of content (truth) and are propelled by the right kind of energy (love), they become life-words to others. This is why Paul avoided words that sprang from error (the absence of truth) or impure motives (the absence of love) in his counseling (1 Thessalonians 2:3). God forbids us from using argumentative words to force or coerce sufferers to do things they don't want to do (Philippians 2:14-16). That's an encroachment on their dignity (the gift of self-determination that God gives to each person).

Can you remember the last time a friend spoke life-words to you? What made them life-words?

THE NATURE OF DEATH-WORDS

But I tell you that men will have to give account on the day of judgment for every careless word they have spoken. For by your words you will be acquitted, and by your words you will be condemned. (Jesus to false teachers, Matthew 12:36-37, NIV)

Job pled with his counselors to say something that would give him hope (see Job 17:10-14): "How long will you torment me and crush me with words?" (19:2, NIV). Job said he'd prefer strangling to listening to them (7:13-16)! Death-words always make it harder for hurting people to grow in the midst of trials.

The tongue has the power of life and death (see Proverbs 18:21), and God holds us accountable for the way we use it to influence others (see James 3:1). Our words do great damage or good in the life of someone who is in great pain! They're like powerful medicine, "a fountain of life, turning a man from the snares of death" (Proverbs 13:14; 16:24). We must never choose our words arbitrarily, carelessly, or maliciously.

The story of Job is a good example of what can happen in counseling. The more reckless Job was with his words (see Job 10:1), the more reckless his counselors were with theirs (20:2-3). We must be careful to avoid using the rash words of sufferers as a license to speak rashly ourselves. Reckless words "pierce like a sword" (Proverbs 12:18) and do great damage.

The Bible declares that we all have a propensity to stumble and err with our words (see James 3:2). So it's wise, at first, to hold our tongues (see Proverbs 10:19), listen carefully (see Proverbs 18:13), and exercise a lot of discernment when counseling others (see Proverbs 17:27, James 1:19-20). Death-words always come easier than life-words.

When's the last time you caught yourself speaking death-words to a friend? How did you recognize them as death-words?

THE WORD-FACTORY IN OUR HEARTS

You brood of vipers, how can you who are evil say anything good? For out of the overflow of the heart the mouth speaks. (Jesus to false teachers, Matthew 12:34, NIV)

Jesus said our words are a product of our hearts, reflecting what's inside us. Within the hidden cellars of our hearts, our sinful human nature creates and stores evil desires, thoughts, and plans. In these cellars, we craft every word we speak. Even when we attempt to help others, our hearts can betray our good intentions and produce words that promote our own well-being at the expense of those we're trying to help. The more conscious we become of this, the more we have to ask ourselves the same question Jesus asked the false teachers: "How can you who are evil say anything good?" (Matthew 12:34).

This is a question I was forced to ask myself during my counseling training. Larry, my internship supervisor, asked me to bring a videotape of my counseling to our meeting each week for review and discussion. At our first meeting, I thought my tape would really impress him. He watched it for just a couple of minutes, then stopped it and said, "Kevin, as I watch you counsel, I see a man talking to his counselee through a Plexiglas shield—like what you talk through when visiting someone in prison." Larry replayed the tape to show me how my words kept the conversation sterile, impersonal, and guarded.

I wasn't sure exactly what this all meant. So I asked, "Do you think this a big problem?" His reply startled me: "As long as you speak to others through a shield, you'll be of little help to them. You may even harm them."

We explored where the "shield" came from. We traced it back to things in my own heart. When I was growing up, my father's career required our family to relocate numerous times. I learned to protect myself from rejection and ridicule as the new kid in school by remaining aloof, self-sufficient, and untouchable. Later, when I became a youth pastor and college chaplain, I used it to keep the kids from getting close enough to break my heart. Without thinking about it, this became my style of relating to almost everyone.

I left that first meeting promising Larry that I'd work hard to change how I used my words. He must have smiled on the inside, knowing that I was like the rich young man who came to Jesus — thinking I could find a way to improve my own character.

That next week, I tried hard to break through my shield, especially when videotaping for Larry. I tried to sound warmer, express greater empathy, disclose more of myself. I brought my tape to our second meeting, certain that Larry would love it. In less than a minute, he turned it off! "Kevin, you're a phony." "What do you mean?" I shot back. He replayed the tape. I began the session telling the counselee *what I thought* she must be feeling after our last session, not inquiring *what she was actually feeling*. Larry asked me what I was thinking about at that moment. I realized I was thinking about how I looked on the tape rather than how I could help this person. My commitment to protect myself superseded my commitment to love.

Each time I met with Larry, I'd resolve to work harder to change, only to return the following week with a tape that revealed I wasn't improving. About six weeks into my internship, my exasperation finally hit the boiling point. We were watching another of my sessions. Larry didn't say a word, but I saw myself still being guarded and stilted in my choice of words. I muttered, "I don't know what I'm going to do. I've tried everything I know to change. I feel like giving up." With a knowing smile, Larry said, "Good, I was hoping you'd come to that. If this was something you could change about yourself, then you wouldn't need God, would you?"

That was the first I realized that there were things about my heart that I couldn't change on my own. My words couldn't change until the energy in my heart changed. And that couldn't happen until God did it for me.

Are you aware of anything in your heart getting in the way of speaking life-words to others?

THE WELLSPRING OF LIFE-WORDS

Each one should use whatever gift he has received to serve others, faithfully administering God's grace in its various forms. If anyone speaks, he should do it as one speaking the very words of God. If anyone serves, he should do it with the strength God provides, so that in all things God may be praised through Jesus Christ. (Peter to the early Christians, 1 Peter 4:10-11, NIV)

Life-words are gifts God gives us to do Christ's work in each other's lives. None of us can speak life-words until we acquire a heart like Christ's (see Philippians 2:5). And we can never acquire a heart like his until God forms it in us.

As King David grew older, he began to recognize how poor he was at loving others. Many of his psalms were desperate prayers for a new heart. In one David pleads "Create in me a pure heart, O God, and renew a steadfast spirit within me. . . . Then I will teach transgressors your ways, and sinners will turn back to you" (Psalm 51:10,13, NIV).

David knew his words could never influence people in a holy way until something deep inside him changed. He prayed, "Wash away all my iniquity and cleanse me from my sin. For I know my transgressions, and my sin is always before me. Against you, you only, have I sinned and done what is evil in your sight, so that you are proved right when you speak and justified when you judge." (Psalm 51:2-4, NIV). David penned this prayer shortly after his friend Nathan used life-words to help him get a glimpse of the true condition of his own heart.

God is never moved by casual prayers to change our hearts. He doesn't want us to approach him for a Band-Aid for our souls or an aspirin for our character. He wants us to ask him for nothing less than a *heart transplant*. He wants us to seek it from him as if our lives depend on it — earnestly, desperately, and whole-heartedly.

We'll never pray earnestly for our own hearts until we come to recognize our desperate condition. In the same way David needed Nathan, and I needed Larry, we all need help to see the destructive patterns we're doomed to repeat unless God graciously intervenes. Only God is able to shatter the self-protective shields we put between ourselves and other people. Only he has the power to change the energy behind our words — from fear to love. Paul knew this all too well: "For the Holy Spirit, God's gift, does not want you to be afraid of people, but to be wise and strong, and to love them and enjoy being with them" (2 Timothy 1:7, TLB).

The Bible tells us that speaking life-words requires two things: the right kind of character and the right kind of skill (see Psalm 78:72). We develop *the character* to speak life-words by bringing the broken parts of our heart to God for reconstructive surgery. We develop *the skill* to speak life-words by training to speak the way Jesus speaks. When we cultivate the two simultaneously — character and skill — we gradually become "a workman with nothing to be ashamed of, and who knows how to use the word of truth to the best advantage" (2 Timothy 2:15-17, PH).

What's your most desperate prayer about yourself right now? What do you most desperately need him to change about your heart?

The Skill of Crafting Life-Words

All spoke well of him and were amazed at the gracious words that came from his lips. (Witnesses of Jesus' first public ministry, Luke 4:22, NIV)

Learning to speak life-words begins with an in-depth familiarity with the way Jesus spoke. Jesus' conversations in the Bible are like rare jewels. The longer we gaze at them the more we come to appreciate the sheer power, love, and wisdom of his words. Imitating him seems beyond our wildest aspirations, but that's exactly what Christ wants us to do.

Life-words need to be custom-tailored for each person according to what he or she needs at the moment to grow (see John 16:12). Just as golfers have a variety of clubs to choose from for each shot, we have a variety of words to choose from for each encounter we have with our friends. We choose the words best suited for where our friends are in their spiritual journey.

When we first encounter hurting people, most are still at the beginning of their spiritual journey, handling life as *reactive victims*. Focusing solely on the problems in their world, they come to us nursing their injuries, asking, *"How can I change my world?"* Their automatic reaction to circumstances is to change the cause of their suffering. The words we offer at this stage determine whether our relationship will focus on the troubles in their world or the troubles in their heart. Will it help them find an external or internal solution to their struggles?

A few come to us as *reflective rebels,* a little farther along in their spiritual journeys, aware to some degree of the problems in their hearts. They need encouragement to put the question in their hearts into words: *"What am I doing wrong?"* They're beginning to suspect that the troubles within their hearts are a greater threat to their survival than troubles in their world. They're discovering how their own response to suffering is the greatest obstacle to the life they really want. Life-words lead them to advance beyond this point by helping them understand the destructive choices they're making.

Sufferers enter the third stage in their journey when they ask, *"How can I change myself?"* Their motivation to change is fueled by disillusionment and disgust over the person they've discovered themselves to be. As *repentant seekers,* their determination to continue to live the way they've been living has been broken. They're realizing what they really want will never be theirs as long as they continue functioning the way they are. They want to be different, but they don't know how. Life-words help them visualize how to change, even if their circumstances never do.

In stage four, people begin to recognize they don't have what it takes to be the person God wants them to be or even who they want to be. Life-words help them realize that reconciling their heart with God's is their only hope, provoking a new question: *"How can I get God to help me change?"* As they pray to him in their brokenness, they experience an intimacy with God they've never known before. In the process, their hearts grow in their resemblance to his — in the ways they think, choose, desire, and feel. As *reconciled worshipers* their hearts change dramatically even though their circumstances don't.

The process of transforming sufferers into servants culminates at stage five. As they exercise their new hearts, they start to ask the question only servants ask: *"How can I serve God?"* Their circumstances haven't changed, but their ability to cope with their circumstances has. As *responsible servants* they're excited about the opportunities their circumstances afford them to display God's character to the world. Life-words encourage them to take responsibility for serving God in the situations they encounter.

Because hurting people have different questions at each stage in their journeys, friendship-counselors must deliberately craft their words to speak to the character need at each stage.

Each stage offers temptation for counselors to speak words to sufferers aimed at helping them improve their self-centered strategies instead of their character. These are death-words because they inhibit character growth. Jesus' model for speaking life-words is the only map we have to avoid this hazard.

JESUS' MODEL FOR SPEAKING LIFE-WORDS

The Stages of Our Friend's Journey	THE QUESTION THEY'RE ASKING	WHAT THEY NEED TO GROW	LIFE-WORDS	DEATH-WORDS
Reactive Victim	How can I change my world?	Shifting from an external focus to an internal one	Words that shape the counseling relationship	Words that offer immediate relief
Reflective Rebel	What am I doing wrong?	Understanding the trouble in their own hearts	Words that guide their reflection	Words that coach them to manipulate relationships
Repentant Seeker	How can I change myself?	Visualizing who they could be in Christ	Words that cultivate their repentance	Words that direct them toward self-repair
Reconciled Worshiper	How can I get God to help me change?	Praying in spirit and in truth for a new heart	Words that promote their reconciliation	Words that promise them rescue
Responsible Servant	How can I serve God?	Choosing bold new ways to serve God	Words that encourage their responsibility	Words that discourage them to risk

The rest of this chapter gives an overview of this model, explaining and illustrating each stage with Jesus' conversations with hurting people.

LIFE-WORDS FOR SHAPING THE HELPING RELATIONSHIP

Words that establish the kind of relationship with our friends that help them achieve a goal that is important to them without helping them achieve a goal that is destructive.

Someone in the crowd said to him, "Teacher, tell my brother to divide the inheritance with me." Jesus replied, "Man, who appointed me a judge or an arbiter between you?" Then he said to them, "Watch out! Be on your guard against all kinds of greed; a man's life does not consist in the abundance of his possessions." (Luke 12:13-15, NIV)

Jesus' goal is never just to help people get along better. When a man came to him with a complaint about his brother, Jesus refused to be his arbiter. This man was convinced that his brother had the power to ruin his life. He wanted to change or control his brother instead of himself. If Jesus offered him a relationship that helped him do this, it would have meant joining him in a destructive goal and reinforcing his foolish belief. While it might have provided temporary relief, the man would continue relating to his brother out of self-interest instead of love.

The first words we speak to a hurting friend are critical. Jesus' first words to this man gave direction to their relationship: "Watch out! The real danger isn't with your brother. It's right here in yourself. That's the problem I want to help you with." Jesus invited him to shift his focus from the troubling behavior of his brother to the troubling intentions of his own heart.

This example teaches us that the first task in friendship-counseling is to clarify the nature of the relationship with the person asking for help. This requires life-words that establish the boundaries for our work together — what our goal will be and what we can expect from each other. How effective we are depends on shaping the relationship around a goal that's important to our friend and beneficial to his character-growth. If we can't agree on such a goal, it's unwise to begin a friendship-counseling relationship.

If we merely help our friends feel better by engineering changes in their world, we'll be speaking death-words. This doesn't mean that if we have the resources to immediately relieve their suffering we should never use them. The Bible asks "how can the love of God live in someone who has the resources to help his brother but shows no compassion toward him?" (1 John 3:17). Compassion should always dictate when and how we respond to hurting friends.

But relieving people's suffering is not always the compassionate thing to do. Jesus certainly had the resources to make the man with the stingy brother rich. But that wouldn't have been compassionate. It wouldn't have addressed his most important need — his need to draw life from God instead of his possessions. That would only have supported his rebellion — his practice of valuing riches more than his relationship with God.

According to Jesus, helping a friend gain the whole world (or even a part of it) at the cost of forfeiting his soul is not loving him (see Luke 9:25). Life-words at this stage carefully direct the focus of counseling — from altering our friends' circumstances to altering their response.

Have you established a clear goal with each of the friends you're presently helping? Are they goals that focus on changing their circumstance or their response to circumstances?

LIFE-WORDS FOR GUIDING REFLECTION

Words that draw out what's in the hearts of our friends without becoming their rescuer or persecutor.

As Jesus and his disciples were on their way, he came to a village where a woman named Martha opened her home to him. She had a sister called Mary, who sat at the Lord's feet listening to what he said. But Martha was distracted by all the preparations that had to be made. She came to him and asked, "Lord, don't you care that my sister has left me to do the work by myself? Tell her to help me!" "Martha, Martha," the Lord answered, "you are worried and upset about many things, but only one thing is needed. Mary has chosen what is better, and it will not be taken away from her." (Luke 10:38-42, NIV)

When people come to counselors, they often have their minds made up about what they need. Like Martha, they're sure that the solution to their troubles is to control their world more effectively. They're asking the question, "What am I doing wrong?" They expect their counselor to supply the know-how, muscle, or coaching to improve or repair their strategy for making their world a more benign place. People always regard this as their greatest need until they understand the trouble within their own hearts.

Martha thought she knew what her problem was — not getting enough accomplished. She even knew the solution: the people in her world needed to cooperate more, especially her family. She was right in a way. Something *was* wrong — but not with her world, with her heart. Jesus' words guided Martha to see this. He handed Martha a "mirror," knowing she could never grow or change until the wrong she saw in her own heart was bigger and more real to her than the wrong she saw in her sister.

Jesus invited her to reflect, first calling attention to what she was feeling. He wanted her to understand how her emotions were misleading her—attaching vital significance to things that weren't vital at all—treating them as if her life depended on them. Her inappropriate emotions reflected a belief system that set her up to feel abandoned by everyone in her life

Martha believed that her life depended on controlling her world at all times. So she had no time to enjoy the people around her. "If they're not working with me to keep things ordered," she thought to herself, "they can't possibly care about me." This even made her doubt Jesus' love for her. It robbed her of the freedom to sit and enjoy Jesus the way Mary did. Her state of mind is aptly described by the words of George MacDonald: "It is very sad for those who cannot trust in him (God); it is a miserable slavery."[1]

Jesus wanted to help Martha experience freedom. Freedom from fear. Freedom from the lies that fueled her fear. And freedom from the behavior patterns designed to protect her from her fear. Without freedom Martha couldn't trust or love anyone. Before she could bring these things to God and find freedom from them, however, Martha had to become aware of them. That's why Jesus guided her to reflect—to see herself as he saw her. Only then would she ask a different question: "How can I change my heart?"

How do you get to know what's in the hearts of your friends? How do you help them uncover what is controlling them at the deepest levels?

LIFE-WORDS FOR CULTIVATING REPENTANCE

Words that cultivate in our friends a vision and
desire for the kind of heart they cannot possibly

produce on their own (the same kind God desires
for them), without shaming or pressuring them.

*Jesus said to his disciples . . . "If your brother sins, rebuke him, and if he
repents, forgive him. If he sins against you seven times in a day, and seven
times comes back to you and says, 'I repent,' forgive him." The apostles said
to the Lord, "Increase our faith!" He replied, "If you have faith as small as
a mustard seed . . . Nothing will be impossible for you." (Luke 17:1-6;
Matthew 17:21, NIV, emphasis added)*

From infancy, each of us develops a mental strategy for coping with suffering—for avoiding it, alleviating it, and protecting
ourselves from it. As we get older, the strategy becomes more
refined and sophisticated. By the time we're adults it becomes so
second-nature that we're barely aware of the control it exerts
over us. Life-words that cultivate repentance help us envision a
new strategy—a fundamentally different way of responding to
suffering. They cultivate a desire in us to deal with adversity in a
way that only God can make possible.

Jesus knows that our psychological health depends on how
we choose to respond to suffering. When he counseled his disciples, he enticed them to imagine what it would mean to manage
their suffering by the principle of love instead of the principle of
self-protection. He helped them visualize a revolutionary new
way to respond to someone who repeatedly hurts them. As soon
as they heard it, they cried out for help: "Increase our faith!" They
knew Jesus was describing a strategy for living that was out of
their league, requiring far more faith in God's ability to protect
them than they possessed. They couldn't imagine loving in such
vulnerable ways unless their trust in God deepened. Jesus' life-
words cultivated repentance in their hearts—the vision and
desire to be someone they couldn't be without God's help.

When we repent it means we change our mind or attitude
about the kind of person we want to be. Instead of living to pro-

tect ourselves, we want to live to love. Repentance doesn't mean we're free to do it yet. It means we want to be.

Death-words obstruct our repentance and cause us to aim too low, visualizing only those ways of dealing with difficulties we can do in our own power. Death-words strengthen our resolve to rely on old strategies for protection, instead of God. They cultivate despair; in the end, our self-protective strategies always fail to produce the pain-free existence they promise.

Jesus didn't give his disciples a strategy for developing more fulfilling relationships or avoiding painful ones. Instead, he gave them a strategy for staying involved with people — even loving them in the worst of circumstances. Jesus told a parable about a man who began to envision a character change only after he became disillusioned with the strategy that was supposed to make his life pain-free:

"[He] got together all he had, set off for a distant country and there squandered his wealth in wild living. . . . When he *came to his senses*, he said . . . 'I will set out and go back to my father and say to him: Father, I have sinned against heaven and against you. I am no longer worthy to be called your son; make me like one of your hired men.' So he got up and went to his father" (Luke 15:13-14,17-20, NIV, emphasis added) .

The young man became a repentant seeker when he "came to his senses" and started to envision a new way to live. He knew he had to change, but he needed help from someone greater than himself — his father. His story teaches a vital spiritual truth: No matter how much we want to change the kind of person we are, we can't without our Father's help. We can envision what it means to be a servant, but only God can make us into one.

In the Old Testament book of Hosea, God tells his people how to repent: "Return, O Israel, to the LORD your God. Your sins [your wrong strategies] have been your downfall! *Take words with you* and return to the LORD" (Hosea 14:1-2, NIV, emphasis added). Repentance requires putting into words the changes we desperately desire God to make in our hearts. When God hears them, he says, "Then I will cure you of idolatry and faithlessness, and my love will know no bounds, for my anger will be forever gone!" (Hosea 14:4, TLB). We cultivate repentance in our friends when we help them acquire the words to talk to God about the changes they want him to make in their hearts.

What do you say to friends who come to you, disillusioned about the self-protective strategy they're using? How do you help them put into words the changes they need to make in their hearts?

LIFE-WORDS FOR PROMOTING RECONCILIATION

Words that call our friends to use the trouble in their world and the trouble in their hearts to pursue God and reconcile their hearts to his, without raising expectations that this will change their circumstances or make their lives easier.

[Jesus said], "Simon, Simon, Satan has asked to sift you as wheat. But I have prayed for you, Simon, that your faith may not fail." . . . But he [Peter] replied, "Lord, I am ready to go with you to prison and to death." . . . [later that evening] He took Peter and the two sons of Zebedee along with him, and he began to be sorrowful and troubled. Then he said to them, "My soul is overwhelmed with sorrow to the point of death. Stay here and keep watch with me." Going a little farther, he fell with his face to the ground and prayed, "My Father, if it is possible, may this cup be taken from me. Yet not as I will, but as you will." Then he returned to his disciples and found them sleeping. . . . he asked Peter, "Watch and pray so that you will not fall into

temptation." (Luke 22:31-33; Matthew 26:37-41, NIV, emphasis added)

In the midst of suffering, our greatest temptation is to use our pain to justify coping with our troubles our own way instead of God's. We go into survival mode. Whatever we need to protect ourselves becomes more compelling than our desire to serve God. Our sinful nature prevents us from holding onto our integrity in the face of adversity—from being the person we want to be.

In the face of adversity, the only hope we have to be free and healthy is God. Only God can reconcile our weak wills to his iron will. Jesus knew this. When Peter claimed, "Lord, I am ready to go with you to prison and death," Jesus discouraged him from putting any confidence in his own ability to live up to this claim. Before the night was over, both he and Peter would face trials that neither of them could endure without their Father's help. This is why Jesus urged Peter to reconcile his heart with God while there was still time.

We offer life-words to our friends when we teach them to pray in the midst of their troubles like Jesus prayed: "My Father, if it is not possible for this cup to be taken away unless I drink it, may your will be done" (Matthew 26:42, NIV). Jesus saw no value in suffering needlessly. So he began by expressing his preference. But he didn't stop there. He turned over to God the decision about when and how he would suffer.

Jesus put himself at God's disposal, with no demand or expectation that God would change his circumstances or make his life easier. By offering himself as a servant to God at a time when, humanly speaking, he lacked the power to be one, Jesus was asking that his Father's will become his will. This put Jesus in a position to be wonderfully helped by his Father: an angel from heaven appeared to him and strengthened him (see Luke 22:43).

God's help didn't come in the form of deliverance from suffering (it rarely does). It came in the form of strengthening

Jesus for suffering, enabling him to endure torture, humiliation, and crucifixion for all of us. Jesus' model for finding help
from God in the midst of suffering is praying for reconciliation
even more than rescue: "Father, I want to entrust when and
how I suffer to you. But I don't have the power to do that. Give
me the heart to accept this suffering as your will and endure it
like you want me to—for as long as you want me to."
Reconciling our will to God's will enables us to experience
something far more valuable than rescue. As George
MacDonald said, "It is worth all suffering to be at length one
with God."[2]

Jim, a young man I know, has struggled for years with
severe depression. It may be biological since many of his rela-
tives struggle with the same symptoms. Medication and therapy haven't helped. At first Jim prayed fervently that God
would take the depression away. When he didn't, Jim decided
to punish God with silence. Eventually, Jim turned to other
Christians for help. Their words guided him to reflect and
repent about the ways he was dealing with his depression.
Gradually, he started praying in a different way. Instead of
demanding that God take away his depression, he offered himself to God: "Heavenly Father, I don't know why I'm depressed.
All I know is that I don't know how to make it better. So I'm
bringing it to you. I'm still kind of angry that you won't just
take it away, but I don't want to be angry. I want to believe that
something about this depression is good, because you're good.
I want to use this depression for some good purpose. I don't
want to use it to hate you or take out my pain on others. But I
can't do this without your help. I need your power to be your
servant. Please help me."

Months after he started praying this way, Jim still struggles
with depression. But he's no longer "stressed out about feeling
depressed." God provided a number of ways to use his sadness to

reach out to others. The depression has become the place where he meets God, worships him, and enjoys God's fatherly affection. He and God are reconciled even though the pain continues.

Our reconciliation with God in the midst of our pain doesn't come only by the words we say, but how we say them. Jesus once counseled a woman, "Yet a time is coming and has now come when the true worshipers will worship the Father *in spirit and truth,* for they are the kind of worshipers the Father seeks" (John 4:23, NIV, emphasis added). *In spirit* means coming to God with our desires to serve him that we can't carry out in our own strength. *In truth* means coming to him with character weaknesses we can't overcome without his help. Reconciliation occurs when God brings the two together—enabling us to be in truth who we desire to be in spirit. Reflection equips us with the words we need to pray *in truth.* Repentance gives us the words we need to pray *in spirit.*

We can't make the journey from victim to servant without first becoming a worshiper. Paul counseled Christians who were suffering at the hands of a ruthless dictator, "Do not be overcome by evil, but overcome evil with good" (Romans 12:21, NIV). The only way we can keep from becoming evil is by immersing ourselves in goodness. This isn't our own goodness, which is too weak to offset the withering effect evil has on our souls. Instead, as we immerse ourselves in worship of God, his goodness becomes more real and more potent than any of the bad things that happen to us. By worshiping him in spirit and truth we acquire the character to display his goodness to an evil world.

What's the ultimate message you want your friends to get from their counseling with you? Where and how do you assume the role of Christ's ambassador, calling your friends to surrender their will to his?

LIFE-WORDS FOR ENCOURAGING RESPONSIBILITY

Words that encourage our friends to exercise their new desire and ability to be the kind of people who display the character of Christ to the world, even though it exposes them to more suffering.

Peter was hurt because Jesus asked him the third time, "Do you love me?" He said, "Lord, you know all things; you know that I love you." Jesus said, "Feed my sheep. I tell you the truth, when you were younger you dressed yourself and went where you wanted; but when you are old you will stretch out your hands, and someone else will dress you and lead you where you do not want to go." Jesus said this to indicate the kind of death by which Peter would glorify God. Then he said to him, "Follow me!" (John 21:17-19, NIV)

A heart reconciled to God's is a heart eager and able to serve him. It's preoccupied with the question, "What's the best way I can love God at this time and in this place?" This heart no longer questions whether it's responsible to serve God — only how.

By the time Peter's conversation with Jesus occurred in John 21:17-19, his heart was reconciled to Christ's. Following his denial of Jesus, Peter experienced great remorse (see Matthew 26:75). After Jesus' resurrection, Peter was among the first disciples to worship him (see Matthew 28:17). At this stage in his journey, Peter's heart was ready to serve Christ. But he needed help to know where and how to begin.

Like Peter, our friends need encouragement at this stage in their journey to translate their growing love for God into action. Jesus found Peter killing time; he was fishing with the other disciples and waiting for someone to tell him what to do next. The last time Peter took initiative to serve God, he recklessly cut off someone's ear (see Matthew 26:51). From this experience he learned not to trust his own instincts — a wise decision as long as his heart remained unreconciled to God's! But this was no longer the case. It was time for Peter to start listening to his new heart. Jesus' life-words that morning on the beach encouraged him to do just that.

At their breakfast meeting, Jesus' words built a bridge for Peter between passion and action. Three times Jesus emphasized Peter's responsibility to make his actions toward others match his passion for God. Serving God always requires sufferers to translate their love for him into tangible acts of love toward others. Peter had learned how to love God, but now he needed encouragement to love others.

Jesus' words encouraged Peter to express his love through a ministry of shepherding and strengthening others: "Feed my sheep!" Peter might have wished (as most sufferers do) that Jesus' counsel was more specific. "Exactly what should I do next?" But Jesus didn't give him a detailed map. That would have inhibited Peter's growth and freedom. Giving him a script would have robbed Peter of the joy of creating his own script — putting his new heart to work choosing where and how he could best serve Christ.

Jesus invited Peter to serve him "in the new way of the Spirit, and not in the old way of the written code" (Romans 7:6, NIV). He didn't want Peter to follow a set of rules that would stifle creativity, individuality, and ingenuity. He wanted Peter to trust the work of the Holy Spirit in his heart. That's the challenge of speaking life-words to people with reconciled hearts: encouraging acts of love — not by telling them what we want them to do, but by affirming them in what *they* want to do. The former produces dependents, the latter disciples.

Life-words at this stage affirm what sufferers already know is true: when they live by the principle of love, instead of the principle of self-protection, their suffering will inevitably increase. Jesus warned Peter that he would be *arrested and crucified* for loving the way God was calling him to love. His words encouraged Peter to listen to his new heart, to trust it and exercise it, even though it exposed him to danger.

Death-words at this stage do the opposite. They discourage taking risks in the face of suffering. Before Peter's heart was reconciled, he tried to persuade Jesus to protect himself instead of serving God (see Matthew 16:22). Jesus sternly rebuked him: "Get behind me, Satan! You are a stumbling block to me; you do not have in mind the things of God, but the things of men" (Matthew 16:23, NIV). In no uncertain terms, Jesus told Peter his words were the counsel of an enemy, not a friend.

At this stage, it's impossible to encourage sufferers to follow their hearts without also encouraging them to take risks to love in bold new ways. Although God's Spirit may not call every sufferer to serve him in ways that result in crucifixion or death, he does call everyone to do things for Christ that risk the everyday "little-deaths" of scorn, rejection, humiliation, loneliness, and persecution. Life-words at this stage strengthen sufferers for this eventuality.

During the years I served as a youth pastor and college chaplain, I discipled a number of young men and women. Speaking life-words to them at this stage of their spiritual journey was hard for me. Encouraging them to order their lives around what they heard God saying—rather than what they heard me saying—required a great deal of trust both in God's ability to lead them and in their ability to follow him. Yet, as their friendship-counselor, it was my job to help them establish God as the source of their wisdom and strength instead of me or anyone else.

Life-words at this stage encourage responsibility by communicating to our friends confidence both in God's ability to lead them and their ability to choose for themselves the most effective ways to love him.

What is your strategy for helping your friends become independent and responsible servants of God? What does this require of you?

p A r T t H r E e :
JESUS AND HUMAN
COUNSELING

"Go out and train everyone you meet, far and near, in this way of life . . . instruct them in the practice of all I have commanded you. I'll be with you as you do this, day after day after day, right up to the end of the age."

Jesus, Matthew 28:19-20, MSG

By now you might be saying, "This is way out of my league. I'd need the mind and heart of God to counsel like Jesus!" That's true! And we should keep it in mind whenever we try to give hope and direction to hurting people. But we should also remember that Jesus never commands us to do something without giving us everything we need to do it. Just before he ascended to heaven, he offered us a promise, as well as a command: "Go out and train [disciple] everyone you meet . . . I'll be with you as you do this . . . right up to the end . . ." (Matthew 28:19-20, MSG). *Jesus makes it clear that friendship-counseling is something he expects us to do for him, but never without him.*

In the next five chapters, you'll watch me counsel "Randy," a fictitious friend who is suffering. I recorded and transcribed my conversations with him from a series of role-plays I did for my university students. I portrayed a counselor working in a church setting with Randy, who was played by an actor. I'm providing these edited conversations, along with my running commentary, to demonstrate how Jesus' model can guide our counseling conversations whether they're with people we've just met, like Randy, or with friends we've known for years.

As I said before, we can adapt Jesus' model to nearly any setting where we encounter hurting people. But it's important to understand that Jesus' model isn't a formula that guarantees a certain result. The road it encourages sufferers to walk is called a "narrow road" for a reason (see Matthew 7:13-14). While it offers them the hope and direction they ultimately want, it's never an easy road to travel. When we invite people to walk it, many will resist. Only a few will end up taking it. Yet guiding or counseling them with Jesus' map can lead to some of the most powerful interactions with people we'll ever have. With the right kind of heart (I'll say more about this in chapter 10), Jesus' model expands our ministry to hurting friends.

Attempting to demonstrate something as profound and

magnificent as Jesus' model of friendship-counseling gives me great reason to pause. I can't give it justice. I'm only a coping model. Jesus provides the only mastery model of counseling we have. In a few sentences, he accomplishes things in people's lives that we can only hope to accomplish in hours or days or months. Our work can only faintly resemble his — even then, only because of the grace, wisdom, and guidance he provides. If we ask him, he'll guide our work with hurting people no matter how "out of our league" we might feel.

5

$$\left[\; l \,\text{I}\,f\,\text{E} - w \;\text{o}\;\text{r}\;\text{d}\;\text{s}\quad f \,\text{O}\;\text{r} \;\right]$$

[life-words for SHAPING COUNSELING RELATIONSHIPS]

Jesus answered, "If you knew the generosity of God and who I am, you would be asking me for a drink, and I would give you fresh, living water. . . . anyone who drinks the water I give will never thirst — not ever. The water I give will be an artesian spring within, gushing fountains of endless life." The woman said, "Sir, give me this water so I won't ever get thirsty, won't ever have to come back to this well again."

John 4:10-15, MSG

The key to shaping a discipleship-counseling relationship is getting the person-in-need to ask for the right kind of help. Jesus' conversation with the Samaritan woman serves as our best guide for doing this.

When they first met, the only way the Samaritan woman could conceive of Jesus' "living water" helping her was to improve her material circumstances: "If these claims about 'living water' are true, I'll never have to come back to this public well where everyone scorns and shuns me for the life I lead." She was more than willing, as most people are, to accept the counsel of a stranger as long as it promised to relieve her suffering. Jesus, however, wanted their relationship to serve a higher purpose. He offered friendship, guidance, and "living water" to bring her life, not just relief.

We shape and define our human relationships, including friendship-counseling relationships, by the needs we expect them to fulfill. Remember that hurting people, at the beginning of their spiritual journeys, are asking only one question: "How can I change my world?" Of course, they expect the answer to be something they find in the world—some material tool or resource they lack (such as money, education, success, opportunity, status, religion). They pressure their friends and counselors to help them identify and secure something that will improve their material existence. This expectation governs their relationship with anyone who offers help unless it is expressly discussed and altered.

What kind of help are you most excited about giving to hurting people? How do you respond when they don't want that kind of help?

Transforming a Request for Help into a Quest for Life

"Sir," the woman said, "I can see that you are a prophet. Our fathers worshiped on this mountain, but you Jews claim that the place where we must worship is in Jerusalem." Jesus declared, "Believe me, woman, a time is coming when you will worship the Father neither on this mountain nor in Jerusalem . . . true worshipers will worship the Father in spirit and truth." (John 4:19-21, 23, NIV)

The Samaritan woman thirsted for something that would relieve her suffering. Instinctively, she realized she needed more than water to improve her plight. She was a member of a despised and disadvantaged minority, a Samaritan. She was poor, she didn't have a family to nurture and protect her, and she was a five-time loser at marriage — presently living as an adulteress with a sixth man. She knew she needed something. When she realized she was talking to a Jewish holy man, it clicked. "I need religion," she thought. "Maybe Jesus can tell me how to tap into the material blessings the Jews enjoy." So she guided the conversation to the subject of worship.

Yet from the first words they exchanged, Jesus wanted to establish a different relationship with the Samaritan woman than the one she had in mind. Jesus faced the same obstacle that threatens to sabotage all counseling relationships from the outset: conflicting goals between the person wanting help and the person offering it. Conflicting goals often pit hurting people and their would-be helpers against each other in a fruitless struggle of wills. Jesus kept this from happening, however, by helping the Samaritan woman focus on something that was even more important to her than her immediate material concern — something ultimately more attractive and life-giving to her than escaping oppression and poverty.

When pressed, hurting people can usually put into words their *immediate* goal for coming for help — get the person or thing that's causing their distress to change. But few can tell you what they hope these changes will ultimately accomplish for them — the *ultimate* difference they think it will make in their lives. They've spent little time thinking about what their souls thirst for even more than these things.

This was certainly true of the Samaritan woman at the beginning of her conversation with Jesus. What she ultimately wanted wasn't just a way to get people to treat her more respectably. It was to be respectable. It wasn't relief from the pain of living in a sinful world, but relief from the shame of living a sinful life. Her ultimate goal was not to research alternate forms of worship. It was to restore her soul. She ached for what Eve enjoyed before her fall into sin — where God could gaze into her soul and say, "You are good. You are very good!" (see Genesis 2:31).

Consciously pursuing this, however, was too painful. Since it required things the Samaritan woman knew she could never achieve on her own — forgiveness, redemption, and inner transformation — pursuing them would only make her more aware than ever of her moral bankruptcy. It was easier to focus on controlling her circumstances. At least that would give her an outer veneer of virtue. This felt more "doable" than removing the evil in her own heart — the pathway to true virtue.

While this woman wasn't thinking about what she ultimately wanted, Jesus was. He wanted to help her pursue something that she wanted more than immediate relief from her circumstances. Jesus knew the key to turning ordinary friendships into discipleship-counseling relationships was helping people pursue their *ultimate* desires instead of their *immediate* needs.

What distinction do you make between ordinary helping relationships and discipleship-counseling relationships? How do you help friends who come to you shift their attention from immediate material concerns to ultimate spiritual ones?

Awakening the Spiritual Appetites of Hurting People

But the time is coming — it has, in fact, come — when what you're called will not matter and where you go to worship will not matter. It's who you are and the way you live that count before God. . . . That's the kind of people the Father is out looking for . . . those who worship him must do it out of their very being, their spirits, their true selves, in adoration. (Jesus, John 4:23-24, MSG)

When people first come for counseling, they often limit their requests for help to what they think will increase control in their relationships, especially the ones that are causing them the greatest pain. That's why the Samaritan woman was concerned about worship. She wanted God to change the way he was dealing with her — to bless her instead of punishing her. Her immediate goal was to use worship to change God, not herself.

Our first task when beginning friendship-counseling relationships is the same as Jesus' with the Samaritan woman: securing agreement to a goal directed at changing the character of our friends' response to suffering rather than the character of who or what might be causing their suffering. This requires more than getting them to agree verbally to such a goal. It requires awakening in them a hunger for this kind of change — so they'll want it more than anything else we could offer. This is the same challenge Jesus faced when counseling the Samaritan woman — persuading someone who's determined to change others, to instead seek deep and profound changes in themselves.

START WITH THE CONCERN(S) OUR FRIENDS WANT TO TALK ABOUT.

Jesus used the concern that was of most interest to the Samaritan woman at the time (worship) to help her discover *something about her own heart* she desperately needed to change. Jesus' first sentence to the woman affirmed her for her concern about worship and her courage in asking him, a Jew, about it: "You Samaritans worship what you do not know; we worship what we do know, for *salvation* is from the Jews" (John 4:22, emphasis added). With this sentence Jesus expressed his willingness to discuss her concern and his confidence that something behind it was beneficial for her to pursue.

Jesus knew that she wanted information from him that she could use to manipulate God. But this didn't deter him from using her question about worship as a starting place to help her. Any problem a hurting person initially brings is connected both to an *immediate goal* (short-sighted and destructive) and to a deeper *ultimate goal* (eternal and spiritual).

Our responsibility at this first stage of a friendship-counseling relationship is to tune into our friends' goals on both levels and build an alliance that turns their ultimate concern into a goal for our work together. Failure to do this results in helping them pursue a destructive goal. This is what Paul warned us to avoid when he wrote, "Brothers, if someone is caught in a sin, you who are spiritual should restore him gently. But watch yourself, or you may also be tempted" (Galatians 6:1, NIV).

LISTEN FOR THEIR ULTIMATE CONCERN AND USE IT TO GIVE THEM HOPE.

Jesus put into words something the Samaritan woman wanted more than any other kind of help he could give her. And then he gave her reason to believe it was possible to obtain it. He gave her hope — not that her immediate goal was achievable, but that her ultimate goal was.

Jesus knew he was speaking to someone who felt, as most hurting people do, like an orphan — like someone who has no family, parents, or husband to love her. And he knew material help would never satisfy what an orphan really hungers for: a Father to love her, pursue her, and enjoy her forever. Although she wasn't aware of it, he knew this hunger was in her heart — coloring every word she spoke with desperate urgency. And he knew which life-words could draw it out and entice her to pursue it: "Yet a time is coming and has now come when the true worshipers will worship the Father in spirit and truth, for they are the kind of worshipers the Father seeks" (John 4:23, NIV).

These words were designed to arouse an orphan's yearnings. Jesus dared to call God "Father" in her presence, even though she was a woman of ill-repute on the lowest social rung of a group that her culture thought was permanently cut off from God's affections. Jesus dared to speak of the possibility of her being a daughter her heavenly Father seeks and takes delight in. He dared to tell her that nothing stood in her way to becoming God's daughter if that's what she genuinely and passionately wanted. Jesus' words encouraged her not to set her sights too low or lose sight of what she wanted most.

EXPOSE THEIR IMMEDIATE GOAL AS INADEQUATE TO ACHIEVE WHAT THEY WANT MOST.

If what the Samaritan truly wanted most was the Father's love, Jesus helped her see she would never find it worshiping a weak god she could manipulate. She would only find it worshiping a strong God who loves voluntarily and freely, never out of pressure or need.

Jesus knew that the Samaritan woman was suffering far more from an impoverished theology than impoverished circumstances. As long as she believed God was like her string of husbands and lovers — men who "loved" only to get their own needs met — she'd never be able to really trust or enjoy his love. She'd feel like an orphan or a prostitute, even while worshiping him.

Jesus' words made it clear that God was different from anyone she'd ever dealt with before. "God is spirit, and his worshipers must worship in spirit and in truth" (John 4:24, NIV). Trying to relate to God with the same strategy she used in her other relationships wouldn't work since God is pure spirit. He's not governed by the same laws or motivated by the same concerns as the material world. If she wanted him to be her Father, she needed a way to change herself — deep within. *She had to approach him with a daughter's heart.* This required more than the cosmetic changes she'd make to get a new man to love her. It required vast subterranean changes in the things that governed and motivated her deep within the caverns of her heart.

HELP THEM START THE JOURNEY TO FIND WHAT THEY ULTIMATELY WANT.

When the woman realized that the key to having the Father she ultimately wanted depended upon changing things within herself that she couldn't possibly change on her own, her mind turned to the Messiah. He was the only person who could help her get a new heart: "The woman said, 'I know that Messiah (called Christ) is coming. When he comes, he will explain everything to us'"(John 4:25-26, NIV). This gave Jesus the opportunity to reveal the true Messiah to her: "I who speak to you am he."

As the meaning of Jesus' words sunk in, the woman felt like a little child again. Her long-forgotten dreams of a father's unconditional love came flooding back and filled her heart with new energy. Instead of fear and shame, she felt hope and courage: "Then, leaving her water jar, the woman went back to the town and said to the people, 'Come, see a man who told me everything I ever did. Could this be the Christ?'" (John 4:28-29, NIV).

Something told her that this was just the beginning of a new relationship! Jesus launched her on this journey by simply offering her a different kind of relationship — one that had a different focus and goal from any she'd experienced before. He used *her immediate concern* to shift her focus from what she thought was ruining her life (the poverty of her circumstances) to what was actually ruining her life (the poverty of her soul). He used *her ultimate concern* to shift the goal of their relationship from changing her circumstances to changing her own heart. This is the model Jesus gives us for turning our friendship-counseling relationships into crucibles for spiritual growth.

How do you begin helping someone who comes to you in pain? How is it similar or different from the model Jesus gives us here?

FOLLOWING JESUS' MODEL FOR SHAPING FRIENDSHIP-COUNSELING RELATIONSHIPS

Shaping a relationship the way Jesus does requires great skill. We learn it by breaking the process into several concrete steps. Once we practice and master each step individually, we can use them together to seamlessly shape the nature and direction of our friendship-counseling relationships. The conversation below with Randy illustrates and explains how this is done.

CLARIFY OUR FRIENDS' IMMEDIATE CONCERN.

Like the concern of the Samaritan woman, the immediate concerns of those who turn to us tip us off to what they ultimately want. So I begin my relationship with Randy by clarifying his immediate concern.

Since you asked for this meeting, Randy, I'm wondering how I can help.

I've been married about three years now. I'm a youth pastor at a church not far from here. Actually, this is my second go-around. I graduated from Bible college a few years ago and took my first youth pastorate right away. It was a rough experience. My wife and I were there just ten months before quitting and moving back in with my parents. Then we got a call from this church. I was a little apprehensive about taking it because of the experience I'd just had. But my wife, Mallory, was enthusiastic and thought this would be a good opportunity. So I took the position and I've been in it now for almost a year.

Now Mallory is pregnant. Actually, it's our second pregnancy. We lost the first one about five months ago. This ministry isn't going very well, either. The youth group isn't really bonding and I feel a lot of stress about Mallory. She's been in the hospital several times. And my pastor said I can't talk

*about the pregnancy because of the nature of it. So I have to
put on this face every Sunday that everything is fine and that
we're doing well when we're not. The board has already said
that I'm on probation. The church isn't aware of it. There's a
possibility I could lose my job, but the board's going to keep me
until at least the pregnancy's complete.*

*So I guess I made the wrong decision about going into the
ministry. Now my wife's pregnant, and I have no idea where to
go. I'm coming to you before I become a total failure. I'm here
to find out what I should do.*

As Randy describes the troubling events that bring him to counseling, his desire to escape "total failure" emerges as his immediate concern. He's concluded that the cause of his suffering is
his failures, and he selectively reports events that support this
conclusion.

His immediate goal is also apparent: to get away from
people and places that make him feel like a failure and go some-
where he can be a "success." At this point, I just want to
acknowledge his concern and how much pain it's causing him.
Then I want to get more details and examples. It's too soon to
challenge Randy's immediate goal or suggest a different one
until I know more about both the troubles in his world and the
troubles in his heart.

This must be an incredibly difficult time for you — feeling like
you're on the verge of being a total failure.
*Yes, and you're the first person I've told all of this to because I've
had to keep it to myself.*
Can you give me any more examples of these struggles you've had
to keep to yourself?
*Sure. I told my pastor we had to go through a procedure for infertil-
ity. When we got pregnant, he told us we shouldn't let anyone*

know about it. I guess he thought people wouldn't approve of the procedure we used to get pregnant.

And when is the baby due?

Sometime in the fall — the beginning of November.

So you're only a few months into the pregnancy right now?

Yeah. We lost the last one about this time . . . in the fourth month, I think. Mallory had to be in the hospital for several days. The people in the church found out and were curious as to why she was in the hospital.

And you still couldn't tell anybody at church about the pregnancy or miscarriage?

Right. I have to try to make everything look like it's going great for the church. It's been really hard for me to prepare lessons and keep the youth ministry going. Several kids in the group are deacons' kids and if I don't spend time with them, I hear about it. One night, Mallory needed me to be home. But I had to visit this boy because he was giving his parents trouble and his father is a big supporter in the church. I was getting a lot of pressure from the pastor to meet with him that night. So I chose to meet with him and left my wife crying. I felt terrible.

You're really feeling caught. Whenever you try to please one person, you fail another.

That's me. Ever since I went into youth ministry my life has been a disaster.

As I listen, I look for opportunities to put the essence of what Randy's telling me into summarizing sentences. When I'm able to do this, a light bulb turns on in his mind, like when Randy lit up: "That's me!" This signals to both of us that I'm beginning to understand what's troubling him. It helps him trust me and gives him hope that I not only care, but that I may be able to help him.

It's important at this stage in our relationship that I not only listen carefully to what Randy is telling me, but I must also be an active listener. I explore for more details, clarify what he's saying, summarize to make sure I understand him correctly, and let him know I not only hear his words, but his feelings too. Often, I turn his emotionally charged words into exploratory questions to invite him to take me deeper into his experience. As the conversation continues, I use the word "disaster" to do this.

Can you be more specific about the trouble you're having now? Maybe a few concrete examples of how your life has been a disaster since you went into youth ministry?

When I started at the church, the junior and senior highers met together. I separated the groups because we had twelfth graders in the same group as sixth graders. What I soon found out was the group was actually being run by some senior high students whose fathers were on the board. These kids didn't like the changes I was making. They no longer want to come to the group, but their parents make them. So they do everything they can to undermine the sense of community I'm trying to build.

What exactly do they do?

Disrupt meetings. Talk while I'm teaching. Turn other kids against me. I've tried spending time getting to know them one-on-one. But they want nothing to do with me. One positive thing is that I've been able to connect with some of the other kids who've been in the woodwork. And they're excited about the changes. But the pastor tells me that the parents who give quite a bit to the church are unhappy with me, and I have to find a way to keep their kids happy and involved. They're the kids who are causing the trouble. Coupled with that pressure, I'm feeling pressure about Mallory being pregnant—especially since I might lose my job.

So I'm questioning what God is trying to do in all this. I can't let my guard down anywhere. I can't tell my wife that I didn't really want her to be pregnant after we just lost a baby. The problems at church and at home seem to just feed each other. The pastor has even been telling people in the church that I'm not a youth man. He has two of his own children in my ministry—his son in my senior high group and his daughter in the junior high group. I've developed a really good relationship with both of them. So I don't understand why he's telling everybody I'm not a youth man.

Tell me some more about your relationship with your pastor.

I'm pretty quiet around him. He's not the kind of person you can really talk to.

Exploratory questions are one of our best tools for clarifying our friends' concerns. These questions invite them to talk more about some aspect of a problem they're experiencing. The best way to ask an exploratory question is to begin it with the phrase "I wonder about . . ." or "Tell me more about . . ." The best exploratory questions solicit more than just "yes" or "no" or a few words. The objective is to invite the person to take us deeper into their concern, giving whatever details they consider important.

Exploratory questions should be used in conjunction with summarizing sentences. Putting what we sense our friends are saying and feeling into our own words gives them frequent opportunities to confirm, correct, or amplify the meaning of their words.

All this feels hopeless to you . . . like you have no power in this situation to keep more disasters from happening. *(Summarizing sentence)*

Yes. I wasn't brought up in a Christian home. When I became a Christian in high school, I thought being part of a church family would change everything, you know, make my life a whole lot better. I never thought it would be like this.

Tell me more about what it's been like. *(Exploratory question)*

Even worse than growing up. Sure, I felt bad about myself then, but never like I do now—a total failure.

I wonder about what makes this worse? *(Exploratory question)*
There's nowhere I can go to escape the pressure. I feel it at church. I
feel it at home. I feel it with God. I feel like I'm going in cir-
cles . . . or like I'm barely treading water.
It's like you're trapped! You can't escape the feeling of being a failure no matter what you do. You thought that becoming a
Christian would rescue you from this feeling. Instead, you're
immersed even more in failure, and you feel like you're drowning. *(Summarizing sentence)*
Exactly.

In order to understand the trouble others are experiencing in
their world, we have to get enough details to write a miniseries
about their life. But it's important not to get bogged down listening for hours to stories that echo the same concern. This only
extinguishes what little hope they still have. Usually, three
detailed examples are enough to clarify the nature of their concern. With each successive example, we're able to put our friend's
concern into more graphic words. After one example I knew
only enough about Randy's struggles to state his concern in general terms: "You're feeling like a failure." As I heard more examples, I could paint it with richer colors and more detail: "You feel
trapped . . . can't escape . . . no matter what you do . . .
immersed . . . like you're drowning."

Practice Exercise

Reread the above conversation. This time skip my commentary and
read only the dialogue. Carefully observe the way I use exploratory
questions and summarizing sentences to help Randy clarify his immediate concern. Choose any three of the questions or sentences that I
used and write them down. Now write one or two alternative questions or sentences that could help clarify Randy's concern (see the
sample below).

Kevin: Tell me more about your relationship with your pastor.
Alternatives: What's your relationship with your pastor like?
   It sounds like your relationship with your pastor is causing you
   some distress.

BRIDGE FROM THE TROUBLE IN THEIR WORLD TO THE TROUBLE IN THEIR HEART.

Although the goal of friendship-counseling is to address what's going wrong in our friends' hearts, we must start with exploring what's going wrong in their world. Since the troubles in their world bring them to us in the first place, taking time to carefully understand these concerns is a gift to our friends that goes a long way to foster hope and trust. At the same time, we must be careful not to slip into trying to rescue them from their troubles, rather than using their troubles to help them grow. To prevent this, we must deliberately build a bridge from the troubles they're having in the world to the troubles they're experiencing in their heart.

Building this bridge starts with helping our friends put into words the internal struggles that grow out of their external problems. We do this by inviting them to talk about the way they're handling these problems.

You've used the word failure several times. Feeling like a failure
   around your family growing up, and now around your wife and
   your church. How are you handling all this failure? How do
   you live with it?
Not well. Anything I do just seems to make it worse.

Like what?

Doing what I always do, I guess. Please everybody as best as I can. Don't rock the boat. Don't make waves.

I guess that's where the "pressure" comes in. That's the other problem I hear. To avoid feeling like a failure, you give in to the pressure to do what everybody else wants. Your pastor, the deacons, the kids — even your wife.

Mallory does pressure me a lot. When we took this new church position, I wanted to wait before we tried to get pregnant again. But she was afraid that if we waited too long maybe we could never have children. She made me feel guilty and selfish about wanting to wait. So we went ahead with it.

Even though I've asked the same basic question twice already ("How are you handling all this failure?"), I'll continue to ask it until I get a fuller answer. It's the kind of question that meets with resistance because it requires counselees to shift their focus from what others are doing to what they're doing themselves. From experience and Scripture (see Proverbs 18:7), I know that if I gently and persistently keep Randy talking about the way he's handling hardships, his words will ultimately expose the struggles going on in his heart.

So, if you don't do what people want you to do, you feel like you're screwing up again. But if you do what everybody wants you to do, it means you're weak and being pushed around. *(Summarizing sentence)* How do you live day-in and day-out in such a lose/lose position? *(Same basic question a third time)*

Right now I fantasize a lot. From early on I learned to escape my problems by fantasizing about . . . well . . . sexual things — about women. Obviously, if I can't talk about the other things going on in my life, there's no way I can talk about battling with lust. I struggle with lust every day.

Does it ever move beyond fantasy . . . into sexual activities . . . relationships with other women, pornography, phone or Internet
sex, anything like that?

*Not yet . . . not that I haven't been tempted. I'm too afraid I'd get
caught. Or afraid of what God would do to me. Sometimes I
think that's why my life is such a disaster.*

Your life is a disaster because God is punishing you for lusting?

Yeah. That thought goes through my mind a lot.

Like most of us, Randy is troubled even more inwardly than outwardly. He longs to be both virtuous and free, but finds the
people in his world quite unwilling to grant him one without
requiring him to surrender the other. The only place he's able to
find both at the same time is in the fleeting world of sexual fantasy. But that only leaves him feeling like even more of a failure.

In the next stage of our work together, Randy and I will
explore his inner struggle more. At this point, it's enough just to
touch on it — to help him acknowledge that it exists and
describe it in general terms. Without some awareness of troubles
within them, our friends will have little interest in pursuing a
goal focused on their own growth.

Because Randy perceives God to be as exacting as his parents, wife, and pastor, talking to him about God right now
would offer little hope (even though God is his only hope). His
current image of God bears little resemblance to the true God of
the Bible. As his friend, it's my job to help him discover, over
time, who God really is. Right now, he wouldn't believe me, and
he probably wouldn't come back. I have to model the true God
to him before I can interest him in coming close to the true God.
This is done the same way Christ did with the Samaritan
woman — through the kind of relationship I offer him. It must
be a relationship that is fundamentally different from what others are offering him.

Early in a counseling relationship, it's wise to clarify *why* the person is asking for help now, to make sure he's not facing any immediate life-threatening circumstances. It's best to ask about this directly. If life-threatening circumstances do exist, it becomes top priority to help the friend find immediate help from the appropriate source (local police, the nearest hospital emergency room, the family doctor). Friendship-counseling can resume as soon as any immediate threat to life is removed.

It takes a lot of courage for you to talk openly to me about your struggles. Why do you think you decided now was the right time to find help?

Like I said, I don't have any pride left. I've already failed at everything. What do I have left to lose, except my family? I can't lose that! When Mallory and I were dating, my father-in-law said that I would never amount to anything. I guess I'm starting to believe it.

That thought is very painful to you — like your worst fear coming true. "I'm never going to be anything more than the screw-up everybody expects me to be."

Yes. That's it.

And if you can't figure out a way to change, you might even screw up your marriage and lose your wife.

Yes. I'm starting to think I'll never be able to change.

Randy, I know you said that you've been handling this pain and the pressure by fantasizing. In the midst of this, have you thought about doing anything drastic or perhaps violent, to yourself or anyone else?

No. I haven't thought about that at all.

Have you ever been suicidal or violent?

No. I don't think I could ever do anything to hurt myself or another person.

Practice Exercise

1. In one sentence summarize the nature of the trouble in Randy's world:

2. In one sentence summarize the nature of the trouble in Randy's heart:

3. Describe how the two are related:

4. In what ways are the troubles in Randy's heart a response to his troubles in the world?

CHAIN FROM THE IMMEDIATE TO THE ULTIMATE GOAL.

I now have a general idea of what Randy wants from me. But I can't assume that I know his goals for seeking counsel until he tells me explicitly. This is critical to establishing our relationship on a firm foundation, and it's best accomplished by using the simple question I ask next:

What kind of help were you hoping to get from me?
I guess it comes back to the practical thing: What do I do to get out of this mess? I studied four years in Bible College, and I can't go out and get an accounting job. I even thought about going to a business school to learn another trade. With two big failures in the ministry, I've obviously misread what I can do. Yet I don't feel like I can change jobs right now. At least they've told

me they'll keep me on until my child's birth because of the
health insurance. And with Mallory being pregnant, I've got to
be careful not to create any more stress for her.

So you want me to help you get into a different line of work, even
though it would be hard to change jobs right now because of
the interruption it would cause in your health insurance and
the stress it would put on your wife?

. . . or at least start the ball rolling toward finding a new career.
You know, maybe get something lined up to do as soon as the
baby comes.

This is Randy's *immediate* goal: "Find a new career." But if I agree
to help him pursue this, I'll reinforce the notion that his life
depends on avoiding failure at all cost. Besides, his fear of failure, conflict, and displeasing others would sabotage a different
job the same way it's sabotaging his ministry, marriage, and relationships at church. If I really want to help Randy grow, I must
resist the temptation to help him escape the current troubles in
his world. Instead, I must help him develop the character to
respond to them in a healthier way. I can only do this if I help
him pursue the one thing he *ultimately* wants and needs more
than a successful career: the ability to live freely and fearlessly
regardless of how others treat him. This requires shifting his
focus from the only goal he's aware of (his immediate goal) to a
goal he has little or no awareness of (his ultimate goal). I'll help
him "chain" from his immediate goal to his ultimate goal by
asking him what he hopes his immediate goal will accomplish.

If I could help you find a new job or career, what would that
accomplish? What difference do you think it would make in
your life?

I guess it would prove to everybody that I'm not some loser . . . a
big failure.

Prove it to . . . ?

I guess Mallory, her dad, my dad . . . maybe myself.

So you want me to help you prove to all these people that you're not a loser?

Chaining brought us to a goal more important than merely getting a new job — proving to himself and the world that "he's not a loser." As important as this is to Randy, it's probably not his most important goal — his *ultimate* goal. His ultimate goal will become apparent when he starts to describe virtues of the heart he's always longed to possess but stands helpless to acquire without God's help. We're not there yet. Randy's aim is still to change others (how they view him), not himself. So I must continue to chain these lesser goals to get to his ultimate goal.

And if you could prove to these people that you aren't a loser, what would that accomplish?

They'd respect me. I wouldn't feel so much pressure and guilt around them. They'd see me as a man who knows what he's doing . . . someone who has it together.

And if they started seeing you as this man, what do you think that would accomplish?

I know I'd feel better . . . I wouldn't have to be afraid of losing — you know — their love.

And if I could help you be with people without being afraid of losing their love, what do you think that would do?

I wouldn't be a loser then.

What would you be instead?

Strong, I guess. My own person.

You want to be a person controlled by something other than fear?

Yes.

What do you want to be controlled by?

What I believe is right.

By your own convictions?

Yes.

Anything else?

Courage. I guess. Courage to stand up for what I believe.

This is Randy's *ultimate* goal. He wants to be the strong, free, and principled man God created him to be. Even though it terrifies him, he wants this far more than a new career. Since I'm sure God also wants this for Randy, we now have a goal I can help him pursue. If Randy agrees, we can shape our discipleship-counseling relationship around this goal.

Practice Exercise

Write an imaginary dialogue with a friend you're currently helping. Begin with the initial exchange below. Continue by using the skill of chaining until you uncover the person's ultimate goal—one you could, in good conscience, enthusiastically commit yourself to helping this person achieve.

You: What kind of specific help were you hoping to get from me?

Friend: I guess I was hoping that you could help me control my anger better.

You: If I could help you control your anger better, what difference do you think it would make?

Friend:

You:

Friend:

Keep chaining until you uncover the ultimate goal.

SECURE AGREEMENT ON A GROWTH GOAL FOR YOUR RELATIONSHIP.

Agreeing on an appropriate goal for discipleship-counseling requires three things. *First,* it requires helping our friend clearly identify some change he wants to make. I did this when I helped Randy chain from his immediate concern (finding a new career) to his ultimate concern (becoming a man of strength and courage).

Second, it requires framing the desired change into a goal directed at altering our friend's response to what's troubling him rather than altering the troubling things themselves. If people or circumstances trouble him, the goal is to help him find the freedom or power to respond to them in a new way. If it's his own behaviors or emotions, the goal should be to help him find the freedom or power to handle these unwanted impulses or feelings in a different way. If it's something about God or life itself, the goal should be to help him find the freedom or power to respond to these disappointments or frustrations in a different way. The purpose of a growth goal is to give your conversations ongoing direction and purpose, so you need to frame it in a sentence you both can remember and articulate.

Third, agreeing on a goal requires supplying our friend with a compelling rationale for making this goal the focus of our work together. The rationale must be more compelling than his fears.

Randy, let me suggest that before we work on finding you a new
    career or job that we first help you develop the ability to be that

man of strength and courage you want to be — to find the freedom to respond with strength and courage to the people who look at you with disappointment, disapproval, and even disgust. No matter what line of work you go into or how successful you are, you'll always encounter people who don't like what you're doing. If you don't develop a different way to respond, you'll quickly end up feeling and acting the same way you do now in the youth ministry. You'll end up in the same dilemma. Does that make sense?

It makes sense, but I wonder if it's really possible for me to respond to somebody out of strength or courage. I'm so used to trying to give people what they want.

I offer to help Randy develop the ability to respond in a fundamentally different way to the most important people in his life. This objective has all three ingredients of an effective friendship-counseling goal: (1) It is critically important to both him and God. (2) It doesn't require him to change anything or anyone but himself. (3) It requires him to change things in his heart that he can only change with God's help.

Wanting to give Randy a rationale for pursuing this goal, I suggest that reordering his priorities is a logical necessity. He can't achieve his immediate goal (finding a job in which he succeeds) until he first accomplishes his ultimate goal (becoming a man of strength and courage). This understandably arouses great fear and confusion — two things he must be willing to endure in order to pursue this goal. I can't say anything at this point to alleviate these feelings. I can only show him why pursuing this goal is worth enduring all the fear and confusion it creates.

Randy, what has trying to give people what they want accomplished for you? Has it made people view you the way you want them to?

[142]

Not really.

How hard have you tried?

Very. That's almost all I think about.

So you've discovered that it's just not possible to control or change the way people view you, no matter how hard you try?

That's about it.

If I had a magic wand I could wave for both of us and make all the people in our lives think we're wonderful, I'd enjoy that as much as you would. But since I don't have a magic wand, I'm in the same boat as you. Neither of us has the power to control anyone but ourselves.

So what you're saying is I shouldn't care about what other people think . . . only what God thinks?

No, not at all. It's natural and probably healthy that you care about what other people think. What gets you in trouble is trying to *control* what other people think. That's trying to control something that you can't control. And it sets you up to feel like a failure, every time.

But if I can't change what people think, what am I supposed to do when they look at me like I'm a loser? I can't just act like it doesn't bother me.

I don't want you to. It should bother you because that's not who you really are. But if you try to change the way others view you, it gives them tremendous power over you. It's like you're saying to them, "My life depends on your good opinion of me. To be a whole man, I've got to get your approval." That just causes them to see you as weak . . . as a loser.

I don't know what else to do. I don't know what it means to respond to them out of strength or . . .

I don't know exactly what it'll mean for you to respond with strength and courage either. We'll work together to discover that. I do know it means something other than trying to escape or appease people when they bully you or treat you with contempt. That's backfiring. Instead, it will mean finding a way to stay involved with them and love them, even when they dislike or disrespect you. It will mean finding a way to be who you want to be when people try to frighten or intimidate you, instead of hiding or retreating into a fantasy world where everyone gives you what you want, whenever you want it.

I see where you're going and it scares me to death. But I think you're right. What I've been doing isn't working. The more I try to please people, the more I hold back. The more I hold back, the more I fantasize. And then I feel guilty and hold back even more when they're around . . . and that makes them see me as an even bigger loser.

What do you hold back?

Me, I guess. What I'm thinking. What I'm feeling . . . I guess you could say my heart.

I know it's frightening to think about making that our goal. Instead of holding back around the critical people in your life or trying to prove something to them, feeling free to offer them some genuine part of your heart — maybe even a part they won't like, or a part that shows them your strength or courage.

That's really different from what I thought we were going to work on.

This is just one possibility. We can explore others. But counseling won't be helpful unless we're working toward a goal we both agree is vital to your growth and health as a man. And that's probably always going to involve a goal that feels scary, at least at first.

I do think I'd like to work on that goal, being strong and real with people instead of holding back. But I guess I'm afraid to fail again. Letting people down is a tough thing. I've been hurt enough to know that it can be dangerous. That's the only thing that makes me hesitate.

It's amazing to me, given what you've been through, that you're willing to consider this goal at all. That takes great courage. I think you're wise, too, to hesitate and really weigh this. Moving this direction could result in more pain.

That's the first time anyone has ever called me wise or courageous.

That's how I see you. You know, you don't have to make this decision right now. Why don't we take a few days to think about it and get back together on Thursday, about this same time? With the urgent things going on in your life right now, we probably shouldn't wait a whole week to meet again.

That sounds good.

My desire at this early stage is to offer Randy a relationship that respects his right to choose for himself the kind of person he wants to be in his circumstances. This means giving him all the information and time he needs to make his own decision about the direction our counseling takes. We'll never come to a sincere agreement if I make him work on something he doesn't really want.

I do sense real interest on Randy's part in the goal I've suggested. But there's no reason to hurry. Securing agreement to an appropriate goal is sometimes achieved in one conversation. Other times it requires numerous talks over several weeks. However long it takes, we can't start a friendship-counseling relationship until we reach agreement on a growth goal. I won't know for sure until our next meeting whether Randy's ready to pursue the goal we've discussed.

This is a goal he both desires and fears at the same time. If he decides he doesn't want help to be the man of strength God created him to be, friendship-counseling won't be very fruitful. Although it's too early in the relationship to pray with Randy about his decision (for reasons I'll go into later), I will pray fervently on my own for him as he's deciding.

Before ending a meeting, clarify any assignments that you've given. This is how I end my meeting with Randy.

Before we adjourn, can you put into a sentence the goal you're
going to be weighing between now and Thursday?
*Getting free to offer people my heart, instead of . . . hiding from
them or trying to please them.*
Yes. I like how you put it. You know how to reach me if anything
comes up between now and Thursday?
Yes. Thanks. See you on Thursday.

Practice Exercise

For each of the following concerns (brought by four different friends),
construct a goal you could use to shape a friendship-counseling relationship. Remember, it must be a goal that focuses on changing their
response to the thing that troubles them instead of the thing itself.
Write a few sentences explaining the rationale you could give each
person for pursuing the goal you constructed.

"I want your help to get my teenage son to obey and respect me."

"I need help to stop lusting after people at the office."

"I need help with my lack of motivation. Since my husband died, everything feels so futile to me. If things like this can happen, life doesn't even
seem worth living."

"I don't understand why God lets people get away with doing these terrible things to me. What am I doing wrong that God would let them do
this to me?"

6

[*l* I ƒ E - *w* o r d s ƒ o r]
GUIDING REFLECTION

I know your deeds . . . You say, "I am rich; I have acquired wealth and do
not need a thing." But you do not realize that you are wretched, pitiful, poor,
blind and naked. I counsel you to buy from me . . . white clothes to wear, so
you can cover your shameful nakedness.

Jesus, Revelation 3:15, 17-18, NIV

The goal of your discipleship-counseling work with your friend is
now established: to change the nature of his response to the troubling events in his life. The next step is to engage him in reflection
about the ways he's *currently* responding to these events. Reflection
is nothing more than "giving thought to the ways" we're living our
lives (see Proverbs 14:15; 21:29) — the actions we choose, the
emotions we feel, the thoughts we think, and the passions we pursue. Guiding others to reflect means helping them recognize and
understand how these forces in their hearts control and direct
their responses to life events (see Proverbs 20:5).

Remember the rich young man came to Jesus asking, "What
good thing must I do to get eternal life?" (Matthew 19:16, NIV).

He was vaguely aware that something about the way he was living life wasn't quite right. He didn't really know or understand what it was, but presumed he could take care of it himself.

He wanted his counselor to tell him how to repair a small defect or two that tarnished what he thought was an otherwise stellar character. But if his counselor had done that, it only would have strengthened the man's belief that his life depended upon his own resources. Instead, Jesus guided the young man to discover a character deficit so great that his illusions of self-sufficiency were shattered. The young man "went away sad" (Matthew 19:22, NIV), reflecting upon the void in his heart that kept him from loving others the way Jesus was calling him to. He was one step closer to understanding what his heart really lacked — the ability to be the servant God created him to be.

Imagine how different this man's next meeting with Jesus would be after he'd had time to reflect. I imagine him speaking words to Jesus that echo our Lord's own words in Revelation 3:15-18: "I came to you the first time saying, 'I am rich; I have acquired status, reputation, and independence and need nothing from anybody.' But I was wrong. I'm the opposite of how I presented myself to be. I'm wretched, pitiful, poor, blind, and naked. I can never be truly clean, healthy, or good on my own. Only you can take my hideous heart and transform it into something virtuous. Would you make me into a different kind of person?"

Our friends can never speak life-words like these to Jesus until they spend time reflecting upon their own hearts. That's our objective as we interact with friends who are asking the question, "What am I doing wrong?" It's to offer words that guide them to take a long look at the troubling things they're doing in their own hearts that they're doomed to repeat unless God graciously intervenes.

The questions we use to stimulate this kind of self-understanding are life-words to hurting people. Through reflective

questioning we help them get insight into the desperate condition of their own souls, their best tool for developing a life-
changing connection with God. Without insight into who they
really are, our friends will never have a clear picture of who God
really is.

**What does God use to help you get Revelation 3:15-18 glimpses of
yourself? What role does reflective dialogue with others play in these
discoveries?**

WHEN PEOPLE DON'T KNOW
WHAT THEY'RE DOING

*Father, forgive them, for they do not know what they are doing. (Jesus on
the cross, Luke 23:34, NIV)*

People are most dangerous and destructive when they're
ignorant of the real nature and impact of their choices. The men
who crucified Jesus didn't understand what they were doing. If
they'd understood, Paul tells us, "they would not have crucified
the Lord of glory" (1 Corinthians 2:8, NIV). People seem capable
of their most heinous acts when they're least aware of the forces
in their hearts that drive them to do what they do. When the disciples wanted Jesus to senselessly destroy a whole village, he
rebuked them saying, "You wouldn't ask me to do this if you
could see what I see — if you could see what's in your hearts
right now — the will to destroy people. I don't have that in my
heart. I have only the will to save them" (Luke 9:55).

When we don't know what we're doing, we can easily
become murderers of one kind or another. The slightest sense of
injury can become justification to "murder" anyone who gets in
our way — if not physically, at least verbally or psychologically —
while not even noticing what we're doing. Hateful thoughts and

feelings make us murderers in our hearts (Matthew 5:21-22; 1 John 3:15). Imagine what damage we do to others when we live our lives oblivious to the murderous forces in our hearts. Reflecting upon our responses toward others, especially when they injure us, is our best window for getting a glimpse at these forces.

Most of us have a vague idea that something isn't right in the way we treat others. We suspect that our impulse to lash out, deceive, or cut people out of our lives when they cause us problems is wrong. Yet we usually don't grasp the depth or significance of our actions. This is why reflection — the way we "examine ourselves" — is imperative. Paul commands us to discover what controls us at the deepest levels (2 Corinthians 13:5). This gives us the information we need to put into words what we desperately need God to do in our hearts (1 John 1:9). Without reflection, we remain blind to who we are and what we're doing (1 John 1:8,10), unable to communicate with God about the help we really need from him.

What's the most painful truth (or character flaw) you've ever had to face about yourself? How would your life be different if you'd kept going, ignorant that this character flaw even existed?

HELPING FRIENDS IN NEED REFLECT

Why do you look at the speck of sawdust in your brother's eye and pay no attention to the plank in your own eye? (Jesus in Matthew 7:3, NIV)

Why is it so easy to spot the character flaws of others, but overlook our own? Jesus' question helps us realize that we can never see others clearly until we first attend to our own character flaws.

The same is true for friends who turn to us for counsel. Character flaws that escape their notice blur their moral vision and distort the ways they think about themselves and others. They need our help to see and understand themselves, warts and all, in the searching light of a committed friend's probing questions. King Solomon observed what the wise use to bring to light the hidden contents of people's hearts: "The first to present his case seems right, till another comes forward and *questions* him" (Proverbs 18:17, NIV, emphasis added).

Jesus frequently used this tool — probing questions — in his conversations with struggling people. He didn't use it to uncover things *he* needed to know, but things *they* needed to know. Jesus' questions always took people beneath the surface of their own lives into the inner workings of their souls (their emotions, actions, cognitions, and passions). He did this to make them conscious that the real threat to their ultimate well-being lay in the way they chose to govern their lives. By asking them to reflect on what they were feeling, doing, thinking, and desiring at a given moment, Jesus helped them discover how inadequate they were to govern their lives without his help.

Who do you turn to for help to understand the significance and meaning of what you're feeling, doing, thinking, or desiring? What kinds of words from others help you do this kind of reflection?

REFLECTING ON EMOTIONS.
Why are you so afraid? (Jesus to his disciples, Mark 4:40, NIV)

Jesus never devalued people's feelings. Instead, he used emotions as a point of entry into their souls. When his disciples were terrified that their boat might capsize during a storm at sea, Jesus asked them to think about what their fear at that moment meant (Mark 4:35-41). What did it mean about their hearts?

Jesus knew that emotions provide vital information about what's going on in people's hearts. Our emotions tell us at any given moment the meaning and significance we assign to events.

Joy means that we see an event as beneficial. *Fear* means we perceive something as dangerous or threatening. *Anger* means seeing an event as an injury or insult of some kind. *Shame* or *guilt* indicates we feel a moral failure on our part. And *sadness* or *grief* means we sense an irretrievable loss. The intensity of our emotions tells us how much importance we attach to the event. The more intense our feelings, the more significant the event is in our thinking.

Our emotions can mislead us if we incorrectly evaluate an event (mislabel an accidental slight as a deliberate offense, or see a small setback as a catastrophe). Any emotion that attaches a different meaning or significance to an event than God does is inappropriate and destructive (Luke 16:15). We come to attach the same significance to events that God does only through the work of his Spirit in our hearts. The more God shapes our character to resemble his Son's, the more his Son's thoughts and emotions become ours.

Believing that God doesn't have the ability or willingness to care and provide for us is the root of the destructive emotions that plague our souls. Helping our friends grow through their trials requires guiding them to recognize the true meaning of their emotions.

Can you identify at least one recent emotion you've had that is inappropriate or destructive? In what way does it attach a different significance to an event than God does? What does it reveal about what's in your heart?

Reflecting on actions.

Why do you ask me about what is good? (Jesus to the rich young man, Matthew 19:17, NIV)

Jesus often asked questions that made people think about their actions — or the purpose behind their actions. Jesus questioned the young man who wanted to be perfect, "What's behind the action you're taking in coming to me? What's the goal behind the question you're asking me?" (Matthew 19:17). Jesus knew that we select our behavior as part of a plan to achieve something we value (Proverbs 16:9). The more we value it, the more stubbornly we pursue the course of action we believe will achieve it. Like emotions, actions are windows into our belief system (see Matthew 6:21).

Jesus also knew that people are seldom fully aware of the purposes behind their actions. Most of our behavior patterns are chosen early in childhood and perpetuated automatically into adulthood. That's why Jesus asked a probing question to get the rich young man to reflect about what he was up to. Jesus wanted him to fully understand the "method behind his madness." In the young man's case, he wanted total control of everything that happened to him — even after death — without understanding how unachievable it was.

Jesus' question was designed to help him recognize the nature of the goal he was pursuing, "Why do you ask me about how you can be good? There is only One in all the universe who is truly good. Do you realize what you're trying to do?" (Matthew 19:17). Jesus often responded to questions by asking questions of his own to encourage people to reflect on the purpose or goal behind their question. Until we understand the goal that drives us to do what we do, our actions won't seem like a choice. Our behavior, for reasons we don't understand, will feel like compulsory duties that we must fulfill to avoid some undefined danger. Only by reflecting on the goal behind our actions — especially on that goal's frustrating and futile nature — will we realize that we're free to choose a different action. We don't have to go on living the way we're living.

As distressing as this kind of insight can be, it's absolutely necessary. Without it, our friends will never experience real brokenness or change of heart. Friendship-counseling always helps people gain insight into their own actions.

What actions do you most frequently use to achieve what's important to you? What's the goal you're pursuing with these actions?

REFLECTING ON COGNITIONS.

Why are you thinking these things in your heart? (Jesus to the Pharisees in Luke 5:22, NIV)

Jesus often asked people to think about the significance of their thoughts at a given moment. Jesus asked the Pharisees what was behind their cynicism as they watched him forgive a paralytic man. Why did they refuse to believe in his authority to forgive sins? After his resurrection, he asked a similar question of his disciples: "Why does it trouble you to think that I've risen from the dead? What causes you to doubt me in your hearts even as you stand here looking at me?" (Luke 24:38).

Jesus knew that people often hold beliefs for reasons they spend little time thinking about. Even when we believe things that seem irrational or unfounded, we have reasons for doing so. During our earliest and most painful experiences we make assumptions and develop convictions about how to survive and protect ourselves from future suffering. We mistakenly attribute our survival to something we can control, instead of God, and bestow on this thing godlike ability to protect us from our greatest fears. Once convinced that our lives depend on obtaining or controlling this thing, it serves as the *god* or *idol* that commands our deepest devotion, ignites our strongest passions, and dictates our most intense reactions.

We seldom pause to question the truth or effectiveness of our early convictions. Even when the thing we value fails to deliver or protect the way we assumed it would, we continue to faithfully regard it as the only thing that can rescue us from our problems. We resist renouncing or replacing it in any wholesale way as long as the slightest hope exists that it still might give us what we want.

This is why Jesus guided the Pharisees to reflect on their thoughts. Spiritual growth requires insight into the reasons we believe what we do. Any event important enough to alter our emotions or behaviors also triggers thoughts important enough to warrant reflection. As automatic or as superficial as our conscious thoughts seem during an event, reflective questions can help us recognize and evaluate the nature of the beliefs that fuel or color our thinking

If one belief superseded your belief in God (at least some of the time),what would it be? How do you know when this is happening?

REFLECTING ON PAST EXPERIENCES.
No one who puts his hand to the plow and looks back is fit for service in the kingdom of God. (Jesus to a would-be disciple, Luke 9:62, NIV)

Jesus often encountered people who wanted to follow him but didn't feel free to. They wanted to go complete some unfinished business of their old life before they began a new one. Jesus said that they couldn't follow him if they felt any compulsion to hold onto the life they were leaving behind. Paul taught a similar principle about Christian discipleship:

> No, dear brothers, I am still not all I should be, but I am bringing all my energies to bear on this one thing: Forgetting the past and looking forward to what lies ahead, I strain to reach the end of the race and receive the prize for which God is calling us up to heaven because of what Christ Jesus did for us. (Philippians 3:13-14, TLB)

Looking back hinders serving and obeying God. We lose our energy, precision, and concentration when we focus on the things that are *behind us* (past experiences, relationships, wrongs, failures, and choices we can't undo or change). Instead, we must conserve our energy and concentration for the things *before us* that we still have opportunity to make choices about.

Some people wonder if the teachings of Jesus and Paul mean that it's hazardous to reflect at all on past experiences. Does "forgetting the past" literally mean never thinking about past experiences — especially negative or hurtful ones? Maybe this is what Paul is getting at in Philippians 4:8, NIV: "Whatever is true . . . noble . . . right . . . pure . . . lovely . . . admirable . . . excellent or praiseworthy — think about such things."

If Jesus and Paul meant for us to avoid all reflection about negative things in our past, they violated their own counsel on many occasions. In Philippians 3:6, Paul recalls past experiences when he arrested and murdered Christians, thinking he was doing God a service. He recounts hurtful experiences and the lessons he learned from them to instruct and encourage other Christians who would one day face similar trials (2 Corinthians 1:8-9). Jesus, as well, helped his disciples reflect upon past experiences, even their failures, so they'd be sure to draw the correct lessons from them (Mark 9:14-29).

Jesus' model for friendship-counseling always involves reflection on past experiences. In urging us not to look back, Jesus and Paul were simply teaching that we shouldn't let things in our past get in the way of obeying and serving God in the present. Past events interfere with the way we presently live when we allow the flawed assumptions and convictions we formed when these events originally occurred to govern the way we respond to things today.

Whatever's in our past, it's exactly the past God wants us to have. He doesn't want us to try to change it or forget it. He wants us to learn how to use it to serve him. Paul learned to use his past as a murderer of innocent people to teach others about God's power to deliver them from the evil in their own hearts. And he used his experiences of being mistreated and persecuted to teach others about God's power to deliver them from the evil in the world.

We can use our past to strengthen our belief in God's power and goodness, or we can use it to strengthen our justification to trust no one's power and goodness but our own. Only by asking and answering some hard questions about our formative experiences can we start making deliberate choices about the lessons we draw from them. Do these events really mean what we thought they did at the time—that we can get along better in the future by trusting in our own care instead of God's? Or do these events have a different meaning than we once thought?

People who choose to live their lives without giving any thought to how their past influences their current choices aren't yet free from the false assumptions that make them slaves to their past. In the words of Christ, they're not yet "fit for service in the kingdom of God." We can help our friends find freedom from their destructive beliefs, forged in past experiences, only by helping them review these experiences. Then they can reflectively decide what influence they'll allow them to have on their present choices.

Are you aware of any experiences in your past that make you wary today to trust and serve God as fully as you could? What destructive lessons did you draw from these experiences?

REFLECTING ON PASSIONS.

You don't know what you are asking. . . . Can you drink the cup I drink or be baptized with the baptism I am baptized with? (Jesus to James and John, Mark 10:38, NIV)

James and John, two of Jesus' closest friends, had a burning desire. But they were reluctant to mention it to Jesus. Putting what they deeply longed for into a direct request to the most important person in their lives probably felt too forward, too vulnerable, or maybe too presumptuous. But they had enough experience with the world and enough insight into their own hearts to know there was no hope of quieting or satisfying this passion any other way. They came to the conclusion that only Jesus had the power to give them what they wanted.

After spending so much time with Jesus, James and John had learned that they could trust him with their hearts. "What's the worst thing that could happen?" they must have said to themselves. "At least we know he'll level with us. If we tell him what we want and it's not good, he'll show us how to change it. But if it's okay, maybe he'll grant it to us like he's been granting food to the hungry, hearing to the deaf, and sight to the blind. What do we have to lose?"

James and John eventually brought their request to Jesus through their mother (see Matthew 20:20-21). Maybe she was better at putting longings of the heart into words or some cultural tradition required her to intercede. We don't know. We do know that Jesus asked James and John to put their request into their own words (see Mark 10:36). That's when they blurted it out: "Grant that we may sit in Your glory, one on Your right and one on Your left" (Mark 10:37, NASB). Seldom encountering such candor, Jesus replied with candor of his own: "You don't know what you are asking . . . Can you drink the cup I drink or be baptized with the baptism I am baptized with?" (Mark 10:38, NIV).

On one level, James and John knew what they were asking for. But on another they didn't. They knew they wanted a whole lot more power and glory than what they presently possessed. They must have spent a lot of time thinking about the glorious things they could do for God if they just had the position and power to do it. What they didn't yet understand was that the power Jesus grants is very different from the power the world grants (see Mark 10:42-43). Jesus doesn't grant power to control what others are doing. He grants power to love others no matter what they're doing. He used James and John's request as an occasion to teach this to all of his disciples: "You know that those who are regarded as rulers of the Gentiles lord it over them. . . . Not so with you. Instead, whoever wants to become great among you must be your servant, and whoever wants to be first must be slave of all" (Mark 10:42-44, NIV).

James and John didn't know that the power they hungered for came through loving others in sacrificial, painstaking ways. Jesus' question to them was designed to help them see this: "Are you sure you understand what you're asking for? Can you handle the responsibilities and consequences that come with exercising this kind of power?" (Matthew 20:22). Jesus wanted them to reflect on how much work God still needed to do in their hearts before they'd be ready to endure the consequences that come with this kind of power.

Without even stopping to reflect, James and John answered, "We can" (Mark 10:39, NIV). Despite their bravado and inflated estimation of themselves, Jesus saw something to affirm in their passion: "Yes. One day you will indeed show me that you can drink the cup I drink, even though I cannot grant you a special place at my right or my left" (Matthew 20:23).

Jesus wanted James and John to recognize — as he wants us to — that there is something both good and bad about human passions. They're good in that they cause us to hunger and thirst for things that ultimately only God can provide. But they're bad to the degree that we believe we can satisfy them with things the world provides. That's how we turn holy and pure passions into corrupt and illicit desires.

We're all driven by passions we barely recognize or understand.

We know they exist, they're hard to satisfy, and they provide the energy and drive for the way we live our lives. Only when we reflect upon our passions do we gain insight to differentiate what's godly about them from what's ungodly. This, in turn, enables us to ask God to make us passionate for those things that drive us to him and dispassionate for those things that take us away from him.

What are you the most passionate about these days? Can you identify anything about these passions that drive you to God? Does anything about them take you away from him?

FOLLOWING JESUS' PATTERN FOR GUIDING REFLECTION

Helping our friends reflect on how they respond to the troubling events in their lives requires a deliberate strategy. The following conversation with Randy demonstrates this. The self-exploration I help Randy to do at this stage in his spiritual journey requires the same kind of reflective questions that Jesus used.

As you continue to read the transcript of my conversation with Randy, please remember that I am condensing the process for the sake of illustration and economy. While the conversation that follows is a realistic portrayal of the kind of life-words our friends need at this stage in their spiritual journey, the process appears more concise and straightforward than it usually is in real life.

Every friendship-counseling meeting after the first one should begin by reviewing and reconfirming the growth goal your friend previously agreed to. If it isn't a goal they still want to work toward, then you need to secure agreement on a new goal before proceeding. It's essential to keep all our counseling conversations with our friends anchored to a shared goal. We do this by simply reminding them of the goal and asking if it still interests them.

RECONFIRM THE GROWTH GOAL.

Randy, it's good to see you. What do you want to talk about today—what did you decide about the goal you left thinking about last week?

After our last meeting, I left afraid to make that next step. But I gave it some thought and realized my life isn't getting any better the way I've been living. So that's why I'm back again today, willing to give it a shot.

What do you think the next step is?

I really need to deal with my fear of failure and trying to please people. In between our last meeting and today, I was in my office and a good friend of mine, Tony, visited me. He shut the door and said, "I just want to pray for you." I didn't know what he meant. So he began talking to me about what I've been dealing with, in terms of the distress with my wife being pregnant, and he said, "I just want to pray for you. I'm concerned about you." At that point I just broke down. I finally just let it all out . . . all the things I've been holding in for so long. I just wept with him.

That doesn't happen very often?

It doesn't. The ironic thing was that during that time my pastor came in and saw me crying. He said "You know, Tony, Randy's really in over his head here. He's really not a youth man." And when he said that, I just clammed up. I swallowed all my feelings because I felt, once again, he's seeing me as a failure. I said I had to do something and went and stayed in the bathroom until the pastor left. Since then I've been thinking I can't keep living like this. I'm dying inside. So that's when I made a decision. I've got to change. I'm tired of being afraid of everyone. I'm tired of having to hide all the time.

So that's what you want to work on? You want to do something different with the fear that you feel around people?

*Yeah. I want to deal differently with my pastor and other people too. It
felt good to finally be honest with someone like Tony. I never let
myself break down like that because I'm afraid I'll be seen as
weak. But it was good. And it felt like Tony really cared about me.*

You were courageous to let someone in to see the real Randy. This
gave Tony an opportunity to love you.

I don't really think of it as courageous.

At this point, I hear a lot of passion in Randy's voice. While some
of it's good, a lot of it isn't. I do sense Randy is passionate about
being a stronger, freer, more honest man. So I affirmed him for
that by calling him "courageous." However, I also sense Randy is
not passionate about being stronger and freer and more honest
so that he can be a more effective servant of God, but so he can
get the kind of love and support from others that he got from
Tony. Randy's passion is tainted by the false belief that his life
depends upon the approval and admiration of other people,
instead of God. This is one of the painful realities I want to help
him discover about himself as we continue to talk. But first, I
want to make sure we still agree on our goal. I have to resist the
temptation to ask reflective questions until this is accomplished.

So it sounds like we're back to the same goal we discussed at our
last meeting? Finding the strength and courage to be honest —
to be who you really are in a situation where you might be
judged or criticized. Is that what you want to work on?

Yeah. I do.

Practice Exercise
Before we start guiding Randy to reflect on the way he's handling life,
think about what it would require of you to be his counselor:

How are Randy's struggles of the heart similar to or different from your own?

What difficulties would you have counseling someone like Randy?

What kind of growth or change would be required in your own life for you to be ready to work effectively with Randy?

FOCUS ON ONE CURRENT TROUBLING EVENT.

The best way to help your friend reflect is to ask him to describe, in intricate detail, his response to one current troubling event. A description of his general response to his problems in life won't give a very accurate picture of what's happening inside him. The picture becomes much clearer when you ask him to reflect on just one event — maybe one that has already come up in conversation or one that stands out in his mind as a vivid example of the concern that originally brought him for help. The best mirror for reflection is usually an event that is current, intense, or emotional — and closely connected to important relationships.

The best place to start would be to go back to the last significant time you felt fear gripping you. Maybe this week when the pastor walked in on you and Tony. Or maybe another time recently that stands out more.

Another time this week I remember feeling the fear. On Sunday, I was leading a youth meeting. One of the kids who is really disrespectful to me — one of the deacons' sons — made a derogatory gesture toward me in front of the whole youth group. He acted like he was going to pull down his pants and moon me. Everyone laughed. And I just kind of laughed it off with them.

But deep down inside I felt extremely humiliated. I remember wondering why I was working with youth.

I can see why that would stand out in your mind.

I can only imagine what the kids told their parents. I keep hearing everyone laughing at me. But I couldn't do anything except pretend it didn't matter and end the meeting as soon as I could to get out of there.

We can spend some time looking more at that event to understand how fear stops you from being the person you want to be in those situations. Or we can look at the incident where your pastor walked in on you weeping. Since your pastor's such a significant person in your life, it might be good to look at that event. It's probably best to choose the time your fear was the strongest.

That would be the time he caught me weeping over the fact that my wife's pregnant and I'm wondering whether she'll carry our baby full-term this time. I can't believe he used that as an opportunity to stick a knife in me again! How can I do my job when he doesn't believe in me, when he treats me like that?

Well, it might not be possible to make him believe in you, but it is possible for you to be the person who you really want to be when you're with him, no matter what he says or does. That's the goal of our work together, right?

Right.

Practice Exercise

Identify two or three recent events that offer you a good glimpse at the way your own heart operates in the face of trouble or danger.

Event 1:

Event 2:

Event 3:

EXPLORE YOUR FRIEND'S EMOTIONAL
RESPONSE TO THE EVENT.

This step requires the gentle, yet tenacious, use of probing questions. There are two ways to pose probing questions: low-structured and high-structured. Low-structured questions cast a broad net, allowing your friend's reflections to go anywhere he wants to take you: "When this troubling event happened, what were you feeling?" High-structured questions clarify or get more detail about information he's already provided: "You say you felt embarrassed. Embarrassed about . . . ?" or, "It sounds like you're feeling pressure . . . I wonder what that's like . . . is it like . . . ?" I use both kinds of questions as my conversation with Randy continues, being careful to keep our exploration of emotions anchored to the one event we agreed to focus on.

Going back to that day, what do you remember feeling when your pastor interrupted your conversation with Tony?
Embarrassment. I felt extremely embarrassed by what he said.
Embarrassment about . . . ?
He saw me crying and gave me that look — you know, the one that says "what a loser."
What is that like? As I imagine what it would be like to be in that situation, I think I'd feel like I was being seen as weak or caught without having my act all together. Is that what it's like?
Yes. In his eyes I'm a big failure. I feel embarrassed around him a lot.

Reflective dialogue requires two active participants. I don't want to do all the work to uncover Randy's feelings nor do I want to abandon Randy to do all the work by himself. To be effective, our relationship must be a collaboration of two equally invested parties. From time to time, I try to match Randy's self-disclosures with my own, offering him any of my own thoughts and feelings that might shed light on his. That's what I did with my last comment.

We can't fully know everything about any part of someone's heart — their feelings, thoughts, or desires in one conversation. When you're helping a friend reflect on his emotional response to an event, you're asking him to articulate feelings he can recall during that event. Over time, his awareness and understanding of his emotional life will deepen and become one of his most valuable tools for worshiping and serving God.

While we can't make our friends aware of everything they're feeling, we can help them put feelings they do recognize into words. That's why I persist in asking Randy if he's aware of any other feelings.

Are you aware of feeling anything else the moment he walked in
    and gave you that look?
Hopeless . . . because I didn't know what to do. I can't be some-
    thing that I'm not. And I'm trying my hardest to be what he
    wants me to be. But he doesn't see it. He doesn't give me any
    credit for even trying.
You feel like the pastor has his mind made up about you; there's no
    way you can change his mind. Hopeless in that way?
Yes. Exactly.
At the same time, it sounds like you were feeling pressure too.
Big time. Tons of it.
Pressure to . . . ?

*Prove myself to him . . . over and over again. I feel that around
him constantly.*

So when he walked in and you heard him say in so many words,
"There's Randy, the loser, being weak again," you felt
hurt . . . embarrassed . . . hopeless . . . pressured . . . I wonder if
you were feeling anything else?

*Anger, too. But, I think more at myself than him. I felt
like . . . there I go again, not being the kind of pastor I should
be. More evidence that I just can't do it.*

Anger at yourself for failing again . . . that you can't perform like
everyone wants you to or like you're supposed to?

That's right.

So when he walked in and gave you that look, then said what he
said, you were churning inside with all kinds of things: anger,
embarrassment, hopelessness, pressure. How about fear? I think
I sense some fear too, as I hear you describe what it was like.

Yes. I feel that a lot too.

What kind of fear were you feeling at that moment?

What we talked about before . . . fear that I'll fail again.

Of all these different emotions you were feeling, which would you
say was the strongest?

That's hard to say. The fear, I think.

If you tried to measure the fear you were feeling in that moment on
a scale of one to ten, one being the mildest form of fear possible and ten being the greatest fear you've ever felt, what number
would you give it?

*I think a seven or eight. I was really afraid he might fire me on the
spot. There we'd be . . . no job . . . no income . . . no maternity
benefits. More disappointment and stress on my wife. It could
have ended the pregnancy again!*

So it felt like there was even life-and-death stuff on the line for you
at that moment?

Yes!

So you were flooded, it sounds like, with all kinds of feelings — the strongest being fear. Were you feeling anything else?
I can't think of anything else.

As I help Randy reflect on his emotional response to this event, I'm consciously doing two things. I communicate that I take his emotions seriously and recognize how difficult and painful they are for him. And I avoid affirming or rebuking Randy for any of his emotions. Affirming his feelings now would communicate that his feelings are healthy and appropriate when they obviously aren't in many ways. Rebuking his feelings at this time might shut him down and end any further exploration of the troubles in his heart.

By helping Randy describe what he felt during a critical event, I've learned at least one important thing about him: Something in his heart causes him to evaluate his own and other people's actions differently than God does. Randy emotionally reacts to any event that brings others' disapproval as if it had "life-or-death" significance. This indicates a destructive belief that distorts his perception of events and relationships. Although he has little or no awareness of this yet, it will come as we continue to reflect. For now, Randy and I have enough insight into his emotions to move on and explore his actions.

Practice Exercise
What's your hunch about Randy at this point? What do each of his emotional responses to his pastor's disapproval tell us about his heart?

Embarrassment:

Hopelessness:

Pressure:

Anger at himself:

Fear:

EXPLORE YOUR FRIEND'S BEHAVIORAL RESPONSE TO THE EVENT.

Guiding a friend to think about his actions starts with helping him recall each of his words and behaviors during and after the event. To truly understand your friend's heart, you need a "blow-by-blow" reconstruction of what he was doing — in enough detail to write a movie script. You want to help him identify the set of behaviors he uses as a way of coping when he feels threatened.

How did you behave when all this was going on . . . your pastor walking in on you and Tony? If I'd been watching you through a video monitor at that moment, what would I have seen?

I was weeping, and then when the pastor walked in I remember just swallowing everything I was feeling. And the tears stopped right away.

Did you say anything to him?

Not a word.

So you shut down . . . retreated into yourself?

Yeah. At that point it was over. I wasn't going to let him see me like that.

Is that when you excused yourself and went to the bathroom?

Yep.

What were you doing in the bathroom while you were waiting for
him to go away?

*I remember trying to daydream. Nothing sexual. But I couldn't. I
couldn't get my mind off what had just happened. So I guess I
just sat in a stall and prayed.*

Do you remember what you prayed?

*Just that God wouldn't let him fire me. That God would give me
another chance.*

How long did you stay in the bathroom?

Only a few minutes, I think. But it seemed like an eternity.

So what happened next, after you came back from the bathroom?

*The pastor made a few more condescending comments — like the
reason God appointed men to lead in the church, instead of
women, is because emotions get in the way of good judgment.
And that's why I'm not cut out to be a pastor.*

He was still there in your office when you came back?

*Not at first. After Tony left, he popped back to check up on me.
That's when he said I wasn't cut out to be a pastor — because
I'm emotional like a woman.*

What did you do?

*I didn't say anything back. When he left, that's when I started — you
know — what I talked to you about last time. I started thinking
about things I shouldn't. That's usually when I fantasize — when
it seems like there's nothing I can do to make things better. I
think about someone I can be with who wants me.*

It sounds like this is your way of coping. You try to keep the people in
your world off your back. And when you fail at that, you retreat
to a pretend world where there are fantasy people and no hassles.

That sounds sick . . . doesn't it?

Proverbs 18:7 is really true: "A fool's . . . lips are a snare to his
soul" (NIV). The more Randy talks about how he relates to others,

the more the true contents of his heart spill out. His words make the goal of his actions quite clear. His goal (even including his prayers) is to please the people in his world. And when he fails to do it, he escapes into a ready-made fantasy world where everyone admires him and he never fails. His behavior reveals that Randy sees his fantasy world as a better hiding place or shelter in time of need than God. Fortunately, his last comment tells us that he's starting to understand the nature of what he's doing.

Before I help Randy get more insight into his behavior, I want to gather a little more information about his use of sexual fantasy. I want to communicate that I'm not afraid to help him face this struggle, no matter how ugly or repulsive it might be. And I want to find out how far-reaching the problem is. It may be necessary to enlist the assistance of others to address this problem, depending on how much control he's exercising over it and whether it's endangering anyone else.

Do you use anything to help you fantasize?
I don't use porn, if that's what you mean. I'd be afraid I'd get caught! So I don't do that. I just fantasize about different women. I've done that as long as I can remember.
Is it usually accompanied with masturbation?
No. I don't masturbate that much anymore. I feel very guilty when I do. So a lot of times I fantasize to the point where I think I'm going to masturbate, but I don't. Certainly when I'm in the church office I'd never do that. I'm very aware of where I'm at.
Who do you fantasize about?
Usually someone I knew in the past. Maybe someone that I knew in high school or maybe a friend. I just imagine being with them. It's usually more like flirtatious banter that leads up to being sexual. But then I get worried about how I'm committing adultery in my mind . . . and feel too guilty to take it any further.

It's impossible to know at this time how complete Randy's description of his sexual problem is. People with sexual problems often leave out details or minimize them when first telling them to a friend or counselor. Without evidence that Randy's doing this, I grant him the benefit of any doubts I have about the veracity of his account. For the time being I will work under the assumption that no other forms of intervention beyond our friendship-counseling are required. In the future, when I see Randy's heart start to change, I may encourage him to talk to Mallory about going together for couple's counseling.

Randy needs to understand the style of coping he uses and the goal it's designed to accomplish before we shift our focus to his way of thinking. While we've already touched on these, I want to return to them now to be sure they're clear to Randy.

So you're fantasizing about being with someone who's crazy about you, thinks you're great, and wants you with no expectations, no pressure, no rejection, no disappointment?

Yes! It doesn't matter whether I'm a successful youth man or not. We can be together and there's no pressure.

And that's something you don't have in your real life right now?

I wish that's how it was with Mallory. But it's hard to feel that with her now because I've disappointed her so much.

When you look into her eyes, are you afraid you might see the same disappointed look you get from your pastor?

I try not to look into her eyes. I don't want her to see how I'm feeling. Because of the pregnancy, I don't want to burden her with my problems. So I try to keep them from her.

I don't believe for a minute that Randy keeps Mallory in the dark for loving reasons. He's furious with her, but isn't ready yet to acknowledge the rage or anger he feels toward her. This is perhaps the hardest of all his emotions to express since it's the most unacceptable to others. The goal of Randy's fantasy life isn't just pain-relief. It's also revenge. His fantasies give him a safe way to defy and betray all those who won't give him the approval he seeks. And because they don't even know he's doing it, he does it without having to fear their reprisals — the perfect revenge for a man committed to self-protection above anything else. Eventually, I'll need to expose this goal. But for now, insight into just one of his foolish goals ("pleasing everyone") is all the exposure he can handle. This is enough to keep him moving on his spiritual journey.

Do you think that's true about the way you handle other relationships too? When you're feeling ashamed, afraid, or angry — like you're not measuring up — you shut down. You retreat into a fantasy world for a few minutes of relief, and then you put your mask on and try to act however those around you expect you to act.

Yes. That's me. I guess it makes me feel better and, like I said, I don't even have to masturbate to feel better. The fantasies alone take the edge off.

The edge off what?

Hmmm . . . I guess my anger. It calms me down so I can be around people without saying or doing something that would get me into even more trouble.

So it saves you from dealing with difficult feelings or relationships, and keeps you from saying or doing anything risky around those who could hurt you?

Yes . . . but sometimes when I'm doing it, I lose a lot of time. I can be there in the office thinking about it for an hour or so, and I don't get my work done. I lose time I could be spending with my wife or the kids in the youth group. I just end up digging the hole deeper for myself.

So it has drawbacks?

Yes.

Practice Exercise

What are the principal behaviors that make up Randy's style of coping?

What is Randy's style of coping primarily designed to accomplish?

What did I do in the above dialogue to guide Randy to discover the answers to the above questions?

EXPLORE YOUR FRIEND'S COGNITIVE RESPONSE TO THE EVENT.

The purpose of helping friends reflect on their thoughts during an event is to uncover their core beliefs. To accomplish this, I rely heavily on the same skill of chaining I used in chapter 5. In this conversation, however, I use it to help Randy chain from a conscious thought to the core belief beneath it.

Let's go back to that day when your pastor walked in on you and
    Tony. We've talked about what you were feeling and doing
    when that happened, but what were you thinking? What was
    going through your mind when this was happening?
*I can remember thinking, I can't believe this is happening. I just
    wish I could die or be invisible right now.*
I wish I could die because . . .
*Because this is so mortifying. I can't believe I could be so stupid to let
    myself get into this situation — to let the pastor see me like this.*
For him to see you like this is awful, because . . .
*Because it just confirms what he says about me — that I'm weak,
    I'm a loser, and I don't have what it takes to be a youth man.*
And if everything he's been saying about you is true, that you're
    weak, that you don't have what it takes, that would mean . . .

There's no hope!

No hope of . . .

No hope . . . of . . . of ever being somebody . . . who others can respect or love.

And if you could never pull that off — being somebody that others could respect or love that would mean . . .

Life wouldn't be worth living. What would be the point of doing anything if no one appreciated it? The fact that people look at me now and say that I'm not amounting to anything — that's devastating. But to think it will never get better . . .

To think that you'll never be somebody who's lovable, somebody who's worthy of respecting — that feels unbearable. Because your life depends on becoming somebody that others can look at and say, "Wow you're good, you really have it together!"

Yes. Well, I don't need the whole world to see that . . . just a few people.

Just a few . . . like your wife, your pastor, maybe the kids and parents at church?

Them. And our parents — my parents and Mallory's parents too. It's important how they see me too.

So if you can't get these people to see you differently, it means your life is doomed. It's not worth living.

That's what it boils down to I suppose. I don't see any other way.

Your life literally depends on getting the important people in your life to see you differently.

Yes.

Using phrases like "that would mean . . . ", and "because . . . " prompt Randy to complete his thoughts until he identifies the one thing he's depending on to fulfill his strongest passion. When I was able to capture this in one succinct sentence, I uncovered his core belief. Identifying this opens the door to explore the passions that give this belief its tenacity.

Practice Exercise

What if Randy reported his conscious thought to be, "Why do these things always happen to me?" Write an imaginary conversation with Randy in which you help him chain from this thought to the core belief we uncovered. Feel free to use any of the phrases or questions I used to help Randy chain.

You: What was going through your mind when the pastor walked in on you and Tony?

Randy: I can remember thinking, "Why do these things always happen to me?"

You:

EXPLORE THE PASSIONS THAT FUEL YOUR FRIEND'S RESPONSE TO THE EVENT.

Our most painful experiences arouse our strongest passions. Exploring them requires recalling things that happened when we were our most vulnerable and dependent — still children, growing up in our families-of-origin. Suffering is always painful, but never greater than when we're too small and defenseless to do anything about it. That's how we experience insult, injury, and inattention as children. Our first response is to cry out for the relief we can't provide for ourselves. When it doesn't come, we assume we're at fault. Something is wrong with us, and relief depends on fixing or changing it. Our minds grope to understand what makes us so unlovable or unworthy that no one will rescue us. Then we compare ourselves to others. Anything different or unique about us is likely to be labeled the culprit. Whatever we finally decide is our "fatal flaw," it becomes our strongest passion to rid ourselves of it or convince others that it no longer exists.

I begin to explore Randy's passion by guiding him to reflect about where he acquired his core belief. By helping him vividly relive early events in his life, the pain and passion connected to them will emerge.

I'm curious, Randy, do you remember when you first started to
believe this — that your life depended upon getting the people
in your life to see you differently?
*I know it's a pressure I felt even as a kid. No matter how hard I
tried, people would always catch me screwing up.*
Can you give me an example of what you mean?
They're so many, I wouldn't know where to start.
Maybe a time that was especially painful to you.
*Hmm . . . okay. I remember one time when my cousin was at
our house. She was younger, and I was probably about ten.
And she tried to kiss me. Since I was only ten, I didn't want
a girl to kiss me! I said, "Stop it, Gale!" and then I pushed
her. She accidentally hit her head on the table. She started
to cry, and when my father came in she told him that I
pushed her. He looked at me and said something like, "You
make me sick, Randy. Anybody who beats up little girls must
be a little girl himself. Come here little girl, and I'll teach
you . . . " Then I just started running. I remember running
out of the house not knowing what to do. I was scared to
death! I just ran and ran, and he didn't catch me. Finally,
our neighbor came looking for me and took me home. When
I got there, my father didn't say a word to me. My mom sent
me to my room. Later she came up and told me that both of
them were angry at me for pushing Gale down and running
away. I remember saying "I'm sorry. I'm sorry. I'll never do
it again." But she didn't want to talk about it. She told me
to go to bed.*
What was it like the next morning?

Terrible. I didn't know what to expect. We never knew whether Dad would come down on us, forget it happened, or just make a joke about it. I guess it depended on how much he had to drink.

Which did he do that time?

He ridiculed me again for acting like a little girl.

Do you remember any of the sentences he said to you?

Not that time. I just remember him always saying things like, "You can do better than that. Come on, try to hit the ball like a man instead of a girl."

I remember one time, I think I was about twelve, he was taking my brother to get a haircut. He said, "Why don't you come along?" I'd just gotten a haircut and didn't want another one. He told me I didn't have to get one; he just wanted me to come along. But once we were there, he forced me into the chair. He lied to me! I'll never forget being in that chair screaming, "I don't want a haircut!" And he said, "Sit down and quit crying like a little girl." He told the guy to keep cutting it, even after he said he was done. I just kept asking myself, "Why is he doing this?" By the time he finally let me out of the chair, my hair looked ridiculous. Nobody wore their hair like that at my school. When I got home, I told my mom what Dad had done. I said that when I turned eighteen I was moving out and getting as far away as I could. That was the first time I remember just wanting to die. Why would he lie and hurt me that way?

At twelve, Randy asked himself some character-shaping questions: "Why does Dad hurt me the way he does? Why does Mom let him get away with it? What am I doing wrong that I can't get them to stop?" In his immaturity, Randy came up with the best answer he could: "They treat me this way because I'm bad." This only added to his pain. He knew the pain of his parents not caring, but also the pain of his not deserving their care. What a heavy burden for a man to carry, let alone a child. To help Randy carry this burden as Jesus commands (Galatians 6:2), I must respond to his pain in a fundamentally different way than his parents did. I must show him the same compassion and gentleness the Good Samaritan showed his wounded neighbor (Luke 10:33-34).

You're feeling some real pain right now.
Yes (tears).
Can you put it into words?
It never mattered to them what I felt, what I said, or what I did. It didn't make any difference to them.
No matter what you did, it didn't make any difference. You couldn't get them to . . . ?
Care (tears). I couldn't get them to care.
So the pain of that feels like . . . what? How would you describe it?
I wasn't worth their bother. I was good for nothing in their eyes.

Only by understanding Randy's deepest pain, can I understand his strongest passion. The pain he's been describing is what he still lives his life to avoid. And whatever offers protection from it arouses his strongest passions. To help Randy see this, I must now make two shifts in our conversation: from past events to current ones and from understanding Randy's pain to understanding how he tries to protect himself from it.

(Shift #1) The pain you felt growing up sounds like the same kind of pain you feel now around your pastor, the deacons, your wife.
Yes (tears). Just once I wish I could prove to them that I'm good for something.
That's something you haven't tasted much — not growing up, and not now as an adult.
That's for sure.
You tasted it a little bit that day with Tony, though. He saw something good in you and told you so.

That's why it felt so good.

(Shift #2) I wonder if that's why you fantasize? It's the one place
you're guaranteed to get a taste of what you're starving for.

*That is why I do it. It started off with nothing sexual—like imag-
ining myself scoring the winning basket. The one time I tried
to play basketball, they told me I was too short. So I started to
imagine soaring over everybody and scoring the winning basket
and everyone just standing and cheering for me.*

And that's what you still want most from your mom and dad, your
pastor, your wife. You want them to see something in you that
makes them just want to stand and cheer.

But that doesn't happen!

That's what really hurts.

It kills me (tears).

You're starving for the people in your world to do what your mom
and dad never did: Recognize that you're good for something
and stand up and cheer for you.

*If I had that, it would make all the difference in the world. I'd be a
different man.*

And you work hard to get it, don't you?

(Nods in agreement)

Do you have any insight into how you try to get it?

Knock myself out to give people what they want.

I think that's right. You want everybody to see you as a good guy
instead of a bad guy.

That's what I want.

Practice Exercise

Think of someone you know well. What's their strongest passion—the
thing that motivates them to live and work and relate the way they do?

What is it about their life, their choices, their behavior, or their words that lead you to this conclusion?

From what you know of their history, what kind of pain might be behind their passion?

What would you say to them if they came to you asking, "What am I doing wrong? With everything that's happening to me, I know I have to make some changes. What should I do?"

INSTILL HOPE AND DESIRE FOR A CHANGE OF CHARACTER.
Randy has growing insight into his response to the troubling events in his life — what he's feeling, doing, thinking, and wanting. However, he won't progress to the next stage in his spiritual journey until these insights give birth to two things: motivation to change the fundamental way he's responding to these events and hope that change of this magnitude really is possible. Instilling this kind of motivation and hope is the last major task before this stage of the journey is complete. I begin by going back to the way his current way of coping backfires.

So how well does the strategy to give people what they want work?
(Laughs) I've tried and tried and tried. It never works.
You've never been able to be the person everyone wants you to be?
No.
What happens when you try?
When I hold in what I really feel and think, and I just pretend, I come across as weak. People don't take me seriously.
Maybe that's why the guy in your group didn't think twice about threatening to moon you, to ridicule you.

He knew that my hands were tied because his dad is on the board.
Yes, your hands were tied. But not by the board or even the pastor.
You tie them yourself with your commitment to always look
like the good guy. The kids in your group have figured that out.
They know they don't have to respect you. Do you suppose
you've tied your own hands in other relationships too?
All of them.
So your strategy not only fails to get you what you want, it also
backfires by getting you what you don't want. You get from oth-
ers the exact opposite of what you want.
Why do I do this? It's stupid. I'm really tired of living this way.
I think you're busting to break out of that commitment you made
as a kid. It weighs you down like a heavy suit of armor. You
want to break out of it and be the man you want to be instead
of the man everybody else wants you to be.
I'm ready to break out of it.
I think you are. And I think it's going to happen. You're going to
come out of this cocoon — a cocoon you learned to wear when
you were a kid to keep people from destroying you. But you
don't need it now that you're a man. No one has the power to
destroy you like you thought they did as a kid. It's time to break
out. That's our goal. Next time we meet, I want to start exploring with you what it will look like to break out of the armor
you wear.
I definitely want to.

Practice Exercise

What would you say to Randy to strengthen his desire to change the
way he's handling life?

How would you give him hope that deep character changes like these really are possible?

KEEP REFLECTION GOING BETWEEN MEETINGS.

When hope starts to bloom, people impetuously launch self-improvement campaigns. It's smart to counsel your friends against this. Try-harder attempts at self-repair only create more frustration and discouragement. Lasting character change can never precede repentance and reconciliation — the next two legs in their spiritual journey. Until then, it's better to keep your friends so engaged in self-reflection that they have no time for self-improvement. That's why I give Randy homework as we conclude.

> You've really done some good work today talking with me about some really hard stuff. What do you think you want to do when you leave here, especially with what you've been learning about yourself?
>
> *I want to find a way to live outside the cocoon.*
>
> You know, I don't want you to try to break out of it quite yet. First, we need to explore what it will look like and cost you to break out. So between now and the next time we meet, I'd rather that you just keep studying the cocoon or armor that you wear. I want you to study it every time it holds you back from being the man you want to be this week. I want you to study what it's made of, what you're feeling, how you behave, what you think. Write down the things you learn. If you're going to break out of this cocoon, you'll need to know everything you can about it first. How do you feel about this assignment? Does it make sense to you?
>
> *It makes sense.*
>
> How do you feel about doing it?
>
> *It'll be hard, but I think I'm game.*

Can you put what I'm asking you to do into your own words?

Study the cocoon this week. Keep a record of the ways it keeps me from being real with people.

That's it. And don't forget to study what it's made of — the feelings, behaviors, and thoughts that it uses to keep you bound up. And then bring that record with you next time we meet. Okay?

I think I can do that.

Okay. See you next Thursday.

At this time Randy seems to have enough *self-awareness, motivation,* and *hope* to proceed to the next stage of his spiritual journey. It's possible, but rare, for someone to actually acquire these as quickly as Randy appears to. We won't know if he has, though, until we see how he responds at our next meeting when I invite him to repent. If he's unwilling or unable, I'll guide him to reflect on another troubling event — using the same process I used in this conversation. I'll continue to do this until he's willing and able to proceed to repentance. The best way to bring our friends to repentance is to encourage them to keep reflecting on their hearts.

Practice Exercise

Design a reflective assignment for yourself, similar to the one I've given to Randy.

Record everything you learn about yourself—the feelings, behaviors, thoughts, and passions that get in the way of your being the person you want to be.

Observe what this assignment does to your motivation to be a different kind of person.

7

$$\left[\begin{array}{c} \textit{l} \text{ I } \textit{f} \text{ E - } \textit{w} \text{ o r d s } \textit{f} \text{ o r} \\ \text{CULTIVATING REPENTANCE} \end{array}\right]$$

Two blind men were sitting by the roadside, and when they heard that Jesus was going by, they shouted, "Lord, Son of David, have mercy on us!" Jesus stopped and called them. "What do you want me to do for you?" he asked. "Lord," they answered, "we want our sight." Jesus had compassion on them and touched their eyes. Immediately they received their sight and followed him.

Matthew 20:30-34, NIV

*E*ven though the two men who cried out to Jesus were blind, they still had a clear vision of what they wanted Jesus to do for them: "We want our sight," they said.

What would have happened if they'd said, "Well, we're not sure what we need. You have any ideas?" How absurd. Why would they go to the trouble of getting Jesus' attention, braving an angry crowd, if they didn't know what they wanted?

But don't we commit this same absurdity when we pray without a clear vision of what we want God to do for us? I'm not speaking about the way we pray for our outer worlds — our circumstances. I'm speaking of the way we pray for our inner worlds — our passions, thoughts, intentions, and emotions.

Ever wonder why Jesus asked these blind men what they wanted? Wasn't it obvious? Perhaps this is why we invest little time developing a vision for what we want God to do for us — we figure he already knows. When Jesus taught his disciples how to pray, he said, "Your Father knows what you need before you ask him" (Matthew 6:8, NIV). But he told them this so they'd understand that putting their requests into words was for their sake, not God's.

God asks us to verbalize our personal requests before he grants them because of the principle of choice (see Matthew 7:8). He refuses to change us without our full consent. Of course, full consent to change is possible only after we picture what that change entails and envision its implications before we ask God to produce it in us.

This is the essence of biblical repentance — imagining character changes so substantial that only God can make them. Repentance is the process God uses to prepare our hearts for life-changing encounters with him (see Matthew 4:17, Acts 3:19).

When did you last ask yourself, "What do I want God to do for me?" Take time to answer this question now.

ENVISIONING THE HEART JESUS WANTS US TO HAVE

Blessed are the poor in spirit, for theirs is the kingdom of heaven. . . . Blessed are those who hunger and thirst for righteousness, for they will be filled. . . . Blessed are the pure in heart, for they will see God. . . . Blessed are those who are persecuted because of righteousness, for theirs is the kingdom of heaven. (Jesus' Sermon on the Mount, Matthew 5:3-10, NIV)

After withstanding numerous temptations in the wilderness, Jesus returned to Galilee to begin his preaching ministry. Matthew summarizes the theme of Jesus' sermons in one sentence: "From that time on Jesus began to preach, 'Repent, for the kingdom of heaven is near'" (4:17, NIV). Matthew then gives us our first detailed record of one of these sermons (Matthew 5–7). It was designed to cultivate repentance in the hearts of those present. Jesus helped his hearers envision two things: the kind of heart he wanted them to have and the kind of behavior he wanted them to display.

This vision boggled their minds. By describing both the inner and outer life he wanted them to have, he set the standard higher than the Pharisees did (Matthew 5:20). Jesus was unveiling a new vision for how to live. Without this vision, they would perish (Luke 13:1-5).

To repent literally means to change our mind about the kind of person we want to be; to exchange our present vision of who we want to be for a bold new vision that requires our hearts to function very differently than they naturally do. The vision Jesus imparted through his teaching is the same vision we want to impart through our counseling. When our friends come to us disillusioned about themselves — telling us who they *don't* want to be and asking how they can be different — our first duty is to help them develop a clear vision of who they *can* be (inside and out). Only then will they be in a position to decide what it will take to become this person.

How do you help your friends develop a vision for becoming a different kind of person? How do you help them envision what it would look like to operate with the heart described by Jesus in Matthew 5:3-10?

ENVISIONING THE BEHAVIOR JESUS
WANTS US TO DISPLAY

I tell you the truth, anyone who has faith in me will do what I have been doing. He will do even greater things than these. (Jesus, John 14:12, NIV)

Changed behavior always follows a changed heart. This is why Jesus wanted his disciples to envision the changes even a little faith made in the way they lived their lives. When his disciples asked why they failed in their attempts to help a family, Jesus said, "Because you have so little faith. I tell you the truth, if you have faith as small as a mustard seed, you can say to this mountain, 'Move from here to there' and it will move. Nothing will be impossible for you" (Matthew 17:20-21, NIV). Jesus knew that insight into what was wrong with their old hearts would never be enough to motivate his disciples to passionately pursue God for a new heart. They also needed a vision for what they could be with a new heart.

Imagine the impact of these words if Jesus spoke them to you. You're doing your best to live a good life but failing miserably at it. Jesus picks you up, brushes you off, and helps you envision — in the most concrete and graphic way possible — things you'll soon be doing a hundred times more powerful, loving, and virtuous than you ever dreamed you'd do. What would life-words like these do to your willingness to let him make you into this kind of person?

True repentance always increases our motivation to pursue God — not out of shame or fear over who we are — but out of longing and expectation for who we can be by his grace. It's God's kindness, not his judgment or condemnation, that leads us to repentance (see Romans 2:4). Jesus gave his disciples opportunity to see him love in many ways and settings. Now he was helping them envision how their opportunities to love, if they had new hearts, would be even greater than the opportunities he'd had in the three short years they were together. Jesus gave them a vision not only for the new hearts they could have but also for the new behavior they could display.

Pick a difficult relationship you have with a friend and envision what it would mean (what specific behaviors it would require) to love them this week the way God is calling you to love them.

ENVISIONING THE EMOTIONS JESUS WANTS US TO SHARE

If a man remains in me and I in him, he will bear much fruit. . . . I have told you this so that my joy may be in you and that your joy may be complete. . . . No servant is greater than his master. If they persecuted me, they will persecute you also. . . . I have told you this, so that when the time comes you will remember that I warned you. (Jesus, John 15:5,11,20; 16:4, NIV)

Jesus was forthright about what would happen if his disciples acquired the heart and displayed the behavior he envisioned for them. He didn't want anyone to seek a new heart or behavior unless they were fully aware of both the joy and pain that follows. Paul experienced both and welcomed them: "I want to know Christ and the power of his resurrection and the fellowship of sharing in his sufferings" (Philippians 3:10, NIV). But not everyone does!

On this leg of their spiritual journey we want to do for our friends what Jesus did for his disciples in John 15 and 16 — give a preview of what they'll experience if they respond to troubling events in their life with a new heart and a new set of behaviors. We help them imagine the joy they'll feel living and loving in powerful new ways, as well as the disapproval, rejection, and pain they'll experience when people react negatively to their new ways. We want them to see how Jesus' own bittersweet experience as a man serves as a preview of what lies ahead for them.

How do you prepare friends who are already in pain for the additional pain that comes with living the way God wants them to?

WEIGHING LIFE'S MOST
IMPORTANT DECISION

If anyone comes to me and does not hate his father and mother, his wife and children, his brothers and sisters—yes, even his own life—he cannot be my disciple. . . . No one who has left home or wife or brothers or parents or children for the sake of the kingdom of God will fail to receive many times as much in this age and, in the age to come, eternal life. (Jesus, Luke 14:26; 18:29-30, NIV, emphasis added)

By helping people reflect on the way they live and envision the radically different way they could live, Jesus brought them to the most important decision of their life. What kind of person did they want to be—a person who acts only to protect his own interests? Or a person who places his trust in God and serves his interests no matter what the cost?

Because the consequences of this decision are so serious, Jesus warned people to carefully count the cost and benefits before deciding (see Luke 14:26-28; 18:29-30). When they chose hastily, Jesus gave them reason to pause and think again about their decision: "Peter asked, 'Lord, why can't I follow you now? I will lay down my life for you.' Then Jesus answered, 'Will you really lay down your life for me?'" (John 13:37-38, NIV).

We are responsible to do the same for those we counsel— help them weigh the consequences of choosing to be the person God wants them to be. Authentic change always requires this kind of conscious deliberation and choice.

For his sake I did in actual fact suffer the loss of everything, but I considered it mere garbage compared with
being able to win Christ. For now my place is in him, and
I am not dependent upon any of the self-achieved righteousness of the Law; God has given me that genuine
righteousness which comes from faith in Christ. How
changed are my ambitions! (Paul, Philippians 3:8-9, PH)

**How do you help your friends realistically weigh the costs and bene-
fits of becoming a new person?**

FOLLOWING JESUS' EXAMPLE FOR CULTIVATING REPENTANCE

As we meet again, my goal is to cultivate repentance in Randy's
heart the same way Jesus cultivated it in his disciples. I help him
picture three things: a godly way to think about his suffering, a
godly way to respond to those who cause his suffering, and the
godly emotions that accompany this new way of thinking and
behaving. In other words, I help Randy envision the person he'd
need to be to accomplish his growth goal. I'm only asking Randy
to *envision* this, not embrace it yet. After he's had a chance to
weigh the pros and cons, I'll urge him to decide if this is the person he wants to be. Whenever I help my friends along this leg of
their spiritual journey, I pray fervently that God will use our conversations to cultivate in them the desire for fundamental character changes, and a realization that changes like these are only
possible with God's help.

First I ask Randy about the homework I gave him at our previous meeting. This communicates that he's responsible
between meetings to work on the things we discuss. Following
up on homework is also a good way to gauge his interest in the

growth goal and his readiness to move to the next stage. If he shows little interest in working between meetings, he's probably back at the first stage. Then the goal of our relationship needs to be revisited and, perhaps, renegotiated.

FOLLOW-UP ON HOMEWORK ASSIGNMENTS.

Hi, Randy. I've been anxious to hear about your homework . . . what you learned this week about yourself.

I saw the cocoon a few times, but don't think it was there as much this week. That was surprising, given all that happened. Whenever I did see it, it grossed me out.

What grossed you out about it?

The way it keeps me silent — and passive, I guess. When I try to be strong or honest, I have thoughts like "keep your mouth shut," "it'll just make things worse," and "nobody cares what you think, you loser."

Those are important discoveries. But you said you were surprised you didn't see the cocoon more, given what happened this week.

We had our monthly board meeting at church on Tuesday. I went to give an update on our youth programs. I'd developed a whole plan for what we're going to do for the senior high youth this summer. But before I had a chance to tell them, they told me they've decided to have someone else lead the senior high ministry. They said they'd keep me over junior high youth and some other clerical tasks until our baby is born. After that I might need to look for something else. Pastor said they were doing this as a favor to me, so I wouldn't have to keep failing with the senior high kids.

How did you handle this? Did you crawl into the cocoon?

Oh yeah. It was funny. I can laugh at it now. But at the time I felt like I was going to explode. I wanted to tell them my side, but felt like the cocoon was tightening around me . . . so that I could hardly speak or even breathe.

Correct me if I'm wrong but, as distressing as this must have been,
you don't seem to have the same panic I sensed a couple of
weeks ago when you were worried that this might happen.

*It's almost like I've switched to the opposite reaction. There's
absolutely nothing I can do. I was ready to explain to them
everything that I planned to do to make the youth program successful. But they didn't even want to hear it. It hurt a lot. The
thing that hurt most was when the pastor said they were doing
it as a favor to spare me from any more failures . . . like they
already think I'm a failure.*

It sounds like you're more angry than panicked about this happening.

*I am. How would he know if I'm a failure or not? He's never even
given me a chance.*

I hear two things as I listen to Randy. First, Randy's spent some
time this week reflecting on the way he responds to troubling
events. Second, his motivation to change is growing, but for
the wrong reasons. It seems Randy wants to be free of the
cocoon so he can defend himself against his critics, rather than
display God's love to them. This is why I don't want to help
him break free of his cocoon until his heart begins to soften
and change.

If Randy is still committed to our original growth goal, it
won't be hard to entice him to envision a whole new way to
handle the difficult situation that now confronts him.

RECONFIRM THE GROWTH GOAL.

Do you think we're moving in the right direction if we continue
with the goal we established at our first meeting . . . helping
you develop the freedom and strength to respond to situations
like this with courage instead of retreating into that cocoon?

*I believe so. Like I said, I'm realizing that nothing I do is going to
change their minds. I mean I realize that's the way it's been all*

along. What's the use of staying in the cocoon anymore? How can it make things any worse? I'm just now seeing that whatever happens, happens . . . and you can't control it. If you try, you'll fail. So it's ludicrous to even try.

It's ludicrous to try to control what other people think or do or say because you can't control other people?

Exactly. Sooner or later they'll crucify you. Everybody always does. I should just accept it's going to happen and get ready for it.

I think that's why the goal we've been working on is so important. Since you can't control what others do to you, that leaves you with only one thing you can do. Do you remember what that is?

Be true to myself, I guess. Stop being fake or cowardly. There's not much more they can do to me anyway.

That's true. We certainly know now they don't have the power to destroy you. Right? If they did, Tuesday night would have finished you off. They can hurt you all right. They can take your job away. Make life difficult for you. But they can't destroy you . . . or control what kind of man you choose to be in response to it all. That's the one thing you do control. You alone control what kind of man you'll be at your crucifixion — the kind of man they think you are, or the kind of man you want to be in your heart. It's your decision to make.

All week I've been holding on to what you said you saw in me — that I had courage. That meant a lot to me.

Have you been holding on to the hope that, on the inside, you could be a very different man from what people usually see — that you can be a courageous man?

Yes. That's what I want to be.

That's our goal. We'll keep chipping away at it, helping you find whatever it takes to be that man of courage, even if people are crucifying you.

I want that.

Since Randy still has strong interest in the goal we previously established, I can now ask him to envision what kind of person he'd need to be to accomplish this goal, starting with the inside and working out.

Practice Exercise

Given what Randy has said about the way he's currently responding to the difficult people in his life, what do you think a courageous new way of responding to them would look like?

What would he need to believe?

What would he do differently?

What would he experience emotionally?

ENVISION A GODLY WAY TO THINK ABOUT THEIR TROUBLES.
Think back to Tuesday night when you were in the board meeting.
Things are being said that you don't think are true or fair or loving. At that moment, *what would you have to firmly believe to be free to accomplish the goal we've been working on*— to be a man of courage and strength? Even if you're with people who see you as a big failure, what would you have to believe to be the man you want to be with them?
I guess I'd have to believe that I don't have to measure up in their eyes anymore . . . that what they think or say doesn't matter anymore.

Randy and I have begun to envision a new way of thinking based on truth instead of the lies Randy grew up believing. I use the question I just asked Randy to cultivate repentance because Jesus said, "You are truly my disciples if you live as I tell you to, and *you will know the truth, and the truth will set you free*" (John 8:31-32, TLB, emphasis added). Jesus views "living as his disciple" as the product of a two-step process: knowing the truth and then being set free by it. For now, my focus is the first step — helping Randy know the truth. In the next chapter we'll focus on the second step.

When working with friends at this stage, I depend on God's Spirit to be at work in their hearts at the same time, affirming what's true and convicting them about what's not (John 16:13). That's why I seek to draw truth from them, rather than impose truth on them. As our conversation continues, I again use the skill of chaining.

So, you're saying, "although I'd prefer that the people in my life valued and respected me, I don't need them to because . . ."

I guess because if God accepts me it doesn't matter if they do or not.

You don't sound very convinced.

It's hard for me to conceive that I don't have to do something to be valued. Everything in me says I have to prove that I'm valuable. I know I can't. But still, to believe that God or anyone would value me is something I'm not sure I can do.

That's okay. I'm not asking you to believe anything right now. Just *imagine* what you'd have to believe to be free. I think you were saying you'd have to believe something about God to be free, right?

Yes. To be free around people I can't need anything from them. So God, he's the only one left to turn to.

When helping friends envision a belief that would emancipate them, it's vital to find words that uniquely fit their situation. A new belief should do three things:

1. *It should embrace the true longing their enslaving belief falsely promises to fulfill.* A freeing belief never requires people to pretend life is better than it is or deny the pain of unfulfilled longings.

2. *It should withdraw the demand made by the enslaving belief.* A freeing belief withdraws any demand that people must control or change their circumstances or other people in order to survive or thrive.

3. *It should dispute the demand.* A freeing belief provides one or more sensible reasons for no longer bowing to the demands of the enslaving belief.

Randy and I have begun to construct a new belief that does all three of these. As our conversation continues, we focus on disputing the demand made by Randy's enslaving belief.

So let's see if we can put that into one sentence. Although I wish the church and the kids and my pastor and my wife all valued me *(embrace the legitimate longing),* I don't need them to *(withdraw the demand),* because . . . *(dispute the demand)*

Because God loves me. He proved it on the cross. He saw every-thing that was wrong with me — all my sin, all my failures, and he still did it. He died for me. That proves that he values me. The fact that he died for me proves it.

So at a deep level, you have to be convinced that you don't need the pastor's approval or the kids' or anybody else's because you've got God's love and approval? That's the belief you'd have to firmly hold to be free — to be the man you want to be. Is that what you're saying?

Yeah. But that's not what I believe now. I'm still back believing that I have to prove I'm not a failure.

Would you say it's a tug-of-war between these two beliefs — the belief that you really have to have people's approval and the belief that God's approval is all you need?

The first one is winning for sure. It's stronger. I've always told myself that I need a real person, at least one other human being, to believe in me before I can believe in myself.

That old belief reminds me of that plant in the movie *Little Shop of Horrors*. It keeps looking for something to eat so it can get bigger and bigger. "Feed me. Feed me." The belief that has a hold on you is just like that plant, looking for evidence it can feed on — any screw-up, any mediocre performance, anyone who doesn't like you — to keep you convinced that your life is sunk unless you can make at least one person think you're great. But when someone does think you're great, it's blown off as being insincere. And you have to keep trying to find another. Your belief is like that plant from outer space. It consumes anything you offer it and just wants more. It'll never let you rest.

I'm not sure I follow.

Well, your wife approved of you enough to marry you and make you the father of her child. Right? But that wasn't enough to satisfy your demand for approval. Tony told you he really admired you and I told you I thought you had a lot of courage. But that wasn't enough either. So how many people have to see you as someone of value before you're allowed to think of yourself that way?

I see what you're saying . . . there'll never be enough.

Why won't there be?

Because I'm never sure if people really mean what they say . . . or whether they'll continue to feel positive about me. That's why I can't rest.

So far we've come up with two reasons to dispute Randy's demand for other people's approval. We might call the first one a "biblical disputation." Randy realized that he doesn't need other people's approval because he already has the approval of the most significant person in the universe — God. Christ paid the price to win it, so Randy wouldn't have to.

The second one is a "pragmatic disputation." I proposed it to help Randy see how his demand is insatiable. It can't be satisfied no matter how many people approve of him. He already has approval from people but it doesn't mean anything.

While Randy acknowledges and understands both of these disputations, they don't carry much weight in his thinking yet. That's why I turn the tables on Randy now to put him into hand-to-hand combat with the very thing that enslaves him. I want to help him develop his own arsenal of disputations to fight it. I want him to learn to look right into the eyes of this insidious belief and overthrow it.

Let's do something different for a few minutes. Let's switch roles.
> Let's even switch seats. You be me and I'll be you. Your job is to convince me that my old belief is a lie and the new belief is what I really should believe. Are you game for this?

I'll try.

Let's give it a shot. I'll go first. I'm speaking as if I'm you now.
> (Kevin as Randy) I think I could believe in myself if I could just get somebody to be proud of me — if not my dad then maybe just one other human being. If I could just make someone proud of me, then I know I'd finally be proud of myself. If I can't even get one other person to be proud of me, then I'm a failure and will never be anything but a failure.

(Randy as Kevin) But if someone has to believe in you before you can believe in yourself, where does that leave you if that person changes their mind? You'll never be able to be yourself around him.

> (Kevin as Randy) That's why I took this job. I was hoping I could get a lot of people to believe in me. It wouldn't matter if one or two changed their minds. I'd still have others that believed in me.

(Randy as Kevin) Don't you see that just makes you a slave to a lot of people instead of a few? The more people you try to make proud, the more pressure you'll feel. You'll never be free or

*strong believing like that. You need to build your life on
someone's approval you can never lose. That's the only way
you'll ever be free.*

(Kevin as Randy) I know you're talking about God. But he's never
been enough. I guess if he could come in the flesh and could sit
in front of me and be like a dad to me, maybe that would be
enough. A couple of times a counselor at camp or someone at
church has valued me. And I felt like I must be worth something because somebody believed in me. And that's always
seemed to do it better for me than God. I don't see what's
wrong with that. Timothy had Paul, didn't he? Is it really that
wrong to want a Paul?

*(Randy as Kevin) No, not if that's all you wanted. But you want
much more than a Paul. You want someone to play God in
your life and give you a reason to live. But as soon as you give
people that kind of power — like you've given the pastor — it
doesn't matter how godly they are, they're going to let you
down. They'll become displeased or unfairly criticize you, and
your whole life will fall apart because you built your life on
them. That's not only unfair to you. It's unfair to them!*

(Kevin) Wow! Let's take a time out for a minute. What did that feel
like?

*Really strange. I kept thinking, where are these words coming
from? It didn't sound like me at all.*

You were speaking some incredible truth. And the more you talked,
the more it sounded like you were starting to believe what you
were saying.

It felt that way. I want to believe it.

I know that what I was saying when I was playing you still has a
grip on you too. But it feels to me like the truth you were
speaking is starting to get a foothold. There's a big part of you
that would really like to believe what you were saying.

It would make a huge difference.

Randy's starting to get vision and enthusiasm for a new heart. The role-play paid off. In the thick of battle he dug deep and found pockets of wisdom and conviction he never knew he had — obviously gifts from the Holy Spirit. This is a sign that repentance is growing in his heart. It's time to help him envision the difference a new heart would make in the way he responds to his present difficulties.

Practice Exercise

Think of a current setting where you don't feel free to speak or behave the way you want to. Identify the belief that's enslaving you when you're in that setting. What would you have to firmly believe to be free to be the person you want to be? Write out the freeing belief so it accomplishes each of the three objectives.

Embrace the true longing the enslaving belief falsely promises to fulfill:

Withdraw the demand made by the enslaving belief:

Dispute the demand:

ENVISION A GODLY WAY TO RESPOND TO THEIR TROUBLES.
Helping Randy envision a godly way to respond to his troubles requires going back to one of the troubling situations we've discussed before and projecting how he might behave in it if he firmly held to the new belief we've constructed. My goal is to give Randy a "taste" of what his life would be like living in the

power and control of the Holy Spirit. As we envision these new behaviors, I must be careful that Randy doesn't hear me telling him to go home today and do them. When Randy's heart begins to change, the Holy Spirit will guide him regarding any specific actions he should take. We're on the right track when we envision together behaviors that are at the same time both frightening and enticing to Randy — frightening because they're boldly loving, instead of self-protective; enticing because they embrace who he was created to be, instead of retreating from it.

Let's go back to last Tuesday night when you were in the board meeting. Let's say that as you were hearing about the board's decision, you firmly believed, "I don't need their approval or this job because I know God still loves and uses me no matter how good others think I am. He'll take care of me even if I lose my job just as we're about to have this baby." If you were holding firmly to that belief, what kind of man would you have been at that meeting? What would I have seen if I was watching through a hidden camera?

I wouldn't have apologized for failing as a youth man. That's what I did. I apologized for failing at something I don't really feel like I'm failing at. I know I've made some mistakes and our group has some problems. But I don't think anyone could get the results they're expecting in the short amount of time I've had with these kids.

So what would you have done differently if your heart was sending the signals I just described?

I can't imagine doing anything else in that situation, no matter what my heart was saying.

Some might see this as "resistance" on Randy's part. But I don't. He's probably never seen strong, loving, godly behavior modeled for him. To help him, I need to use a character metaphor — a

familiar image or personality from a story or movie that person-
ifies the character or behavior I'm trying to help him envision.
The most powerful metaphors are ones people come up with
themselves. If I can get Randy to identify one, I can use it to help
him envision how a "new Randy" might behave in this situation.

Imagine what you'd do in that meeting if you were fearless. Who
would you be like — maybe a person from a movie or a story
you know?

I'd be somebody like Russell Crowe in The Gladiator . . . *some
Christian version of him I suppose.*

I like that. So let's imagine for a minute what you'd do in that situation if you were a "Crowe-like" gladiator, only Christian. Instead
of apologizing, I imagine you speaking up and telling the board,
"You know, we've got some real challenges with this youth
group. I don't deny that. And I've made some mistakes. I don't
deny that either. And I don't know how long it's going to take to
turn things around. But there are a few things I do know. One, I
love your kids and have no plans to run away or give up on
them just because things are tough. Two, blaming me for not
having instant success at solving the problems this youth ministry had long before I came isn't going to help your kids a bit.
And three, there's a spiritual battle going on right now in these
kids' lives. What they need right now is all of us going to battle
for them — getting on our knees and asking God to light a fire
in them, us, our church, and our families.

I prayed with you before I accepted this position that God
would bring the right person here to pastor these kids. When you
invited me to come, we all believed this was God's will. Don't you
dare reverse that decision unless you're convinced that God's
directing you to do it. If you tell me that you've sought God and
he's telling you he's closing the door for me to work with the
senior highers, I'll accept that and hand you my resignation. You

don't need to worry about Mallory and me. I serve a big God and he'll take care of us. I won't accept any other position you offer me just because you feel obligated to take care of us."

Whoa (laughter)! Now that's a gladiator! I could never imagine talking to them like that.

So, would you want to talk to them with that kind of freedom and courage? Is it something that confirms what you want to be in your heart?

Even though the thought of it makes my blood run cold, I'd have to say yes.

Why? What appeals to you about being a gladiator?

I know these kids need a gladiator, not a wimp. They need someone who'll go to war for them. They don't need someone to silently take the blame for them. They need a gladiator.

That's right. When you make yourself everybody's whipping post, it takes away the power you need to be a gladiator for these kids, your wife, for anybody. Of course, we're not talking about you acting nasty or mean. But as you're leading a Bible study with your kids, instead of desperately trying to get them to like you, communicating with your presence an entirely different message: "I'm here to make you wrestle with stuff that God wants you to look at even if it doesn't make me popular. I'm committed to be the one adult in your life who's going to tell you how it really is — go to the cross and lose my job for you if I have to." I don't know if those are the actual words you would say to the kids, or for that matter to the church board if you suddenly acquired a gladiator's heart. What I do know is you'd speak with a lot more courage and bold love.

There's something about that that I want. It feels freeing.

This last comment tells me that repentance is indeed taking root in Randy's heart. The work we're doing is fanning his desire to be a different kind of man. I want to keep going until he can do for himself what I've been doing for him — envision a new way he might behave in a situation he currently faces.

Now let's go back to the day the pastor walked in on you and Tony, or when he came back to check up on you. If you firmly believed then that you didn't need anyone's love or approval except God's — and as his gladiator you already had it — how would you handle yourself?

I wouldn't just sit there on my hands like I usually do.

That's true. But what would you do instead? Let's say I'm the pastor and I'm worried about my youth man because I walked in the door and he was weeping like a little girl. That's what it felt like to me. So I'm coming back to see if he's pulled himself together. As you encounter me, and you firmly believe you're a man who doesn't need to be ashamed of who you are, what will you do when I walk in and say "I'm glad to see you've pulled yourself together — this isn't the place for that display of emotion"?

I'd want to say something like, "I disagree, Pastor. I don't mean any disrespect, but if the church isn't a place where we can be honest with each other about our pain and sadness, where is? I'm sorry if you think it's weak for me to weep about my child who never had a chance to be born, and for my wife when she's scared to death it might happen again to the baby she's carrying now. But what I was doing with Tony was a strong thing. And I think it's disrespectful for you to say I should be ashamed of it. I'm not ashamed of it at all. When I walked out of the room earlier, I acted like it was something to be ashamed of. But it's not."

Whoa. I wish I had taped that. That was powerful. You sounded like a gladiator!

It was really different. I wish I could talk like that in real life.

Something would have to change deep within. You'd have to have a gladiator's heart before you could talk a gladiator's talk, wouldn't you?

Randy's starting to hunger and thirst for a heart like Christ's. Paul tells us that repentance is characterized by "earnestness," "eagerness," "longing," and "readiness" to change our ways (2 Corinthians 7:10-11, NIV). It's time to help Randy envision one last thing — the emotions that would accompany this kind of change.

Practice Exercise

What character metaphor models the behavior change you most desire for yourself?

What kind of emotions would you experience, positive or negative, if you changed in this way?

ENVISION THE EMOTIONS THAT
ACCOMPANY THESE CHANGES.
Envisioning the emotions — both positive and negative — Randy will experience if he becomes the person we're talking about accomplishes two things. It helps him grasp the significance of choosing to be this kind of man. And it prepares him for the added difficulties and pain it will bring.

You said a few minutes ago that even thinking about being a gladiator makes your blood run cold. What do you think it would be like to think and talk this new way we've been picturing?
I think it'd feel great. Strong and real. But terrifying too.
Being a gladiator for the kids in the youth group, or for your wife, or whoever, would feel different from staying in a cocoon around people?
No comparison.
Tell me what you imagine it would feel like — both sides of it, the strong side and the terrifying side.

I'd feel free to speak my heart and be the man people need me to
be instead of who they want me to be. I wouldn't back down
when things get tough. I'd be there in ways that count.

And what would that feel like . . . being free in those ways?

I think it would feel incredible. I wouldn't feel like a loser, I can tell
you that.

What would it feel like to be that kind of man with Mallory?

I think I used to be sometimes. I know she needs me to be strong
for her. I'd really feel like a man.

Do you think you'd still need that fantasy world and fantasy
women to make you feel like a man?

Not at all.

So, what about the terrifying side of being a gladiator?

I'd probably get fired. A lot of people wouldn't like it. When they
couldn't control me anymore, they wouldn't like it.

Life would be scary or painful? You'd have to face more rejection?
And you'd be in even bigger trouble at church?

Probably. I know gladiators don't have an easy life.

So it wouldn't make life easier than it is now?

Not easier. I think it would be a lot more exciting and rewarding.
But much harder.

Randy's picture seems balanced. He has a glimpse of both the power and the suffering that comes with being the man God created him to be. His understanding of both is still embryonic, but sufficient to prepare him to wrestle with one of the most important decisions he'll ever make.

Practice Exercise

Describe the two kinds of people Randy must choose between. How does each think, act, and feel?

Choice #1 (the "old" Randy):

Choice #2 (the "new" Randy):

HELP THEM WEIGH LIFE'S MOST IMPORTANT QUESTION.

So which kind of person do you want to be? A person who
believes his life depends upon getting the important people in
his life to give him what his mom and dad never gave him,
and chooses then to behave in ways that will win their
approval and avoid their rejection? Or a person who believes
his life doesn't depend on controlling what people think or
do, but only on what God thinks and does — and who is
unleashed by God to speak and act in whatever ways are most
loving and growth-producing? Which kind of person do you
want to be?

*I don't want to be that first guy you described anymore . . . you
know, the cocoon-dweller. I want to be a gladiator. Just role-
playing a little bit actually felt more real than what I usually
do even though it was imaginary.*

How sure are you? What about the complications and pain it's
going to create, how uncomfortable it will make some people —
the kind of backlash it could unleash? It could end your junior
high ministry too, even before it starts.

*I'd say that's likely. I've seen what happens if you make waves. But
what's the point of staying the way I am just to keep a job? As
long as I'm this way, I'm just part of the problem — not a part
of the solution.*

But what about your wife, your growing family? Don't you need a
job, a salary, benefits?

*That scares me a lot. I'd be lying if I said it didn't. But the way the
board was talking I'm going to be out of a job soon anyway. I*

*can't imagine anyone wanting to hire a cocoon dweller, can
you? Mallory needs me to be a gladiator now more than ever.*
You sound like you're champing at the bit to be a different kind of
man.
*I didn't feel like that before we talked today. But that's how I'm
feeling now.*
Would you be willing to hold off making a final decision about it,
though, until you've had a few more days to think about it,
gather some more data, and maybe even discuss it with
Mallory? It's going to mean big changes in her life too.
*I'm willing to do that. But I don't know what you mean by gather
more data.*

Asking Randy to hold off on this decision accomplishes three
things: it provides an opportunity to help him conduct an experiment to get more data about what it means to be a gladiator; it
gives him time to weigh the implications of this decision; and it
gives us a chance to explore where and how he can find the
power to make these changes before he tries to make them in his
own strength.

Practice Exercise

If you were to design an experiment to give Randy more insight into the
changes he's weighing, what would it be?

What do you think would happen if Randy went out and tried to be a
gladiator this week in his own strength?

DESIGN AND ASSIGN AN EXPERIMENT.
At this stage in their journey, it's good for people to experiment
with the new thinking and behavior they're envisioning. To be

effective, an experiment must carry some risk of failure or negative consequences, just like Jesus' first assignments to his disciples (see Matthew 10:5-10). But it shouldn't put people in
danger of harm, irreversible consequences, or certain failure.

It's important to design the experiment for one specific time
and place and provide precise guidelines to prepare and carry it
out. It's also important to meet as soon as possible after the
experiment to evaluate it and learn from it. No matter what the
outcome, a well-designed experiment always sheds light on the
character decision facing our friends.

By gathering more data, I mean conduct an experiment. It'd be a
trial run to try out this new way of thinking and behaving. How
would you feel about planning one time where you make a
deliberate attempt to think, talk, and behave in real life like a
gladiator — to see what it's like, what it evokes from others, and
what it requires from you?

I'm interested, but what would I have to do exactly?

Let's plan one right now. Then you can decide if you want to do it.
Can you think of a good time and place you can experiment
with being a gladiator this week?

*I'm thinking about Thursday night. The board is scheduled to meet
again, and they've asked me to come back with a schedule for
the junior high ministry.*

Let's not do it there. I'd rather meet with you again before that
meeting . . . to talk about it in more detail before it happens.
Would there be any way the two of us could meet on Tuesday
or Wednesday, and for you to conduct the experiment between
now and then?

*I can meet on Wednesday. My last meeting with the senior highers
is Tuesday evening. How about doing the experiment there?*

What's the purpose of that meeting?

I guess to tell them I won't be their leader anymore.

I'd also like us to meet before that meeting if we can. How about
Tuesday afternoon? Can you meet me Tuesday afternoon?

Late on Tuesday afternoon? I couldn't meet before 4:00.

That will work. And how about another time, between now and
then, for the experiment?

*I'm meeting with the pastor on Tuesday morning. It's our regular
weekly meeting. I'm sure we'll be talking about the switch from
senior high to junior high.*

Let's conduct it there. You'll need to spend at least thirty minutes
before rehearsing what you'd need to believe to be God's gladiator at that meeting. I'd also like you to reflect on how you'd
talk and how you'd handle yourself if you were truly God's
gladiator there. Get firmly in mind what your goal will be; if it's
not to smooth things over or to "go along to get along," what
would a gladiator's goal be at that meeting?

*To be honest with him — to tell him how I feel about the board's
decision.*

Tell me if this makes sense to you. I think a true gladiator of God
would be more concerned about the well-being of the kids in
the youth ministry than getting the pastor to understand his
feelings. Does that make sense to you?

*Talking to him about the kids instead of me does sound stronger.
But I'm trying to think what I would say about the kids.*

At the start of the meeting, remind yourself of what a gladiator
believes. Then make it your goal to bring the struggles and
needs of the kids to the pastor's attention. And then passionately offer him — in the words of a gladiator — your perspective
of what these kids need right now from the church, their adult
leaders, and their families.

I can imagine him refusing to listen.

That could happen. If it does, I want you to handle that as God's
gladiator too. Remind yourself again of what a gladiator would
believe and do in that situation. Then respond accordingly.

What do you think? Is this something you're willing to experiment with?

It scares me. But I want to do it.

Good. Take at least thirty minutes preparing for it, and afterward, spend another thirty minutes reflecting on what you learn. Keep notes about what it requires — what it feels like to be a gladiator and how others react. Then bring those notes with you to our next meeting. Sound doable?

I think so.

What'll be going through your mind as you're driving home today?

I've got a lot to think about, and a lot to talk to Mallory about.

Have you told her much about our talks?

A little. But I think I'll tell her more now.

I look forward to hearing from you on Tuesday about how your conversations go with your pastor and with Mallory.

Okay. See you Tuesday.

Practice Exercise

What do you predict will be the outcome of Randy's experiment?

As Randy's friendship-counselor, how could you use each of the following outcomes to help Randy weigh what kind of person he wants to be?

1. Randy falls flat on his face and is not able to think or talk like a "gladiator" when he's with his pastor.

2. Randy is somewhat successful, but his pastor responds very negatively to his new behavior.

3. Randy is somewhat successful, and his pastor responds very positively to his new behavior.

8

[
l I *f* E - *w* o *r* d s *f* O *r*
PROMOTING RECONCILIATION
]

Two men went up to the temple to pray, one a Pharisee and the other a tax collector. The Pharisee stood up and prayed about himself: "God, I thank you that I am not like other men . . . like this tax collector. I fast twice a week and give a tenth of all I get." But the tax collector stood at a distance. He would not even look up to heaven, but beat his breast and said, "God, have mercy on me, a sinner." I tell you that this man, rather than the other, went home justified before God. For everyone who exalts himself will be humbled, and he who humbles himself will be exalted.

Jesus, Luke 18:10-14, NIV, emphasis added

*J*esus went to great lengths to teach hurting people how to have the same kind of intimate and honest communication with his Father that he had. He prayed in front of them, with them, for them and taught them how to pray for themselves. This equipped them to speak to God with their own "life-words." The most important life-words spoken in any friendship-counseling relationship are the ones our friends offer to God from their own hearts.

Teaching people who are estranged from God to do this isn't an easy matter. As long as their hearts mistrust what God's doing in their lives, their prayers consist of dishonest words, much like the Pharisee's in Jesus' parable. His prayer tried to hide who he was and what he really needed from God. This stands in stark contrast to the tax collector's naked seven-word prayer (18:13). These were life-words because they communicated to God who he was and what he needed — without arrogance or pretense.

During this fourth stage in their spiritual journey, people ask, "How can I get God to help me change?" Through reflection and repentance they've realized that they not only lack the power to make their world right, they also lack the power to make themselves right. Without God's help, nothing in their lives can be right. Turning to God now, however, means facing something else that isn't right — their relationship with him.

They feel God is distant and indifferent to their struggles, more of an enemy than a friend. They attribute the accumulated hardships in their lives to neglect or intent on God's part. They have huge differences with God over the way the world is run. To protect themselves from the insecurity this causes, they pretend God doesn't matter or that he's not the all-knowing, all-powerful, and all-judging deity of the Bible. They try to convince themselves that they don't need anything from God. Or they go through the motions of worshiping and serving God to appease him so even worse things won't happen.

Since people at this stage in their journey see and do things quite differently than God, they feel uncomfortable talking to him from the heart. They want to make peace with him, but they fear what God confirms through the prophet Isaiah: their differences with God are too great for him to overlook.

Let the wicked forsake his way and the evil man his thoughts. Let him turn to the LORD, and he will have mercy on him, and [let him turn] to our God, for he will freely pardon. "For my thoughts are not your thoughts, neither are your ways my ways," declares the LORD. "As the heavens are higher than the earth, so are my ways higher than your ways and my thoughts than your thoughts." (Isaiah 55:7-9, NIV)

In order to reconcile himself to creatures with hearts so different from his, God not only had to make provisions to *forgive them* for the evil things they've thought and done, but also to *remake them* to think and act in holy new ways. To accomplish both of these for us, God sent his own Son, Jesus Christ, to provide everything we need to experience full reconciliation with him. Paul explains:

Once you were alienated from God and were enemies in your minds because of your evil behavior. But now he has reconciled you by Christ's physical body through death to present you holy in his sight, without blemish and free from accusation. (Colossians 1:21-22, NIV)

Jesus paid the penalty for the evil we committed in our past and also freed us from the power of the evil still present in our hearts. When we come to God without any pretense about who we are and what we've done, and ask him to receive us solely on the basis of who Christ is and what he's done, God welcomes us to his side. He gives us access to an up-close and personal place in his presence where we can enjoy a reconciled relationship with him. As we spend more and more time in that place baring our hearts to him, he reconciles our character by reshaping us to yearn, think, choose, and feel like Christ.

When Jesus counseled hurting people, he not only helped them recognize their need for reconciliation with God, he showed them how to seek it through prayer. His model requires us to do no less for our friends who feel separated from God because of the great differences they have with him. Equipping them with the life-words they need to reconcile their relationship with God is the greatest gift we can ever give them.

Where and when did you learn how to talk to God in honest and intimate ways? Describe what happened the last time you talked to God about the differences between you.

TEACHING FRIENDS TO PRAY ABOUT THEIR RELATIONSHIP WITH CHRIST

I tell you the truth, my Father will give you whatever you ask in my name. Until now you have not asked for anything in my name. Ask and you will receive, and your joy will be complete. (Jesus, John 16:23-24, NIV)

Jesus taught his disciples to come to God through him — in his name, on his merit, and for his sake. To approach the Father in their own name or on their own merit would be fruitless (see John 15:7-8). To think they could say or do anything to win an audience with the Creator and Lord of the universe would be the height of arrogance. By authorizing his disciples to address God as their "Father in Heaven" (Matthew 6:9), Jesus granted them a privilege no human had previously enjoyed except him — the privilege of talking to God as their very own dad.

Enjoying a personal relationship with God depends upon first establishing a relationship with his Son. Jesus clears or blocks our way to God, depending on what we believe about his identity, words, and death. When we seek access to God, Jesus asks us the same question he asked Peter: "Who do you say I am?" (Matthew 16:15, NIV). He grants us access when we genuinely answer, "You are the Christ, the Son of the Living God" (16:16, NIV).

To help our friends reconcile their differences with God, we must explore their understanding of who Jesus is and how his suffering relates to theirs. Their differences with God begin and end with their incorrect perceptions of Jesus. We want to help them examine anything that stands in their way of worshiping Jesus as the only one who has the power to change the nature of their relationship with God and the nature of their own hearts. We want to teach them to use whatever they think and feel about Jesus (even angry feelings and unbelieving thoughts) as the beginning point for reconciling their relationship with God. When part of their heart wants to worship Jesus, while part violently resists, they can use both parts to talk to God in the same way a desperate father once used both to talk to Jesus: "I do believe, help me overcome my unbelief" (Mark 9:24, NIV). When our friends aren't sure what to believe about Jesus, we can teach them to ask God to show them who Jesus really is (see Matthew 16:17).

How do you get hurting friends to talk about Jesus when all they want to talk about is their pain? How can you help them talk to God in Jesus' name when they have little faith in Jesus?

TEACHING FRIENDS TO PRAY ABOUT THE TROUBLE IN THEIR WORLD

Then Jesus told his disciples a parable to show them that they should always pray and not give up. . . . Will not God bring about justice for his chosen ones, who cry out to him day and night? Will he keep putting them off? I tell you, he will see that they get justice, and quickly. However, when the Son of Man comes, will he find faith on the earth? (Luke 18:1,7-8, NIV)

Jesus taught his disciples to talk to God passionately and persistently about their adversities the same way he did (see Hebrews 5:7). Appealing to God in times of injustice and hardship wasn't just their privilege, it was their responsibility. Turning to God in the midst of suffering—at the very time they had every earthly reason not to—was an act of worship in the truest sense.

The problem with promoting this kind of worship in hurting people is that it often feels phony to them. They mistakenly think their disappointments and doubts about God need to be removed before they can worship him, so they avoid praying. Or out of false respect, they pretend nothing is wrong when they pray.

They fail to realize that talking honestly to God, when they have grave doubts or questions about the way he's handling things, is the most genuine kind of worship they can offer. It requires far more faith than worship offered when God seems to be doing everything "right." In fact, coming to God when things aren't "right" is the remedy Jesus prescribed for emotional distress: "Come to me, all you who are weary and burdened . . . and you will find rest for your souls" (Matthew 11:28-29, NIV).

Jesus knows our best tool for reconciling our troubled hearts with God is the thoughts and feelings that are weighing us down. Disappointment, rage, loneliness, terror, doubts, and questions can all be used to start life-changing conversations with God. When hurting people do this, they encounter a God bigger than their troubles and grace deeper than their doubts and disappointments. This enables their hearts to rest even while their suffering continues.

When people suffer, their natural response is to blame God. But they seldom talk to God passionately and honestly. This is why our hurting friends need friendship-counselors. They need help to talk to God about their suffering.

Have I been wasting my time? Why take the trouble to be pure? All I get out of it is trouble and woe—every day and all day long! . . . Then one day I went into God's sanctuary to meditate . . . I saw myself so stupid and arrogant; I must seem like an animal to you, O God. But even so, you love me! You are holding my right hand! (Asaph, Psalm 73:13-14,17,22-23, TLB)

How do you know when part of your heart remains unreconciled to God? What roles do talking to God about your suffering play in making you aware of this?

TEACHING FRIENDS TO PRAY ABOUT THE TROUBLE IN THEIR HEARTS

Is not life more important than food, and the body more important than clothes? . . . So do not worry, saying, "What shall we eat?" or "What shall we drink?" or "What shall we wear?" For the pagans run after all these things, and your heavenly Father knows that you need them. But seek first his kingdom and his righteousness, and all these things will be given to you as well. (Jesus, Matthew 6:25,31-33, NIV)

Jesus taught hurting people to seek two things from God above all else — his kingdom and his righteousness. These would give them hearts after God's own heart.

Seeking God's kingdom means asking God for a heart that carries out his sovereign will here on earth the same way the angels carry it out in heaven — unflinchingly, willingly, speedily, completely, and joyfully. Seeking God's righteousness means asking God for a heart that sees things like his heart does — accurately discerning right from wrong, truth from error, wisdom from foolishness, what is real from what is false, and what is valuable from what is worthless.

Jesus taught his disciples that the quest consuming them should be quite different from that of those around them. Most are on a quest for nothing more noble than *the protection or enhancement of their material existence:* "What shall we eat? What shall we drink? What shall we wear?" Knowing that being pre-occupied with these things was the main cause of people's anxieties and addictions, Jesus taught his disciples to concern themselves instead with *transforming their spiritual existence.* He told them that this meant acquiring two things: the will to live the way God wants them to live and a mind that thinks the way God wants them to think. But Jesus didn't stop there. He went further and showed his disciples how to seek the will and mind God wanted them to have. He showed them how to talk to God about their hearts.

When is the last time you sought God for a will or mind like his? How do you use your friendship-counseling relationships to help others do this?

TEACHING FRIENDS TO PRAY ABOUT THE TROUBLE OF OTHERS

Listen, all of you. Love your enemies. Do good to those who hate you. Pray for the happiness of those who curse you; implore God's blessing on those who hurt you . . . Then your reward from heaven will be very great, and you will truly be acting as sons of God: for he is kind to the unthankful and to those who are very wicked. (Jesus, Luke 6:27-28,35, TLB)

Jesus taught his disciples that a direct connection exists between their relationship with others and their relationship with God. He taught them to link their prayers for reconciliation with God to their prayers for reconciliation with others. "This is how you should pray . . . forgive us our debts, as we also have forgiven our debtors" (Matthew 6:12, NIV). Jesus knew that his disciples' hearts wouldn't be fully reconciled with God's until they aligned the way they treated their enemies with the way God treated them. That's why he taught them to pray for God to give them the ability to love like he does (Luke 11:5-13).

John tells us that how we relate to others is the best "barometer" of how reconciled to God our hearts really are:

> Anyone who claims to be in the light but hates his brother is still in the darkness. Whoever loves his brother lives in the light, and there is nothing in him to make him stumble . . . If anyone says, "I love God," yet hates his brother, he is a liar. For anyone who does not love his brother, whom he has seen, cannot love God, whom he has not seen. (1 John 2:9-10; 4:20, NIV)

God provides us with this barometer to keep us from deceiving ourselves about how far we've come in our spiritual journey. At any moment, we can gauge the differences that still exist between ourselves and God by merely reflecting on the way we relate to others — especially those who hurt or injure us. We only need to ask ourselves, "How closely does our treatment of others resemble God's treatment of us?"

Jesus taught his disciples to pray earnestly for those who troubled them because it brought their small heart for people into contact with God's large heart. He knew our love only grows to resemble God's when we start to pray as passionately for others as we do for ourselves. When Jesus wanted his disciples to have the same compassion for troubled people he had, he urged them to pray that God would send shepherds to guide them (see Matthew 9:36-38). Of course, his disciples didn't realize that this was Jesus' way of preparing them to be the very shepherds they were praying for!

Promoting the well-being of those who trouble us isn't easy. When our hearts keep us from loving others or even praying for them, our only remedy is to talk to God about it. This is what Jesus taught his disciples to do. And we must teach those we counsel to do the same.

How do you get the people you counsel to pray for those who mistreat them? How do you help someone who's too angry to pray for anything but their offender's demise?

FOLLOWING JESUS' EXAMPLE FOR PROMOTING RECONCILIATION

Prayer is the central thrust of any counseling relationship that empowers hurting people to acquire and display Christ's character. Until the people we counsel learn to commune with God more deeply than they do with other people, their hearts will never be aligned with his. The main task at this stage is to teach our friends to pray in a way that promotes the reconciliation of their mind and will with the mind and will of God.

Even though I prefer not to pray (or even talk about prayer) with those I'm counseling until they've completed the first three legs of their spiritual journey, everything we do during those stages — shaping the relationship, guiding inward reflection, and cultivating heartfelt repentance — is designed to get them ready to commune with God at depths of intimacy they've never known before. Jesus counseled many people without praying with them. He knew the soil in their hearts needed to be plowed, tilled, and cultivated before they'd have the insight, motivation, and words to genuinely and vulnerably speak to God from their hearts. Until I sense this is true in the people I counsel, I don't ask or teach them to pray. I encourage them to continue reflecting on how they're living their lives, and I ask them to envision the way they could live their lives if they had a new heart. That's what I did in my two previous conversations with Randy.

As this conversation begins, I'm curious about Randy's heart. What's happened to it since our last conversation? What did he learn about his heart in his conversations with Mallory and his pastor this week? Is his determination to be a new kind of person still growing? Is he ready to talk to God genuinely and vulnerably about the condition of his heart? This is what I want to assess as I followup on the homework assigned at our last meeting and as I reconfirm Randy's commitment to the goal we agreed upon earlier.

FOLLOWUP ON HOMEWORK ASSIGNMENTS.

I've been anxious to hear about how your homework assignment went.

Well, you asked me to experiment with being a gladiator. What happened actually spanned two days.

The first thing that happened was I gave one of my junior high kids, Rod, a ride home. He lives in this little RV court with his aunt and uncle who never come to church. They invited me into their trailer, and they had a big bottle of liquor on the table. The uncle — the gruff marine-sergeant type — says, "Do you want a drink?" And Rod's aunt says, "No, Randy's not that way." I was surprised by that, wondering what she meant. For a minute, I felt like I wanted to run out of there as fast as I could.

But I forced myself to stay and talk. After some small talk, I actually started to enjoy being there. I shared with them what Rod has meant to our youth group and what he means to me. And it just naturally led into me sharing about Christ. Both seemed really interested and open and asked a number of questions. I ended up talking to them for a couple of hours — I heard their lifestories and told them mine. When I left, I felt like a million dollars — like the Lord really used me — because somehow I broke out of my cocoon. I really felt like a gladiator for God.

Did you consciously plan your visit with Rod's family as an experiment?

No. That part just kind of happened. It was totally unplanned. But it got me in the right frame of mind for my meeting with Pastor this morning. When I met with him, I felt the same way as when I was talking to Rod's aunt and uncle. I wasn't afraid to be myself with him. For the first time, I talked about what's really happening to the youth in our church — the problems they face at school and at home and where they're at spiritually. I was able to communicate — or we were able to communicate with each other — like we never have since I've come to the church. I didn't feel afraid of him like I usually do. I didn't have a chance to. I was feeling too many things for the kids and the families in our church.

I'm not saying everything has changed between us or that I'm not going to lose my job. But it feels like I can work differently with him now for whatever time I've got left. That feels really good.

Both of these events, and the way you handled them, strike me as significant. In these situations, were you consciously choosing to think or do anything different from what you normally do? As part of the experiment I think I had asked you to consciously do that.

You did. And that's what really freed me. Both times, I said to myself that it doesn't matter if they like me or approve of me. All that matters is that I love them like the gladiator God wants me to be. If I do that, God will take care of everything else. I think that's what freed me. And everything just kind of flowed.

So what do you take away from this experiment? What's the biggest insight you've gained?

I don't have to be afraid.

Why? What's changed?

I guess the way I'm thinking about things.

RECONFIRM THE GROWTH GOAL.

It sounds like the answer to the question, "Do you really want to be
a gladiator?" is still yes.

Absolutely.

Even though things could go a whole lot differently for you in the
future than they did this week? This week people responded
positively to you behaving like a gladiator. But many times they
won't.

*I realize that. I already know what that tastes like, and there's no use
living my life to avoid it. People are going to respond negatively
sometimes either way — whether I stay in the cocoon or not. I'd
rather live free even if it means risking getting people miffed.*

That fits the growth goal we've been going after together. Do you
remember how it goes?

*Instead of being stuck in my fears and looking for ways just to
please others, being free to be who I want to be — someone who
has courage and love.*

That captures it pretty well. Where there's a risk of being rejected or
ridiculed, you want to be able to act out of strength and
courage instead of fear. That idea, right?

Yes.

So you're feeling good about this direction? Is this still the most
important thing we can work on for you right now?

I don't have any doubts about that.

Remember the tax collector in Jesus' parable at the beginning of
this chapter (see Luke 18:10-14)? Randy needs two things before
he can approach God like the tax collector did: *repulsion* over the
man he is *now* (operating with a heart largely unreconciled to
God), and *passion* for the man he *could be* (with a new heart).
Without this kind of holy repulsion and passion, he won't be
ready to pray in truth (talk to God about the man he is) or in
spirit (talk to God about the man he wants to be).

Although I suspect Randy is open and ready to learn how to talk to God in a new way, I can't be sure until I ask. To some degree he still looks at his heavenly Father through the distorted lenses of his experiences with his earthly father (and other authority figures like his pastor). He also still feels quite a bit of anger and doubt toward God around major disappointments and losses in his life — such as the miscarriage of his first child and the ministry failures he's experienced. Any or all of these may suppress his God-given desire for an intimate relationship with the Creator and Lover of his soul. I may need to spend many hours with Randy in discussion, tears, and Bible study over the next several weeks or months, exploring and shaping his understanding of God, before this desire returns. I want to plant enough doubts in Randy's mind about the way he's viewing God that he'd risk giving God a chance to show him what he's really like. Hurting people always see God in a distorted way until their encounters with God become more powerful than their encounters with evil.

EXPLORE AND SHAPE THE WAY THEY THINK ABOUT GOD.

I use a question to shift the topic of our conversation to God. It's a question that makes a logical connection between what we've discussed up until now and Randy's pressing need of a power source greater than the one he's been using.

I'm wondering, what do you think it would take to be able to live the way you did this week when you did that experiment? What would it take to live as a gladiator day in and day out — even when the people in your life try to drive you back into the cocoon?

A lot of courage and concentration. I'd need to constantly remind myself that I don't need them anymore.

But wouldn't it take more than just *reminding* yourself that you don't need them? Wouldn't it take getting to the point where you *really don't need* them?

I'm not sure what you mean.

All your life you've been pretending to be who other people want
   you to be to get their approval or applause. Right?

Right.

Would it really change anything if you started pretending instead
   that you don't need people's approval? Wouldn't you still feel
   like an imposter? Wouldn't you still feel alone, empty, worthless?

*You're right. I'm sick of pretending around people. But how do you
   get to the point where you really don't need their approval any
   more?*

That's where that new belief comes in that we talked about last
   week. Although it would be great if I had everyone's approval, I
   don't need it because . . .

Because I've got God's. And that's all I need.

You've got God's what?

His approval.

Wouldn't it be great if that was true? It would be so freeing. He'd be
   your source of fuel, the place you'd go to fillup with the
   strength to be the man you want to be. But what would that
   feel like to put all your trust in God that way?

Mixed, maybe, I don't know.

You've brought up God many times before in our conversations. I
   think there's a big part of you that would like to be close to
   him. But I've also kind of picked up — correct me if I'm
   wrong — that there's sort of a wall between the two of you. You
   feel like either he's angry with you or you're angry at him. And
   the two of you haven't really been on talking terms much.

*I hate to say this, but I think I almost see him as the enemy. If I go
   to him with my need, he's going to chase me like my dad. And
   if he catches me he's going to hurt me. Yes, a part of me just
   doesn't trust him — like he'll lie to me or trick me like Dad
   does.*

If God was anything like that, I wouldn't trust him either. But what
if he isn't like that? What are you missing out on, if he isn't like
that at all?

*I've thought about that before. Sometimes I've started to believe
that God is different. Then, pow! Something bad happens that
just makes me doubt him again.*

Doubt him in what way?

That he loves me, I guess.

So you believe that God can't love you if he lets bad things happen
to you?

*Why would he, if he really loved me? Why would he let my baby
die like that? Why would he put us through all that pain?
Why would be bring me to this new church just to get fired?*

I don't know. If those things had happened to me, I'd probably
have the same questions you have. They're not bad questions to
ask. I've had some really bad things happen to me too. Like
you, I had real trouble understanding why God let them happen.
I still don't know exactly why he did. I only know that God
loves us even when he lets bad things happen to us. You know
how I know that?

How?

Two ways. First, I know how much God loves Jesus. Yet he still put
Jesus through the worst suffering imaginable: crucifixion. That
proves to me that God can love someone even when he causes
them to suffer. In fact, since I'm a dad, I wonder who suffered
more at the cross, Jesus or his Father. I know that as a dad,
when I cause my kids pain — even when I know it's good for
them — it hurts to see them hurt. And the other way I know
God loves me — even when bad things happen — is the way he
responds when I'm suffering.

What do you mean?

Well, I used to hold back. But I've learned that when I'm hurting,
he's never harsh or uncaring if I tell him just how I'm feeling —

angry, disappointed, confused, or whatever — and ask him directly the kind of questions you were just asking. I feel God's love the strongest when I'm the most honest, naked, and raw with him.

I thought I tried that already, and it didn't work. Maybe I didn't, though. Maybe I was pretending then too.

It's probably impossible to know. I'm glad you've tried to talk to him about these things before. What might be different this time, though, is that I'll be here to help you do it. It's easy to get discouraged and give up praying when you're doing it alone — especially if God seems silent. Sometimes he is. We might have to wait days or weeks for his response. I've found that it's always worth the wait. But it's always good to have someone waiting and praying with you. But, I'm not sure what it would mean to you if I helped you talk to God about the man you are and the man you want to be, without any pretending or hiding, asking him for the power to come out of your cocoon.

I know I need to do something to tear down this wall between God and me.

The two of us have spent several hours together the last few weeks trying to understand what's going on in your heart and your life. I think we can use that now to get God's help to tear that wall down.

I want to. I know I need God . . . and I need to tear that wall down.

At this stage, I often alternate in the roles of evangelist, theologian, apologist, Bible teacher, and grief counselor to my hurting friends. I draw upon the spiritual truths I've learned through studying the Bible and reflecting on my life experience to help them develop a more accurate understanding of God.

My goal is to give them a "taste," as Peter puts it, "that the Lord is good" (1 Peter 2:3, NIV). They won't begin to really comprehend the depth and breadth of his goodness until they lay their head against his breast and start to draw their life from him. Only then can our hurting friends start to "grow up mature and whole in God" (1 Peter 2:2, MSG). This is what I want to teach Randy to do, if he'll let me.

When I'm teaching hurting friends how to commune with God in a way that connects and reconciles their hearts to his, I like to spend most of our meeting time praying. I do this by leading them through four seasons of prayer every time we meet. I base these seasons on the four ways Jesus taught his disciples to talk to God: about their relationship with his Son, their trouble in the world, the trouble in their heart, and the trouble of others.

Practice Exercise

Reread the above dialogue and circle the statements or questions I use to explore Randy's thinking about God. Underline the statements or questions I use to shape his thinking about God. What are some alternate statements, questions, or ideas you might use in future conversations to explore and shape a friend's thinking about God?

TEACH THEM TO TALK TO GOD ABOUT HIS SON.

Before we talk to God about the wall, let me ask you a question.
    Why do you think Jesus teaches us to always talk to God in his
    name? What do you think that means?
I guess because he's our Savior. Because of what he did for us.
That's a big part of it. But why do you, personally, need a Savior in
    order to come to God? Why can't you come to him in your
    own name, and say, "Hi, God — this is Randy. You know, the
    youth pastor"?
*Probably because I've done so many things to make him mad —
    like my name is mud or crap to him. That's why I have to use
    somebody else's name. It's like using somebody else's credit card*

because mine is overdrawn. Jesus' card has a big balance in his Dad's bank.

There's a big difference between conviction of sin and self-contempt. The two carry entirely different messages. Conviction draws us to God, using our failures to convince us how much we need him. Contempt drives us away from God, using our failures to convince us how much he hates us. Conviction whets our appetite for God. Contempt spoils it. Randy has the two confused. He mistakenly assumes the contempt with which he regards himself is something noble — the kind of humility and self-evaluation that pleases God. Of course, it's not.

Before helping Randy pray, I want to try to deepen his understanding of the gospel. The more Randy understands the gospel of Christ, the more reason he'll have to question his distorted images of himself and God. The gospel isn't just good news for nonChristians. It not only tells us how Christ's sufferings provide the way for us to *have a personal relationship with God.* It also tells us how Christ's sufferings provide the way for us to *have minds and hearts like God's.*

But what gives you the right to use Jesus' credit card — to ask his Dad to give you money from his account as if you were his son, too?

Because he died for me, right?

Yes. Jesus died for you, for your sins, as well as for the sins of the whole world. But does that automatically give everyone the right to use Jesus' credit card or to pray in his name?

No. You have to accept him . . . accept what he did . . . and ask him to be your personal Savior.

Have you done that?

Yes. Back in high school. I belonged to a group called Young Life. At one of their camps, I asked Christ to be my Savior.

Why did you do that? What motivated you?

*I guess I felt convicted about the way I was living my life. I was liv-
ing it just for myself and making a big mess of it.*

That convicting voice within you back then — that voice that kept
talking to you about the way you were living — whose voice do
you think that was?

*Don't know. Never thought about it. I suppose it was my con-
science speaking.*

Do you mind if I read you a statement Jesus once made? (Randy
nods his head.) It's in John 6:44. "No one can come to me
unless the Father who sent me draws him." I'm wondering if
Jesus' words here shed any light on whose voice was speaking
to you?

God's?

That's what Jesus said. The people who ask him to be their Savior
are the ones the Father chooses and draws and entices. Where
does your mind go, Randy, when I say that God chose you,
then pursued you, and drew you, until you recognized that he'd
sent Jesus to bring you to him? And that's why you get to use
Jesus' name now and get credited for his righteousness.

*It blows me away. I don't understand why he'd choose me to be his
son. Why would he do that for me?*

None of us knows why. None of us deserves it. And none of us
would let him do it for us if he didn't plant in our hearts that
desire to be his child. But let me read one more thing to you
that Jesus said: "No one comes to the Father except through
me. If you truly know me, then you know my Father as well"
(John 14:6-7). Jesus gives us two reasons here to always pray in
his name. One, we're acknowledging that we wouldn't be talking to God at all if it wasn't for Jesus giving us a way to do it.
And two, God would be a stranger to us if it wasn't for Jesus.
By praying in his name, we're praying to the one whose love
and character Jesus showed us on the cross. I'd like us to start
our conversations with God by telling him how we're feeling

this moment about who Jesus is and what he's done for us. How would you feel about starting our conversation with God that way?

It would be different. I might need some help.

I'll be glad to help if you need me. We can do this a couple of different ways. We can talk to God out loud or silently. Either way, I'd like to talk to God on your behalf, so you can hear me. I'll talk to him first this time, and when I'm done, it'll be your turn to talk to him. Out loud or silently — whichever would be most meaningful to you. I'd like to do this a few times with you in the time we have left today, if that's okay. We'll talk a few minutes each time to get ready. Then we'll pray. After we're finished praying, we'll take a few minutes to reflect on it and then get ready to pray again, with a different topic or focus each time. How's that sound?

Good, but hard. I don't have any problem praying out loud, but I'm glad you're going first.

It's important not to rush into prayer without Randy fully understanding and consenting to the procedure. When counseling hurting friends, praying from the heart is the most powerful intervention we can offer them. We're preparing them for a type of spiritual surgery.

If Randy had chosen to pray silently, after he finished I would have asked him to tell me about his conversation with God. People who pray silently at first usually switch to praying out loud within a few meetings.

Why don't we begin, then, by talking to God about his Son?

All right.

Heavenly Father, I come to you right now in the name of someone that both Randy and I call our Savior, the Lord Jesus Christ.

When I think of the way Jesus suffered and died so that Randy and I can have a relationship with you, I want to thank and worship both of you, Father and Son. I can't believe that you want to share with us the love you have with each other. As Randy just stated, that blows me away too. We thank you that because of your Son, Jesus Christ, we can come and talk to you as a loving dad. I'd ask that you'd make yourself known that way to us. Allow Randy to experience you as the dad he's always wanted. I pray that as Randy talks to you, he won't feel a need to hide anything from you — that he'll trust what Christ did on the cross to make things right between him and you. We pray that you'll get pleasure from this time that we spend talking to you. And we pray this in Christ's name.

Dear God. I know I don't deserve to be talking to you right now. But I'm doing it because for some reason you chose me to be your son. I think that's why you took me to that camp when I was in high school and made sure I heard about Jesus dying for me. You wanted me to be your son. I'm sorry, God, that sometimes I have so much trouble believing that. But right now I do believe it. And I want to thank you for sending Jesus to me and loving me even when I don't deserve it. Amen.

How was that, Randy?

I'm glad God and I are starting to talk to each other.

When you say, "you and God are talking to each other," what do you sense God was saying to you just then?

No words, really. I felt him listening and caring.

That speaks louder than words, doesn't it?

It sure does.

Practice Exercise

It's difficult, if not impossible, to teach others to do something you're not doing yourself. Take some time right now to talk to God about your own thoughts and feelings about his Son. Record your observations about this experience after you do it.

Teach them to talk to God about their trouble in the world.

I'd like us to continue our conversation with God by talking to him
next about all the things happening to you that you can't
control — especially the things you're most worried, upset, or
angry about right now. What kinds of things come to mind?

*Number one would be the health of my wife and unborn baby. I'm
really worried about them.*

Okay, let's make them the first thing we talk to God about. What else?

*My ministry to the kids and my future at the church — having a
job so I can support my family.*

Those are very big. We'll be sure to include those. Is anything else
causing serious difficulties or pain for you right now?

*All my relationships — with Mallory, with the pastor, the board,
and with the kids at church.*

I know you're feeling a lot of pressure and rejection in these relationships. Is that what you mean?

*That and conflict, especially if I start to be more of a gladiator with
them.*

Okay. We'll talk to God about your relationships too. Can you think
of anything else right now?

How about my fantasy problem?

Let's hold off on that until we talk to God about your heart. That'll
be next. Okay? (Randy nods his approval.) Would you know
how to talk to God about the problems we just named?

I suppose just ask him to help me and Mallory get through them.

That would be fine if that's all you want from God right now.

What do you mean?

Jesus said you can ask God anything you want. I'm just wondering if
that's all you want from him. If you could have anything, right
now, would all you want be help to get through these problems?

*If I could have anything I wanted from God, I guess I would ask
him for a lot more than that.*

Why don't you then? Even if he doesn't give you everything you
want, what have you got to lose? Jesus taught that everyone
who asks receives, and he who seeks finds. He's telling you that
one way or another you won't be disappointed if you bring
your deepest desires to God.

*I think I'm afraid that I will be disappointed. And then I'd really
feel like he's deserted me.*

But isn't that how you already feel? It seems you have a much
greater chance of feeling deserted if you hold back and ask him
for very little. You won't even know if he's there if you do that.
It's up to you — I'm just throwing it out as a possibility that you
might want to ask him for a little more than you usually do.
How do you feel about going first this time?

I'm okay with that.

One last suggestion. Don't feel like you have to hold back anything
you're feeling either: any questions or any pain you want to tell
him about. God's not fragile. He can shoulder anything you're
feeling or thinking.

*Okay. Here goes . . . Dear God, there are so many things going on
in my life right now that I just don't understand. I've been
struggling not to let them make me bitter and angry toward
you. But sometimes I feel all alone and that you don't care.
What I'm afraid the most about right now — or if I could have
any wish right now from you — it would be for the health of
Mallory and our baby. Please God, I don't know if we could
handle the loss of another baby right now (tears). Please give
us a safe birth and healthy baby. I'm also angry about what's
going on at church. It's not just about losing my job. I am
afraid about that and ask that you would at least make sure I
can support my family doing something. But I'm really angry
about what all this means for the kids in the youth group. God,
please do something to wake up the church and parents and
the board to what these kids really need right now.*

*God, please show me what I'm supposed to do. Help me
to be a better man. Help me to love the people I feel mad at
or afraid of right now. I don't want to be mad at everybody,
but I don't know what to do when they put all this pressure on
me. I don't want to just let them push me around. But I don't
want to fight with them either. I guess I just really need you
right now to keep me from drowning. I feel like I'm treading
water, but I'm getting tired, and there's no land in sight. I
don't even know for sure what all I need. But I know I need
you. Amen.*

Lord, as I listen to Randy talking to you, I'm thrilled that he's
trusting you with what's troubling him the most. Lord, I'm
thrilled that he wants to look at you in a different way — that
you haven't deserted him. Lord, I ask that you answer the
requests that Randy's made to you just now in whatever ways
will accomplish the most good in his life, in Mallory's, in the
kids and parents and board at church. I ask that you will
respond to Randy's requests in a way, Lord, that will speak
loudly to Randy and the people in his world about your love
for him and Mallory and their baby. I pray too, Lord, that you
not only calm the stormy seas that rage *all around* Randy right
now, but more importantly you calm the stormy sea *inside
him.* Give him a sense of peace on the inside that can only
come from you. Thank you, Father, for listening and caring
for Randy. Amen.

*That was really different. I'm not used to telling God anything like
it really is. I'm feeling closer to him too. I feel like my load's
been lightened. Like whatever happens, it will be okay.*

That makes sense. You invited God to take a lot off your shoulders.
But it'll be a big temptation to take it back — especially if things
stay tough for a while, and they probably will.

I can see that.

Practice Exercise

Without rereading the above prayer, write out the prayer you would pray with Randy concerning all the difficulties he's having right now.

TEACH THEM TO TALK TO GOD ABOUT THE TROUBLE IN THEIR HEART.

Praying from the heart — especially for those who are new to it — is strenuous and exhausting. It can feel like holding your breath under water. They have to build up to it to stay there for very long. And praying about trouble in the heart requires the deepest and longest "descent" of all. That's why I conduct this next season of prayer like a "tag-team" dialogue with God. It gives Randy frequent opportunities to "catch his breath" and gather his thoughts. It also gives me opportunity to model for him how to pray with pinpoint accuracy — zeroing in on the specific things he wants and needs God to do in his heart.

Earlier I asked you if you had any idea where you could find the power to be this new kind of person you want to be. As we begin another round of prayer, I'd like you to take the opportunity to talk to God about freeing you to be the man he wants you to be and the man you want to be. Do you feel up for that?

Definitely.

Before we do, let's review the specific things about yourself you need God's help to change — especially the things in your heart that you could never change on your own. Where does your mind go with that?

What I mentioned before — my problem with lust and fantasy.

What deep inside you would have to change for you to be free of the lust and fantasy?

The way I think about a lot of things. The way I doubt God, the way I care too much about what people think, the way I try to get them to give me approval.

Randy has enough insight into the sins of his heart to begin to pray meaningfully about them. Over time, his insight and his ability to pray meaningfully will grow as he keeps talking honestly to God about them. I could help Randy reflect more now and probably deepen his understanding of the trouble in his heart, but a hurting person's time is always better spent talking with God than talking with a friend or counselor — as long as he's talking with God from a reflective and repentant heart.

It sounds like you're ready then. You have a good idea of what to talk to God about. When we pray this time, let's take turns going back and forth until you've had a chance to say everything to God you want to say about your heart right now. Just say "Amen" when you're finished and I'll close. Okay? *(Randy nods agreement.) Father, I really want to ask you to help me change my thoughts, especially those times when I get pressured and I begin to lust and use fantasies about women to escape or run. I really don't want to do that anymore. I pray that you'd help me stop. Help me come to you for help instead. I'm sorry that I turn to fantasy instead of you. That must really hurt you. I'm sorry for all the ways I must hurt you every day. Help me clean up my head, my thoughts. I want to think like you want me to think.*

Lord, both Randy and I struggle with believing that you're enough. We both struggle with believing that we have to take our life in our own hands because we really can't trust you. I'm excited to hear Randy tell you that he's ready for you to cleanse him at the deepest level. God, it's so exciting to hear Randy asking you to give him a new mind — to change him from the inside out. I'm excited, Lord, about what that clears the way for you to do in his heart. Blast the logjams out of his heart . . . the lust, fear, unbelief, and selfishness that keep his strength as a man all dammed up. Help him to cut loose and be bold and alive in real life instead of fantasy.

God, I pray that you'll help me become who you allowed me to be a little bit this week. Help me be strong when I don't know whether I'll have a job and when I get scared about Mallory and the pregnancy. When these things make me afraid, help me, Lord, to trust you more. Help me be more loving, more brave, and more real with people.

Lord, I believe that Randy's desire to be a different kind of man is one you've put in his heart. I know he can't be this kind of man unless you also give him the power to be it in some very difficult situations. Randy faces pressures to conform every day. He risks being ridiculed or completely rejected if he doesn't do what others want him to do. The temptation is there in big ways for him to give in to his fears and to play to the audience, hoping that somehow they'll give him the approval he thirsts for. God, I know that Randy is tired of living that way. He desires to be a man of strength, love, and courage—all things that only come from you. I'm so excited that he's turning to you now, Lord, and asking you to do something in him that he can't do in his own power. I pray that through your Holy Spirit, you'll give him strength to be and do things that he could never do on his own.

God, help me to truly believe that you care about me and Mallory and our baby and that you're my Father. Help me to know that you're not lying to me or tricking me when I trust you. Help me to know who you really are. Amen.

Lord, we're going to keep coming to you as we have today because you're Randy's only hope. If you don't work a miracle in his life, he's doomed to be the kind of man he doesn't want to be. But I'm so glad that he can turn to you as a dad he can always trust. Thanks, Lord, for listening to us. I pray that you'll continue to draw Randy's heart toward you and convince him that you're a dad who can be trusted. We pray all these things in Christ's name. Amen.

What's going through your mind right now, Randy?

I don't remember ever praying that way before.

What's different about the way we're praying?

I'm not just saying words. I'm saying things that are from deep down in my heart. I've always prayed "good prayers" that sounded nice. But this is something I really feel.

As we were praying, I got the picture of the prodigal son returning home, with his dad just clutching him in his arms.

Yes. And he's taking this big weight off my shoulders and telling me I don't have to carry it anymore.

What would that weight be? Can you put it into words?

I don't have to be something I'm not. I don't have to hide who I am. I'm starting to believe he's going to make me different. I don't have to do it myself.

I'm glad you're feeling that the pressure's off. You're asking God to do something that you can't do. It must feel good to give that job to him.

Practice Exercise

Think of someone you know who's come to you in pain. Write out the kind of prayer you'd like them to learn to offer God about the logjams that keep them from being the kind of person God created them to be. After you do, think about how you could teach them to pray this way.

TEACH THEM TO TALK TO GOD ABOUT THE TROUBLES OF OTHERS.

There's one last thing, Randy, I'd like us to pray about before we end our meeting today. We've been praying all about the trouble you're having in your life. But I'd like us to spend some time

praying for the trouble other people are having—especially the
people you have trouble getting along with. Who comes to
mind when I say that?

The first one that comes to mind is my pastor.

Okay. Anybody else?

The kids at church and their parents . . . the board members.

Okay. How about people even closer to home?

Mallory? She should definitely go on that list too.

And your parents? Aren't you still having some trouble with them?

*Tons! They might be the hardest of all for me to pray for. Praying
for them seems futile. I gave up a long time ago on them ever
changing.*

That's a good reminder that none of these people may change because
we're praying for them. So, how do you react to the suggestion
that we end our meeting today praying for this list of people?

I'm okay with it.

Do you want to go first, or should I?

*Can you go first this time? I think this might be the hardest for me
to pray for.*

I'll go first then. But your comment that this will be hard brings one
other thing to mind. As we pray, let's be real with God about
the struggle you're having to love and pray for these people.
Let's just admit that to God up front. Okay?

Okay.

Heavenly Father, we come this time to talk to you about these people
in Randy's life that have struggles of their own. Right now, Randy
doesn't feel very loved by any of them, and he struggles about
praying for them. God, I ask that as Randy comes to you about
them, you'll help him develop the same kind of heart for these
people that you have. I pray that you'll help him get better at
knowing how to pray for them and knowing how to love them.

I ask that you comfort Mallory's heart and help her heal
from the loss of her first baby. Help her know how much you

care about her and the baby she's carrying now. Melt her fears and help her draw strength and nourishment from you to walk through this difficult time with Randy as his partner in every way.

I also pray for Randy's pastor. Shepherding one of your flocks, Lord, is difficult in many ways. I ask that you'll keep drawing this man's heart toward you, keeping it soft and pure in the midst of all the heartaches and trials he experiences every day as a pastor. Help him see each precious person in his flock, including Randy, the way you do. Give him compassion and wisdom to shepherd their hearts toward you.

Father, a big part of me wants what Kevin just prayed for too. I want that for Mallory, Pastor, and for the kids, parents, and board at church. I want to want that for my dad and mom too. God, I haven't said anything to you about my parents for a long time. I'm sorry, God, about the way I've hated them. (Tears.) I need your help to forgive them and to love them. I ask that you'd just open their eyes to who Jesus is and help them believe in him. I'm trying not to ask you this so they'll change just for me, but that they'll stop hurting each other and other people in their lives, and they'll be filled with your love and be the people you want them to be. In Jesus' name, Amen.

What do your tears mean, Randy?

How sad I am about my mom and dad. I'm sad about all the hate that's there, them toward each other and me toward them.

I think your tears are there for another reason. They're like drops running off melting ice. As you put your hard, cold heart out there in front of God, his love and his warmth started melting it. He'll keep doing that as long as you keep putting it out there in front of him. What does that sound like to you — that if you keep praying for others this way, your heart toward them will slowly become like God's?

That sounds like good news.

Randy's starting to understand the gospel. The more he does, the more his heart will resemble the heart that moved Jesus to die on the cross for the very people who deserted, rejected, and executed him. The first indications that this is happening will be in Randy's conversations with God. They'll slowly come to embody the same concern for others that Jesus' conversations with the Father did. Randy's prayer for his parents is the first faint indicator that this metamorphosis has begun.

Randy's choice to concentrate his prayers on the two people who have hurt him the most was a good one. As his heart softens toward them, it will soften toward everyone else in his world and he'll grow in his ability to selflessly pray for each of them. Only as he learns to be a gladiator for others in prayer, will he grow free to be a gladiator for them in life.

Practice Exercise

If Randy's character transformation continues, what changes would you expect to see in the way he prays for the following people?

Mallory:

His parents:

His pastor:

The problem kids at church:

Parents and board members:

TEACH THEM TO KEEP TALKING TO GOD FOR AS LONG AS IT TAKES.

Reconciling a human heart to God's heart requires prayer that is both passionate and persistent. The first time a hurting person speaks passionately to God, his heart will still be out of tune with God's. It's important to help our hurting friends continue to keep talking and listening to God. The more they do, the more the words of their mouth and meditations of their hearts will become attuned to God's. Their concerns will shift from knowing reasons for their suffering to knowing the God behind their suffering; from changing their circumstances to changing their character; from advancing their own interests to advancing his interests; and from promoting their own well-being to promoting the well-being of others.

For as long as this leg of their journey takes, our job is to promote this kind of prayer while we wait with our friends for God to work in their hearts and their world in whatever ways he decides.

I mentioned to you before that God asks us to trust him with when and how the requests we put before him are answered. In the meantime, he asks us to keep talking to him and waiting for as long as it takes for him to answer. What's that going to feel like to keep putting these same things before him for days or weeks or even months, while we wait on him?

In one way it feels comforting, but in another like work.

What do you mean?

It's comforting to know that if God doesn't answer right away that it could be kind of normal. It doesn't mean he's mad or not listening. It feels like hard work because it is. It takes time to talk to God about the things that really matter. Like any other relationship, it requires hard work to keep it healthy.

So is this something you're willing to do — to keep meeting with me weekly to pray intensely like we did today and maybe plan one or two times each week to pray on your own following the same format we did today?

Exactly like we did today?

That's what I'm suggesting. Doing it in four rounds on the same four topics. Do you remember what they were?

Can you remind me while I write them down?

Sure. First we talked to God about your relationship with his son, then about your troubles in the world, then about the troubles in your heart, and finally about the troubles others are having. I'd also suggest that you take a few minutes to keep a notebook or journal on the conversations you have with God, writing down any way God might be speaking to you. How do you feel about doing it that way?

I'm willing to give it a try. How long is it supposed to be?

As long as it takes to talk to God meaningfully and honestly about all four areas. It's probably best not to watch the clock while you're praying.

I like that.

Can you take a minute right now to pick the one or two specific times you'll do it this week? Do you want to do it once or twice or how many?

Maybe just once to start with.

That's fine.

I think I'll do it Monday morning. I'm usually the only one around the church then. I should have plenty of privacy.

Sounds great. Would you be sure to keep a notebook or journal and bring it with you when we meet next week?

Okay.

Do you have any questions about your assignment?

No.

I think we're ready to adjourn then. What do you think?

I'm ready . . . Thanks a lot for today. I really appreciate your time.

You're welcome. See you next week at this same time.

Practice Exercise

Pick a time and place to do the assignment I just gave Randy. Be sure to include all four seasons of prayer and keep a notebook or journal. After you do this, consider asking a friend to do it with you.

9

$$\left[\begin{array}{c} l \text{ I } f \text{ E } - w \text{ o } r \text{ d s } \quad f \text{ O } r \\ \text{ENCOURAGING RESPONSIBILITY} \end{array} \right]$$

This is to my Father's glory, that you bear much fruit, showing yourselves to be my disciples.

Jesus, John 15:8, NIV

*B*ecause others can't observe our hearts directly, they judge who we are inwardly from what they see outwardly. By studying our behavior — especially when we're in pain or distress — they get a pretty accurate "taste" of our hearts. Our behaviors are the fruit that tell others what kind of "tree" we are: good or bad, trust-worthy or treacherous, kind or malicious.

Character is the most graphic tool God gives us to commu-nicate to others who he is and what he's like. When our hearts are reconciled to God's, we bear fruit that gives others a taste of his character. Our behavior patterns serve as proof to the people in our world that he exists, he is good, and he has the power to transform lives.

When it comes to character, Jesus is emphatic with his disci-ples about two things: they do not have the power to generate good character on their own (see John 15:5), but they still have the responsibility to do so (see John 15:8). This is why Jesus never exhorts us to change our behavior as an end in itself, only as a means to an end. He does it to help us discover how incapable our unreconciled hearts are to generate good behavior (as he did with the rich young man and the woman caught in adultery), or to help us employ our reconciled hearts to serve him (as he did with Peter after his denials).

As friendship-counselors, our ministry at this stage is to encourage our friends to do what Jesus encouraged Peter to do: translate their love for God into love for others by exercising their new heart — to love the way it's telling them to love.

The ultimate aim of the Christian minister is to produce the love which springs from a pure heart, a good conscience and a genuine faith. (Paul, 1 Timothy 1:5, PH)

Do you ever catch yourself expecting a friend's behavior to change before his heart does? What effect does this have on your relationship with him?

THE RESPONSIBILITY THAT COMES WITH A NEW HEART

You are the light of the world. A city on a hill cannot be hidden. Neither do people light a lamp and put it under a bowl. Instead they put it on its stand, and it gives light to everyone in the house. In the same way, let your light shine before men, that they may see your good deeds and praise your Father in heaven. (Jesus, Matthew 5:14-16, NIV)

God doesn't want our friends to keep their new hearts a secret. They're responsible to "let them shine before men" wherever God puts them. If this seems unpleasant or laborious, it's a sure sign they don't have a new heart yet! A new heart brings new passions, the strongest being to serve God wherever and however he asks. This is a responsibility they *want to meet* rather than something they *have to do*. They understand what Jesus meant when he said, "Take my yoke upon you . . . for *my yoke is easy* and *my burden is light*" (Matthew 11:29-30, NIV, emphasis added).

That's why at this stage in their spiritual journey our friends ask, "How can I serve God?" This question naturally flows from their new passion to know God and make him known to others. One of Jesus' disciples described it this way:

> We saw it, we heard it, and now we're telling you so you can experience it along with us, this experience of communion with the Father and his Son, Jesus Christ. Our motive for writing is simply this: We want you to enjoy this, too. Your joy will double our joy! (John, 1 John 1:3-4, MSG)

When friends at this stage ask how they can serve God, it's not because they're clueless about what he wants them to do. By now, they know instinctively *what* God wants them to do (see 1 Thessalonians 4:9), but don't know *how* to do it in their complex and precarious world. In order to be lights in these dark places, they need the same kind of preparation and encouragement Jesus gave his disciples.

> These twelve Jesus sent out with the following instructions: . . . "I am sending you out like sheep among wolves. Therefore be as shrewd as snakes and as innocent as doves." (Matthew 10:5,16, NIV)

How do you respond when a friend asks you how they can serve God in their situation? How can you help them do what God is calling them to do?

UNWRAPPING AND UNLEASHING OUR NEW HEARTS

Jesus called in a loud voice, "Lazarus, come out!" The dead man came out, his hands and feet wrapped with strips of linen, and a cloth around his face. Jesus said to them, "Take off the grave clothes and let him go." (John 11:43-44, NIV)

The way Lazarus was raised from the dead and released from the wrappings that bound him parallels the way our friends are spiritually brought to life and freed from the wrappings that bind them. It starts with Jesus speaking words to them that shoot life pulsating through their dead hearts. It follows with the ministry of friends like us, working under Jesus' direction, to unleash them to live the new life Jesus intends them to live. This is our task as friendship-counselors at this stage—helping our friends unwrap their new hearts.

When we first brought our friends to Jesus, their hearts were dead because of differences that separated them from God. They were restricted from functioning the ways God created them to function. Over time, as we helped our friends seek God in spirit and in truth, their minds and wills started to change. When we're with them now, we sense their hearts are coming alive, pumping with new energy, passion, and vision to serve God and love others. Now we need to help them break out of the restrictions that still inhibit them from acting on the inclinations of their new heart.

This is how Paul counseled a group of Christians who let restrictions from their past get in the way of exercising their new hearts:

> Since you died, as it were, with Christ and this has set you free from following the world's ideas of how to be saved — by doing good and obeying various rules — why do you keep right on following them anyway, still bound by such rules as not eating, tasting, or even touching certain foods? Such rules are mere human teachings . . . They have no effect when it comes to conquering a person's evil thoughts and desires. (Colossians 2:20-23, TLB)

Imagine that we can measure human pain and emotion like we measure electrical shock. The smaller disappointments in life sting us with 50 to 100 volts of pain. Greater heartaches send 500 volts or more coursing through our nervous systems. But the greatest blows of all — those that send us reeling and gasping for air — are 1,000 volts!

Growing up in a world "rigged for frustration and disappointment,"[1] we learned very quickly to avoid the shocks of life, especially high voltage ones (100 volts or more). We asked: "How can I prevent this from happening to me in the future?" We looked for rules to follow that would protect us — the kind Paul urged the Christians at Colossae to discard. We created our own or borrowed them from people we admired. Maybe we even found a religion with a ready-made set. While we forfeited our freedom and restricted our choices, it seemed a small price to pay for the illusion of security the rules provided.

But now the weight of our self-imposed rules threatens to crush us. While the rules make our lives safe, they also make them dull, drab, and burdensome. Little freedom exists for creativity, spontaneity, adventure, or love. Caution replaces courage. Fear replaces faith. Ritual replaces risk. Inhibition replaces intimacy.

New hearts need freedom to love boldly and dangerously. They must be unleashed to go wherever love compels them —

into 100-, 500-, even 1,000-volt settings as opportunity arises. This is why our friends need help to identify and strip away the manmade rules that restrict their lives to a 50-volt existence. These rules are the "wrappings" of the old life that Jesus wants them to discard.

It's a sad irony. Many of us seek God for a new heart only to keep operating by our old rules even after he grants it. Jesus said this was like putting new wine into old wineskins. When you do that "the old skins burst from the pressure, and wine pours out" (Matthew 9:17). Imagine the arrogance of attempting to harness, contain, or regulate the work of the Spirit of God in our lives! That's why Jesus' model requires us to encourage our friends to trust, strengthen, and exercise their new hearts.

Are there any rules from your past you should discard to give your new heart room to operate? How do you help the friends you counsel do the same?

ENCOURAGING OUR FRIENDS TO TRUST THEIR NEW HEART

Make a tree good and its fruit will be good . . . The good man brings good things out of the good stored up in him . . . (Jesus, Matthew 12:33,35, NIV)

When we first encounter Nehemiah, he's weeping (see Nehemiah 1:4). But it's not for himself, even though he was the captive of a terrorist dictator, hundreds of miles from his homeland. Instead, he's weeping for the tiny remnant of his countrymen. He just received the first news in years about his country and it was bad — worse than he imagined. All he could do for days was weep, mourn, repent, and pray.

And as he did, God stored up all kinds of good things in his heart for this ragtag group of survivors — compassion, courage, and vision to help them, even if it meant putting his own life at risk. God put it in Nehemiah's heart to do the unthinkable (actually a capital offense) — to ask the Persian emperor for the authority and resources to return to his homeland, rebuild its capital, and govern its territory (see Nehemiah 2:5,12)! To say the least, this was a true 1,000-volt risk.

This is the kind of heart God gives us when we ask him for a new one. It's not timid or cowardly. It's powerful, loving, and determined (see 2 Timothy 1:7). Many, even in Christian circles, are threatened by hearts like these, considering them reckless, foolish, and stubborn. They often discourage us from listening to them or acting on them. They tell us our hearts will get us in trouble and lead us astray. We're taught to suppress and ignore the voice of the Spirit of Life. Rather than trust the Spirit to work in our hearts, we're encouraged to trust only those who speak with caution, reason, and moderation. For all practical purposes, they want us to live disconnected from "the vine," starving our new hearts while they're still in infancy! These words, no matter how well-intentioned, become death-words because they take the place of God's spirit in our lives.

When our friends ask how they should serve God, there's no better response than the question God prompted the Persian emperor to ask Nehemiah: "What is it you want?" (Nehemiah 2:4, NIV). A mentor once asked me that same unexpected and unnerving question. I desperately wanted him to tell me how to serve God in a particularly distressing circumstance. Instead, he simply asked, "What do you want to do?" I pushed harder: "Tell me what to do!" He answered, "Kevin, make sure your heart is close to God's, then do what you want to do." Wisely, he encouraged me to trust my new heart.

Some well-meaning people might object and say they'd rather trust the Bible to tell them what to do than their heart. They argue that the heart is easily swayed by all kinds of influences while the

Bible is objective and never changes. But they fail to recognize three things. First, we can misunderstand what God says in the Bible as easily as we can misunderstand what he says to our hearts (maybe more so). Second, the Bible is meant to help us get and keep a healthy heart, but it isn't to take the place of our heart. And finally, Scripture isn't given to provide specific direction for every decision we make. That's the function of the Holy Spirit. Of course, his counsel never contradicts the Bible, but shows us how to live out the Bible in our everyday lives.

Jesus warned the Pharisees, "You diligently study the Scriptures because you think that by them you possess eternal life. These are the Scriptures that testify about me, yet you refuse to come to me to have life. . . . I know you. I know that you do not have the love of God in your hearts" (John 5:39-41, NIV). Commenting on these verses, Oswald Chambers writes:

> These verses reveal how a knowledge of the Scriptures may distort the mind away from Jesus Christ. Unless we know the Living Word personally first, the literal words may lead us astray. The only way we can understand the Bible is by personal contact with the Living Word; then the Holy Spirit expounds the literal words to us along the line of personal experience.[2]

Ever wonder why Jesus didn't make his instructions to his disciples more explicit? Why did he give them general instructions about their responsibilities and then tell them to wait until they were "clothed with power from on high" (Luke 24:49, NIV)? He was encouraging them to be responsible — not just to follow instructions and rules, but to trust the Holy Spirit to guide and empower their hearts. Jesus' model shows us how to encourage each other to do the same — trust the "good things" God puts in our hearts (see Matthew 12:35).

What precautions do you take to make sure your words never take the place of God's words in a friend's life? What do you do to help them take responsibility to decide for themselves how to serve God in their present circumstances?

ENCOURAGING OUR FRIENDS TO STRENGTHEN THEIR NEW HEART

No branch can bear fruit by itself; it must remain in the vine. Neither can you bear fruit unless you remain in me. (Jesus, John 15:4, NIV)

No matter how our hearts prompt us to serve God, we don't possess the strength to carry it to fruition. That's why Jesus retreated to the Garden of Gethsemane the night before his crucifixion. As he reconciled himself to do his Father's will, he became so anguished that he sweat drops of blood (see Luke 22:44). Even the best heart — a heart reconciled to do God's will at any price — takes pause when facing a 1,000-volt cross-experience. When Jesus cried out to God for strength, God immediately dispatched an angel from heaven to strengthen him for the ordeal ahead (see Luke 22:43).

Jesus also encouraged his disciples to pray for strength that night. He knew they needed a "garden experience" even more than he did. While they had every intention of doing the right thing that evening (see Matthew 26:35), it required more than good intentions to pull it off. Jesus asked them to prepare for what would require superhuman strength of heart: to live as sheep among wolves.

God rarely calls us to love "safe" people. It's no wonder, since there are so few of them around. Perhaps that's why — while Jesus taught his disciples not to fear people (see Matthew 10:28) — he taught them to take precautions when loving others: "Be on your guard against men . . . brother will betray brother to death, and a father his child; children will rebel against their parents and have them put to death. All men will hate you because of me" (Matthew 10:17,21-22, NIV).

Loving others as God intends requires trusting our own hearts. But it doesn't require trusting the hearts of others. The very reason people need our love is because their hearts can't be trusted. Paul advised taking special precautions when loving people with character problems (see 1 Thessalonians 5:14; 2 Thessalonians 3:14-15). Jesus warned his disciples to guard their hearts around others, especially around those they knew were predators (see Matthew 7:6). Jesus always dealt with people shrewdly because "he knew them inside and out, knew how untrustworthy they were" (John 2:24, MSG).

Love inevitably brings us close to the most dangerous creatures on our planet — wounded people with wicked hearts. The only way to love such creatures is with shrewdness — not to keep them from causing trouble in our world (it's inevitable that they will), but to keep them from causing trouble in our hearts. Jesus went to great lengths to prepare his disciples for the consequences of loving sinful creatures — first, warning of the suffering it entails (John 16:1-4), then showing them where and how to find the strength to endure it without sinning (see Matthew 26:36). He never intended the Garden of Gethsemane to be a one-time event for his disciples. They needed to repeat it as often as love compelled them to take high-voltage risks.

> At my first defense, no one came to my support, but everyone deserted me. May it not be held against them. *But the Lord stood at my side and gave me strength* (Paul after his first trial before Caesar, 2 Timothy 4:16-17, NIV, emphasis added).

How do you prepare your friends for the increased complications and pain that loving others inevitably brings into their lives? How can you use "garden experiences" to do this?

ENCOURAGING OUR FRIENDS TO
EXERCISE THEIR NEW HEART

This is a large work I've called you into, but don't be overwhelmed by it. It's best to start small. Give a cool cup of water to someone who is thirsty, for instance. The smallest act of giving . . . makes you a true apprentice. (Jesus, Matthew 10:41-42, MSG)

God's careful to give us responsibility that matches our maturity level. When our new heart is just developing, a 50-volt assignment from God can seem like a 1,000 volts. When we finally encounter a true 1,000-volt risk, we realize how little God asked us to risk at those earlier times in our lives. That doesn't make the early risks less important. Without them, our hearts would never develop the maturity needed for higher voltage assignments.

Jesus encouraged his disciples to start exercising their new hearts as soon as they started forming. He knew it would be detrimental to their health "to know the good they ought to do, and not do it" (James 4:17). He directed Peter to flex the muscles of his new heart by feeding, strengthening, and leading the small group of disciples that remained together during those first weeks following his crucifixion and resurrection (see Luke 22:32, John 21:15). It's easy to imagine how stepping forward to lead this tiny band of believers might have felt like a high-voltage risk to Peter, given that they all knew he'd publicly denied Christ just a few weeks earlier. He needed encouragement to take this risk to be ready for the larger assignment of leading the thousands who'd soon be added to their number (see Acts 2:41,47).

PART THREE: JESUS AND HUMAN COUNSELING

Jesus told two parables about servants who were assigned "high-voltage" responsibilities by their masters (see Matthew 25:14-30; Luke 19:12-27). In each, the master, who was about to go on a journey, assigns several servants to manage parts of his estate while he's away. Their assignment was to "put it to work" until he returned (see Luke 19:13). Upon returning, he finds some were faithful to make their trusts grow, while others — the ones afraid of failing — were not. The faithful were rewarded with larger trusts, while the fearful lost what they'd been given.

Jesus is like the master who entrusts his servants with his assets in his absence. He entrusts us with the heart and power to do his work. When we go to work for him in the ways he asks, we grow richer in our desire and ability to serve him. When we let our fears stop us, our desire and ability to serve him diminishes.

Spiritual insight, maturity, and responsibility grow in direct proportion to how much we exercise our new hearts. That's why Jesus "spurred [his disciples] on toward love and good deeds," and instructs us to do the same for our friends (Hebrews 10:24, NIV).

What high-voltage assignment is God putting in your heart to tackle? Are you aware of any fears that could keep you from exercising your heart in this way?

ENCOURAGING OUR FRIENDS TO MONITOR THEIR NEW HEART

I see what you've done, your hard, hard work, your refusal to quit. I know you can't stomach evil, that you weed out apostolic pretenders. I know your persistence, your courage in my cause, that you never wear out. But you walked away from your first love — why? What's going on with you anyway? (Jesus to the church at Ephesus, Revelation 2:2-4, MSG)

Jesus had an incredible way of looking at his disciples' hearts with "X-ray eyes." He saw both the good and bad parts — the parts that had already been reconciled to God's heart and made new, and the parts that still remained unreconciled — more responsive to the voice of sin and death than the voice of the Spirit of Life. Mercifully, he never revealed everything he saw in his disciples' hearts at any one time (see John 16:12). From time to time, he called both good and bad parts to their attention so they could trust and exercise the good while acknowledging and reconciling the bad.

Jesus encouraged his disciples to continually monitor their own hearts. Since they didn't have "X-ray eyes" like his, he taught them to use their words to assess the health of their hearts:

> It's not what goes in your mouth (what you eat or drink) that tells you whether your heart is good or bad. It's what comes out of your mouth that tells you the true condition of your heart. Bad hearts spout death-words — words that communicate evil thoughts; words that conquer, kill, or seduce others; words that steal what belongs to others or misrepresent the truth — these are what tell you that something's wrong with your heart. (Matthew 15:11,18-20)

One of the most important ways we prepare our friends to live and love independent of our help is to encourage them to continually assess the health of their own hearts. Love requires them to take responsibility for the words of their mouth and the meditations of their hearts before, during, and after every high-voltage assignment they attempt. When they do, they're sure to get a glimpse of what God sees in their hearts — the good and the bad. Both will give them reason to draw near to him — to thank and worship him for what he's made possible, and to grieve and pray for what still needs changing.

How do you monitor your own heart when you're talking with hurting friends? What parts of your heart (good and bad) tend to emerge when you're trying to help them?

FOLLOWING JESUS' MODEL FOR ENCOURAGING RESPONSIBILITY

In my last conversation with Randy, I sensed a new passion to serve God growing in his heart. Now I want to see if that's continued to grow this week as he sought God on his own. Unless it has, I don't want to encourage him to contemplate new ways to serve God. If I do, I'll encounter massive resistance or insincere agreement. By following up on his homework assignment and reconfirming the growth goal for our work together, I get a sense of whether his passion to serve God is growing.

FOLLOWUP ON HOMEWORK ASSIGNMENTS.

I've been looking forward to hearing how things have been going.
Good. The pregnancy is good right now. The last ultrasound showed the baby is doing well. That's a big relief. I'm getting excited about being a father! Things at church are about the same. I'm doing the work with the junior high and it's been going good. I've been able to spend time with some of the kids this week and move into their lives. That seems like where I can best serve God right now.
You seem to have more hope or more vitality than when we first got together several weeks ago.
That could be. I know I'm not feeling as afraid around people. Remember that meeting I was supposed to have with the board? Well, they wanted me to present a whole new plan and schedule for the junior high ministry and also be ready to talk about what my career plans are for the future when I leave

*youth ministry. I started to feel all this pressure to do this. Then
I realized that it was ridiculous. I'm not ready to do either of
these. I just found out that I'm leading the junior high. And
I'm not ready to say that youth ministry isn't what God wants
me to do. So I talked with the pastor and just told him that
I'm not ready and that it might be several weeks before I have
anything concrete to talk to them about.*

You were really risking his disapproval — and the board's.

*Yeah, especially since I didn't apologize or make any excuses. I just
looked him in the eye and told him. I didn't even feel afraid.
And you know, he just said okay. He didn't make a big deal
out of it. He just told me to let him know when I'm ready and
not to worry about coming to the meeting.*

What do you think made it possible for you to do that? Do you connect it to anything we talked to God about last week or maybe
something you've been talking to God about on your own?

*I think it has a lot to do with how we prayed last time and how
I've been praying since. I've noticed that the biggest thing
changing right now is how I'm talking to God. For as long as I
can remember, my prayers have mostly been just pleading with
God to take my problems away. This week, asking for that just
doesn't come up. Even today, I was reading in 2 Corinthians,
and Paul says at one point that things had gotten so bad that
he felt like giving up. But then he figured that God was letting
it happen for a reason — to teach him to not rely on himself so
much. I really related to that. So this morning I was asking
God to help me learn what he wanted me to learn from everything that's happening right now. Somehow, I think that had a
lot to do with how I was able to talk to the pastor like I did.*

From the changes in your conversations with God, it seems like he's
already starting to answer our prayers from last week to give
you a new heart.

It feels like that to me, too.

RECONFIRM THE GROWTH GOAL.

Do you remember the goal we started with? We're been working on
it all these weeks.

*That regardless of whether I feel the approval of others, to be a man
of courage — a man who is real.*

Do you still want to work toward that goal?

I think now more than ever!

We'll keep doing that, then. It feels like the right direction to me, too.

I do sense a new heart growing in Randy enough to make it
appropriate and beneficial to encourage him to proceed in the
direction he's already heading — identifying, planning, and
accomplishing things he feels called to do for God in the midst
of his present circumstances. Since marriage is very high on
God's agenda, I'm particularly interested to hear how God might
be moving Randy to act in his relationship with Mallory. Until
now, he's been avoiding high-voltage risks in his marriage.

EXPLORE THE "NEW WAY" THEIR HEART IS
CALLING THEM TO LOVE.

As our conversation proceeds, I want to encourage Randy to
embrace the unique opportunity his circumstances offer him to
serve God. If a new heart is truly growing within him, he's
already heard God's Spirit calling him to take high-voltage risks.
I assume this will involve loving one or more of the people in
his world in bold new ways. I want to help him explore this. If
I'm wrong, and Randy's heart isn't changing, he'll have little passion to do this with me. In that case, I'll suggest that we continue
to seek God in prayer as we did in our last meeting. Notice the
question I begin with. It's an important one.

I have a question I want to ask you. Since we've been praying for
God to give you the freedom and the strength to be a new man,

and since we're feeling that God is already starting to do this — giving you that kind of heart — I'm wondering, *what do you want to do now?*

Do you mean as a career path?

No. I mean *do you sense any new desires or passions* to live differently or handle life differently?

I have this strong desire now to just be more honest with people — like I was with the pastor and the board. I want to do that with Mallory more, too. This week I started to talk to her a little about my excitement and fear of being a dad. And I told her that I wanted to set boundaries around the time I spend with the youth group kids so I don't neglect our family. Sometimes kids just drop by our house, and I'd been afraid to tell them they can't do that. But this week I told a bunch of them that they needed to call us first and not just drop by anymore. I decided it isn't fair to neglect Mallory just to keep everyone thinking I'm this great guy.

What Randy's describing is more evidence that God is working in his heart. These aren't 1,000-volts risks, but they're very significant. It doesn't surprise me that they involved Mallory. I'm anxious to see where else his new heart might be leading him.

That sounds like a real gladiator kind of thing to do — risking your popularity with the kids for Mallory. Do you hear God saying anything to you about being more honest with her?

Show her more of my heart, I guess. But I'm not sure if that means being honest with her about the fantasies I was having — even though I'm not now. With her being pregnant, I don't know what kind of stress that would cause. Maybe it's something I should do later. At this point, I'm not sure how to talk to her more about my heart without hurting her.

So you're saying you feel stuck. On one hand, you feel like you want to bring more truth into your relationship with Mallory and that's what God wants you to do. But on the other hand, you don't want to tell her things that would hurt her right now. You don't think God wants you to do that, either. Is that what you're saying?

Exactly.

Is it possible that you're hesitating to tell Mallory about the fantasies because you're afraid of what she might do or because of what it could do to your marriage?

I ask this question to explore what's truly behind Randy's reticence to tell his wife about his fantasies. It may very well be that this *isn't* the way God is calling him to love Mallory right now. But I want to make sure he's doing this out of *love,* not out of *self-interest.* If he's acting out of self-interest, then it's not from God — nor from the good part of his heart. In that case, if I went along with him, I'd be affirming something bad.

I think I'm afraid that it will hurt the way she thinks about herself. Mallory is very self-conscious. Her mother was actually a model. And Mallory wrestles with her self-image. I don't ever want her to think I had this problem because she's not pretty enough. She's always been beautiful to me — even more now when she's pregnant. I didn't fantasize about other women because she wasn't pretty enough. I chose to do it because I didn't like who I was. But I'm afraid she'll think it's her.

In that case, what would there be to gain by telling her at all? How would that help her or your marriage?

The one thing it would do is allow me to be honest in an area where I've lived secretly. To live secretly, I've had to cover my tracks sometimes. If she caught me daydreaming or if I wasn't able to do what I said I was going to do, I'd cover with a lie. I don't want to be that deceptive guy any more. I'm tired of having secrets between us. So as I think about how God wants me to move toward my wife in a way that I've never done before, I know the lies are still there, and I can't ignore them the way I used to.

I like the idea of you moving toward Mallory in an honest new way. That feels right to me. But I guess what you need to think through is this: would telling Mallory about your sexual struggles be the best way to promote God's purposes in your life and her life right now? Or would sharing some other part of your life with her accomplish that better?

Wow! That's a different way to look at it.

It may very well be that the Lord's calling you to move in a more honest way toward your wife right now. And it may be that he's calling you to show her some part of your heart that you've never shown her before. But this ugly, lustful part that we've been asking God to pluck out isn't the only part of your heart that you've withheld from Mallory. And I'm wondering which part God is calling you to start with.

It's funny you say that. It's almost like I'd be telling her just to get this off my chest and to get it behind me. But it might just take it off me and put it on her.

It strikes me that you and Mallory have both been living in a desert and feeling very lonely. Perhaps there's a level of connection that you need to develop in your marriage before you decide to bring this struggle into it. You're fighting and winning this struggle without her help anyway. It may be a good idea for you to tell Mallory about this struggle at some point. But for now, I think we need to get back to what it would look like to move into Mallory's life as that man of courage God is calling you to be for her. What would it look like to offer her your strength instead of your failure?

I don't get the part about failure. How do I offer her my failure?

If you think that the most important and deepest part of you is a failure, that's what you'd naturally offer Mallory to connect with her. Your sexual fantasies represent that failure. If you offered that to her right now, maybe she could respond in a forgiving way and you'd feel better. But I'm not sure that would be helpful for either of you, because it's all based on a big lie. The truth is that the most important and deepest part of you is *not* a failure. That most important and deepest part of you is strength and courage and love. That's the part God has his fingerprints on. What would it look like to offer that part of you to Mallory? You already started to offer it this week when you told her you were man enough to be a father and when you asked the kids to start respecting your privacy as a couple.

That's really hitting the nail on the head for me. That's what I really want to do.

Let's take a few minutes to envision how you could do that this week.

As I help Randy clarify how God is calling him to love his wife, there are three criteria I use to guide me. A prompting of the heart has to satisfy all three before I encourage a friend to follow it. First, it must be consistent with biblical commands; it can't go outside the moral boundaries God gives us for our behavior. Second, it must be consistent with the principle of love; it must promote the well-being of *all* involved — not benefiting one person at the expense of others. Third, it must constitute genuine repentance for the person; it must be something that diametrically opposes or contradicts the self-protective strategy he normally uses to avoid pain and suffering. Anything that constitutes genuine repentance will also be consistent with the growth goal for our work together.

Randy's idea of telling his wife about his sexual fantasies doesn't satisfy all three of these criteria. While it doesn't take Randy outside explicit biblical boundaries, it does tend to promote his well-being at his wife's expense. (However, if Randy's immoral activities put him at risk of infecting himself or Mallory with STDs, love would require Randy to immediately disclose everything about his sexual activities to her.) It's also questionable whether telling Mallory really constitutes repentance for Randy. Using his failures to win her sympathy has all along been part of his strategy for keeping her expectations of him as low as possible. The less she expects from him, the less guilt and pressure he feels around her.

When I'm helping friends pinpoint what God is calling them to do, I continue to explore their new desires until a direction emerges that satisfies each of these criteria. This is what I did in my conversation with Randy. When his passions finally connected with the idea of continuing to offer Mallory his strength and courage, I knew we were on the right track. This clearly satisfies all three criteria. Now we're ready to envision in greater detail what this will entail.

Practice Exercise

Think about a difficult situation you're facing. What do you want to do? How do you want to respond to the people involved? Use the three criteria to evaluate your answer. What does your assessment tell you about your heart?

ENVISION THE "NEW WAY" THEIR HEART IS CALLING THEM TO LOVE.

Where does your mind go when you think about offering Mallory more of that good part of your heart — the strong and courageous part God is growing?

Well, I'm not sure how I would do it exactly. But somehow I'd want to communicate that she doesn't need to worry about what's going to happen to us. I'd want her to trust that I can take care of her and the baby, and no matter what happens I'm not going to fall apart or bail out on her.

Yes. That direction feels right to me. Saying to her, as much with
actions as words, "you can really trust and depend on me." One
reason I like it is that it puts you in a place you fear the most.
You give her permission to expect more from you, and that
means there's a greater chance you could fail her. I like that.
Except that I could fail her big time.
But you'd die trying, right? Isn't that what a gladiator does? You'd
never just give up and abandon her. She could count on that
from you, right? That's a hundred times more important to her
than you succeeding at everything you do.
You're right. She could count on that from me.
I think that message would nourish her soul much more than a
message that says, "I'm sorry I'm such a failure, but I want you
to know I'm going to try really hard not to be one anymore. I
can't make any promises, you know, because I am kind of weak
and fragile. But can you at least give me some credit for trying?"
Do you really think that's the message I send her?
I think that's a possibility — until this week. What message do you
think your actions this week sent her?

The farther our friends progress in their spiritual journeys, the
more candid and specific we can be in feedback we give them —
provided we do it with a lot of love and encouragement. I've been
dying to give Randy the kind of feedback I just gave him since we
first started meeting. But it wouldn't have been beneficial before
his new heart started forming. A new heart gives people the perspective they need to handle negative feedback constructively.

At this point in the journey, I also feel more free to bring in
personal observations and insights I've acquired from other settings. I do this somewhat tentatively, clearly communicating that
I'm leaving room for the possibility I could be wrong.

As we continue, I encourage Randy to be more specific in
envisioning the new way his heart is calling him to love Mallory.

It's important that I ask him to envision actually doing it — loving her in this new way — not just talking about it with her. We must never allow *talk about change* to be a substitute for *real change*.

This week, when I was telling her I was looking forward to being a father, and telling the kids to call before coming over? (Kevin nods.) I guess I was saying that whatever's ahead in terms of employment, I'm not going anywhere. I'm with her. I'll be there for her and for our children.

I like that — sending her a strong signal about being there for her. So if God is calling you to be there for her in bigger and stronger ways, how could you actually *do* that for her this week — be there for her? You could sit down, give her a pep talk, and tell her you're going to be there for her, no matter what. But I think it would speak much more powerfully to her if you actually *did* it — if you were actually there for her in some new way that's scary for you, yet in a way that she'd find incredibly nourishing.

I can think of one way, but it seems almost too simple. For nearly a year, since the doctor confined her to bed rest the first time, I've done a lot of the housework. I haven't minded it since it gives me an excuse to keep busy and avoid talking with her so I wouldn't upset her more than I already have. But Mallory often asks me just to come over and sit down with her and talk. I say that I can't because of this whole list of things I have to get done. So I think one way I could be there for her would be just to sit down and talk with her when she asks or even if she doesn't ask.

And when you sit down and talk with her, instead of bringing her into your fears and your concerns, maybe you could enter her fears and concerns.

I don't know if you're like this when you're with Mallory. But one thing I've noticed when you're with me — not in these meetings, but other times around the church — I experience you as someone who is much better at bringing me into your world than you are entering mine. In other words, it's hard for you to draw another person out. You don't send the message that you're strong enough to handle their fears and concerns and that it's okay if they don't take care of you in the conversation or that you'd like to take care of them.

Ouch. That hurts.

I'm sure it does, and I don't say it lightly. But, in a real way, it's a big compliment I'm telling you this. It means I don't see you as fragile anymore. I respect you as a man who's strong enough to handle honest feedback.

Even though it hurts, I think you've pegged me. Instead of just telling Mallory everything I'm feeling, it'd be very different if I invited her to talk and I sat back and listened. I don't know what she'd do. She's so used to me carrying the whole conversation.

Once she got past the initial shock, I think she'd love to have her husband's listening heart tuning into her heart. That would be nourishing. It would be like you saying to her, "Come on. Let me have it. I can handle anything you've got. Give me your best shot — anger, disappointment, or fear. Whatever it is, I can handle it."

I'll tell you something. I'd like to see that Randy myself.

What do you think makes it hard to be that Randy with her?

Fear of what I'm going to hear.

What would you be the most afraid you'd hear?

That she's sorry she married me or she wants out. Something like that.

So, if that's what she feels, to give her permission to say that would be how big of a risk?

That would be huge.

This reconfirms for me that we're on the right track. While sitting and listening to his wife might feel like a small thing to others, it's no small thing for Randy. It is a 1,000-volt risk. That's the funny thing about high-voltage risks. They are different for each of us. A 1,000-volt risk for Randy may be no risk at all for me and vice versa. That's why our work now must be built on good work at previous stages. I must draw upon everything I've learned about Randy in order to know what to affirm and what not to.

Once Mallory realizes that you're strong enough to handle parts of her that no man ever has, you might hear some scary stuff — including a time she considered walking out on you. You might hear about a time she was so furious with you that she was ready to kick you out. I don't know. But I do know this: as she senses that she can trust your strength, you're going to see parts of this woman's soul you've never seen before. And it's going to be so nourishing for her to have someone strong enough that she can be naked with him and unashamed. What an act of love that would be to offer that to Mallory. But I'd never want to encourage you to go in this direction unless you felt that it's where God's calling you to go.

When we started today, I didn't think we'd be going this direction. It's almost like the opposite end of the scale. But I know in my heart it's the right part of the scale for me to move to.

Practice Exercise

Reread the above transcript, skipping over the commentary. How did I move this discussion about Randy's servant-responsibilities from the general to the specific? From low-voltage risks to high-voltage risks? From things that serve Randy's interests to things that serve others' interests?

EQUIP THEM FOR THE "NEW WAY" THEIR HEART IS CALLING THEM TO LOVE.

Our friends may have the heart to do things, but still lack the knowledge and skills to accomplish them. That's where we come in. According to Paul, our job is to come alongside and equip our friends to do what their new heart is prompting them to do: "To some he gave the power to guide and teach his people . . . that Christians might be properly equipped for their service" (Paul, Ephesians 4:11-12, PH).

Some Christian leaders mistakenly believe that equipping others involves only imparting Bible knowledge. But Paul makes it clear that equipping also involves training people to conduct themselves and relate to others in ways that are "in accord" with the Bible (see Titus 2:1, NIV). Fortunately, when someone possesses a renewed heart that's full of passion to love and serve others, they're generally quick-learners.

While God has supplied Randy with the passion and power to love Mallory in bold new ways, he may still lack the social skills and emotional intelligence to do it very effectively. Or he may already have them, and I'll need to do very little to equip him. I won't know until we enact what we've been discussing. I refrain from encouraging friends to take bold new steps to love people around them until they do it with me first in a role-play situation. That's what I ask Randy to do next.

Since you're feeling led this way, why don't we take a few minutes to role-play what that might look like — just to give you a chance to see what you're in for. What do you think?

Okay.

Why don't you set it up? Tell me what our setting and surroundings are.

Say we're in our living room after dinner, and for a change I invite you to just sit down and spend some time with me.

If I was Mallory, how would I be feeling about this?

Taken by surprise. But pleasantly surprised, I think.

So I'm sitting here waiting for you to start. What do you want to do? How do you want to start?

Maybe I'd ask her some kind of question.

Okay, but let's just do it. I'm Mallory now.

Hey, Mal. Thanks for giving me this time with you.

(Kevin as Mallory) Well, I have to admit I'm kind of shocked that you asked.

I guess I haven't asked to spend time like this with you for a while.

(Kevin as Mallory) That's the message I've been getting. So why do you want to talk now?

I guess I've been thinking a lot about our relationship and all the things we've been going through and . . .

(Kevin breaking out of role) Let's take a time out for a second, Randy. I'm wondering if you're sensing what I'm sensing right now. This conversation has just reached a critical fork.

I think so. I guess I could steal the conversation right now and make it all about me.

Right. Or you could steer it right now to enter Mallory's heart. Which do you want to do?

I want to enter hers.

Do you have any idea how you could do that?

Maybe ask her how she's feeling about things?

That would probably work. But maybe you could get a little more specific. What don't you know about her? What would be really scary to ask her about? Maybe something you've never asked her about?

I think I know something. But it's going to be hard (tears). I've never asked her about how she's feeling about the daughter we lost this time last year. We named her Marcie. But see what happens (wiping tears) when I try to talk about it? That's why I don't bring it up. I know I'll cry. Then she'll cry.

Those would be nourishing tears for both of you. Especially for Mallory. Think of it — to have a man strong enough not only to handle her tears, but strong enough to show his own. Wow! That's gladiator territory.

I've been feeling like we need to talk about it, but thought it would be bad if I couldn't do it without crying.

No way. I think it'd be awful if you did it without crying. That could really damage Mallory's heart. I'm guessing she's feeling terribly alone right now in her grief and pain. Maybe even feeling abandoned by you, wondering how she could have married a man who feels no pain at the loss of his own daughter. What a gift it would be for her to find out that she didn't marry a man like that.

I want to show her that. But I'm afraid. I wouldn't know what to say to take her pain away.

Let me relieve you of that. It's not your job to take her pain away. It's your job to share it with her. Pain is much more bearable if you have someone to share it with. How could you share her pain when the two of you are talking about the daughter you lost?

Move closer to her and hold her.

That's good. And listen to her. Look into her eyes, even though you see pain in them, and really listen. Don't worry about your tears. Let them come. But keep her talking to you. And when she's finished emptying her heart out to you, if she asks to see your heart, empty it for her so she can know what you're feeling about everything she just said. What's that sound like to you, Randy?

I want to do that. This is long overdue.

Yes it is. But does it sound doable to you? To approach Mallory the way we just talked about? Is there anything about what I just described that you don't know how to do? I mean, there's no reason you have to do it smoothly or polished. Even if it feels clumsy, can you realistically imagine yourself doing what I just described?

I think so — if I can get my courage up.

Well, that's where God comes in. I want to come back to him in a minute. But first, let's go back to the role-play. I don't want to take it much farther because it will be a special time and I want you to share it only with Mallory. But I do want you to show me how you're going to steer the conversation toward your daughter that you lost. Would you be willing to show me that? (Randy nods) Okay. I'm Mallory again. And you've just told me that you've been thinking a lot about our relationship and all that we've been going through. And now you want to steer the conversation toward the loss of our daughter. Go ahead.

Well, Mal. I guess what I'm trying to say is, how are you doing? How are you feeling about Marcie's birthday coming next week? How are you feeling about that?

Okay, Randy. I don't want to take the role play any farther. I really like how you did that. I think that would be an excellent way to start. How do you predict she'll answer that question?

I don't know. It's hard to say since I've never asked her anything like that. I think she'll go there with me.

You'll have to be ready for it to get messy. Do you know what I mean by that?

She could cry.

Or maybe she'll scream. Maybe she'll get angry that you waited this long to ask her. I don't know. Once you enter your wife's soul, anything could happen.

I'm doing with Randy what Paul tells the older men to do with the younger men (see Titus 2:1-6) — teach them how to love their wives. Randy is ready now to go home and love Mallory in the new way we've been envisioning. Though he has the skills and knowledge he needs for this experience, he'll only be able to carry it out if he prepares for it the same way Christ prepared to go to the cross. He must get away to a "garden" and ask for strength from God to do what he can't do in his own power. That's what I encourage Randy to do as our conversation winds down.

Practice Exercise

What other skills and knowledge do you think Randy needs to serve God effectively in his present circumstances? List them, along with any ideas or strategies you'd use to impart them to Randy if you were his counselor.

ESTABLISH A PLAN FOR THE "NEW WAY" THEIR HEART IS CALLING THEM TO LOVE.

When friends decide to step out and love in bold new ways, I encourage them to establish a concrete plan for where and when they'll do it. This provides them with the opportunity to do three things:

1. Choose a time and place that's most beneficial to the person whose welfare they seek to promote.

2. Design and carry out a "garden experience" to prepare.

3. Schedule their next meeting with me as soon as possible to assess how things went.

Where does your mind go when I say that your heart must be ready to love Mallory no matter where this conversation goes?

It means I can't pull this off on my own. I'm going to need some big-time help from God to do it.

That's true for me too. We can plan these things and role-play them like we just did. But whenever we attempt to love people as God calls us to love, we can't "pull that off" without big-time help from God. How would you feel about creating a place, just like Christ did at Gethsemane, where you can go and call on God for strength right before you initiate this conversation with Mallory? There's no question that this is going to be one of those opportunities to deny yourself and take up your cross in order to love Mallory like Christ does.

That's really what it feels like to me.

When do you want to do it?

I'd like to do it sometime this week. Maybe this weekend. Saturday is my day off. I think that'd be a good time. I think maybe right after breakfast would be best for Mallory. The weather is supposed to be nice, so I could invite her to take a walk with me to a little park near our house.

Is there a place the two of you can sit and even weep without anyone seeing you? It would have to be really private.

I think so. There's a bench in kind of an out-of-the-way place.

Do you feel like it would be considerate to give her a "heads up" a day or so before? Maybe you could ask her for a date and let her know that you want to spend some heart-to-heart time with her.

I think she'd like that. I could mention it to her tonight.

What about the garden experience — a time where you can spend some time seeking God, really getting your heart ready for your conversation with Mallory?

I usually make Mallory breakfast on Saturday, so I already get up earlier than she does. I can get up a little earlier this Saturday and do it then.

Can you get quality time then — at least thirty minutes undisturbed?

That shouldn't be any problem.

The kind of man you're going to attempt to be on Saturday for Mallory isn't going to come naturally for you.

I realize that. I want to be a Randy for her that she's maybe never seen.

As long as it's not just a Randy thing. It has to be a God and Randy thing or it'll never work. Do you know what I mean?

Yes.

I'd like to talk with you as soon as possible after you do this. Could you get together with me this same time on Monday?

That would be good.

So as you're preparing for this and carrying it off Saturday morning,
I'll be praying for you.
I'd appreciate that.
Why don't we also spend some time right now praying for you and
Mallory before we leave?
That sounds good.

I'd spend my next meeting with Randy assessing, in great detail, his conversation with Mallory. I'd help him reflect on both his heart and behaviors throughout the event, paying special attention to how he succeeded or failed to love her in the new way he set out to. This would give us the opportunity to celebrate what God accomplished in and through him, or talk and pray about what he still desperately needs from God. I'd continue to encourage him to listen to his new heart and help him plan and prepare ways to exercise it.

The pattern I used to lead this meeting is the pattern I'd continue to use until Randy—without my guidance—begins to report spontaneously planning and taking bold new steps to love the people in his world. At that point, I'd give him a choice—to schedule less-frequent get-togethers for encouragement or to construct and pursue together a new growth goal. If he chooses the latter, it would give us the opportunity to revisit a lot of the same ground we covered previously. Each successive journey, however, provides the opportunity to deepen Randy's self-understanding, repentance, character, and ministry to others.

10

[*l* I ƒ E - *w o r d s* ƒ o r OUR OWN HEARTS]

First take the log out of your own eye, and then you will see clearly to take the speck out of your brother's eye.

Jesus, Matthew 7:5, NASB

Jesus says the most important preparation for helping our friends is learning to help ourselves first. That's what he means by removing the "logs" that blur our vision, jam our hearts, and impede our growth.

In other words, the insight we have into other people's hearts comes in direct proportion to the time we spend reflecting on our own. The more time we spend envisioning and seeking a heart that's reconciled to God's, the more effective we become at helping others develop vision and passion for a new heart for themselves. And the more time we spend strengthening and exercising our new heart, the better we'll be at helping others do the same with theirs.

This is why I encourage people who want to be friendship-counselors to use Jesus' model to counsel themselves before they use it to counsel friends. I recommend they counsel themselves on paper through the same five stages I journeyed with Randy. Often, people tell me that this is the single most growth-producing experience of their life.

I recommend this same exercise to you, using the guidelines I've given. Don't attempt it until you've read the entire book and completed all the questions and exercises in the previous chapters. When you're ready to begin, carve out five blocks of time from your schedule over a two- to three-week period. You'll need up to ten hours to counsel yourself through all five stages, so look ahead on your calendar for several days that will allow you a good deal of uninterrupted time and privacy.

You can do this exercise with a paper and pencil, although most people find a word processor works more efficiently. For each "counseling session," you'll need a quiet, comfortable setting where you have at least two hours to work without interruptions from people, pets, and machines. Have this book and the friendship-counseling model (see page 286) beside you. If you currently have a mentor or counselor, discuss with them the possibility of doing this assignment before you attempt it. If you're in a counselor-training class or program, you may want to make it a part of your training.

At the first "counseling session" start by simply playing the role of your own friendship-counselor, an old friend who knows you pretty well. Type or write, "I'm glad you asked for this time to talk. How can I help you?" Then switch roles, and write the answer or response you'd give if you were seeking help from a trusted friend. For this exercise to be effective, you have to ask this friend to help you with a current struggle that troubles you. Playing the counselor then, guide the conversation through each step of the process listed on page 286, using the same kinds of questions and statements I used with Randy.

When you finish a stage, save your work and store it in a secure place. As you begin the next session, follow the example and instructions I give you in each chapter to journey through that stage of the model.

Feel free to take breaks as you need them, and reread portions of this book if you become uncertain how to proceed. You may want to make notes on the following outline of key words, statements, and questions you find in chapters 5–9.

As you proceed, be prepared for some surprising things to happen: penetrating questions you didn't expect, revealing answers you didn't anticipate, strong emotions you didn't know you had, insights into yourself that break new ground. You may even forget that this is an assignment and that you're counseling yourself. You'll lose track of time. And your words will pour out faster than you can record them. If it ever feels like more than you can handle, set it aside and decide later if you want to resume. Or you might consider doing the exercise with a trusted friend, mentor, or counselor rather than by yourself.

When you've finished your journey through all five stages, consider asking a friend, mentor, or counselor to read your transcript and discuss it with you. You may or may not find this desirable or beneficial. Your transcript represents an important and vulnerable part of your heart. Protect it as you would your heart.

Pray for yourself as you do this assignment. Remember to offer the same care, compassion, and support to yourself during this process as you would a hurting friend. The way we speak to ourselves when we're hurting is the same way we speak to others when they're hurting. We learn to speak life-words to hurting friends by first learning to speak life-words to ourselves.

JESUS' MODEL FOR SPEAKING
LIFE-WORDS TO HURTING PEOPLE

SESSION ONE:
SHAPE THE COUNSELING RELATIONSHIP (CHAPTER 5)

Clarify your friend's immediate concern

Bridge from the trouble in their world to the trouble in their heart

Chain from the immediate to the ultimate goal

Secure agreement on a growth goal

SESSION TWO:
GUIDE REFLECTION (CHAPTER 6)

Reconfirm the growth goal

Focus on one current troubling event

Explore your friend's emotional response to the event

Explore their behavioral response to the event

Explore their cognitive response to the event

Explore the passions that fuel their response to the event

Instill hope and desire for a change of character

Keep reflection going between meetings

SESSION THREE:
CULTIVATE REPENTANCE (CHAPTER 7)

Follow up on homework assignments

Reconfirm the growth goal

Envision a godly way to think about their troubles

Envision a godly way to respond to their troubles

Envision the emotions that accompany these changes

Help them weigh life's most important question

Design and assign an experiment

Session Four:
Promote Reconciliation (chapter 8)

Follow up on homework assignments

Reconfirm the growth goal

Explore and shape the way they think about God

Teach them to talk to God about his Son

Teach them to talk to God about their trouble in the world

Teach them to talk to God about the trouble in their heart

Teach them to talk to God about the troubles of others

Teach them to keep talking to God for as long as it takes

Session Five:
Encourage Responsibility (chapter 9)

Follow up on homework assignments

Reconfirm the growth goal

Explore the "new way" their heart is calling them to love

Envision the "new way" their heart is calling them to love

Equip them for the "new way" their heart is calling them to love

Establish a plan for the "new way" their heart is calling them to love

NOTES

INTRODUCTION

1. Oswald Chambers, *Still Higher for His Highest* (Grand Rapids, Mich.: Zondervan, 1970), p. 16.
2. Henri Nouwen, *Wounded Healer* (New York: Image Books, Doubleday, 1979), pp. 92-93.

CHAPTER 1

1. C. S. Lewis, *Letters to an American Lady* (Grand Rapids, Mich.: Wm. B. Eerdmans, 1971), p. 49.
2. Joni Eareckson Tada. (Nashville, Tenn.: AACC Soul Conference, 1999), videocassette.
3. Oswald Chambers, *Still Higher for His Highest* (Grand Rapids, Mich.: Zondervan, 1970), p. 55.
4. Corrie Ten Boom, *The Hiding Place* (New York: Bantam Books, 1971), p. 217.
5. *The Hiding Place.* (Minneapolis, Minn.: World Wide Pictures, 1975), videocassette.
6. Richard Wurmbrand, *From Suffering to Triumph!* (Grand Rapids, Mich.: Kregel, 1991), pp. 151-152.
7. Debbie Morris, *Forgiving the Dead Man Walking* (Grand Rapids, Mich.: Zondervan, 1998), p. 223.
8. Lewis, p. 20.
9. C. S. Lewis, *Mere Christianity* (San Francisco: HarperCollins, 2001), pp. 204-205.

CHAPTER 2

1. Harold S. Kushner, *When Bad Things Happen to Good People* (New York: Avon Books, 1981), pp. 83-84.
2. William Glasser, *Reality Therapy in Action* (New York: HarperCollins, 2000), pp. xv-xvi.
3. C. S. Lewis, *Mere Christianity* (San Francisco: HarperCollins, 2001), pp. 47-48.
4. Lewis, pp. 47-48.
5. C. S. Lewis, "God in the Dock," in *The Collected Works of C. S. Lewis* (New York: Inspirational Press, 1996), p. 403.
6. Richard Wurmbrand, *From Suffering to Triumph!* (Grand Rapids, Mich.: Kregel, 1991), pp. 115-116.
7. Wurmbrand, p. 103.
8. Joni Eareckson Tada. (Nashville, Tenn.: AACC Soul Conference, 1999), videocassette.
9. Charles Spurgeon, *All of Grace* (Pasadena, Tex.: Pilgrim, 1978), p. 103.

CHAPTER 3

1. Mary Nicholas, *The Mystery of Goodness* (New York: W.W. Norton, 1994), pp. 12, 222.
2. Eugene Peterson, "The Business of Making Saints," *Leadership Journal* (spring 1997): 24.
3. C. S. Lewis, *Mere Christianity* (San Francisco: HarperCollins, 2001), p. 190.
4. Paul Ferris, *Dr. Freud* (Washington D.C.: Counterpoint, 1997), p. 232.
5. Lewis, p. 142.
6. Mary Pipher, *The Shelter of Each Other* (New York: Ballantine, 1996), pp. 123-124.

CHAPTER 4

1. Quoted M. Phillips, *George MacDonald: Scotland's Beloved Storyteller* (Minneapolis: Bethany House, 1987), p. 254.
2. Phillips, p. 225.

CHAPTER 9

1. Joni Eareckson Tada. (Nashville, Tenn.: AACC Soul Conference, 1999), videocassette.
2. Oswald Chambers, *Still Higher for His Highest* (Grand Rapids, Mich.: Zondervan, 1970), p. 173.

AUTHOR

KEVIN HUGGINS is the associate provost and dean of the School of Church and Community Ministries at Philadelphia Biblical University (PBU) in Langhorne, Pennsylvania. He also serves as a graduate professor of Christian counseling at PBU and trains Christian workers to lead counseling and family ministries in their local churches.

An author of several books and articles on parenting teenagers, Kevin has worked with youth and families over the past twenty-five years as a pastor, family therapist, and college and prison chaplain. Kevin has conducted hundreds of Christian counseling and family living courses, seminars, and workshops across the world.

HELP OTHERS GET FROM WHERE THEY ARE TO WHERE THEY WANT TO BE.

The Biblical Basis of Christian Counseling for People Helpers

This book will guide you to a practical, working knowledge of Scripture and the basics of the Christian faith—the core of what Christian counselors must know to be truly effective in helping others.
(Gary R. Collins, Ph.D.)

Christian Coaching

Coaching is a hot topic today. Dr. Gary R. Collins shows us how to combine the successful principles of coaching with a God-centered application to help others realize their maximum potential.
(Gary R. Collins, Ph.D.)

Words That Hurt, Words That Heal

This book looks at the hurt bragging, complaining, gossip, unchecked anger, and careless remarks cause, and the healing words can bring if used positively.
(Carole Mayhall)

To get your copies, visit your local bookstore, call 1-800-366-7788, or log on to www.navpress.com. Ask for a FREE catalog of NavPress products. Offer #BPA.

NAVPRESS
BRINGING TRUTH TO LIFE
www.navpress.com